CHICHESTER IN 50 BUILDINGS

EDDY GREENFIELD

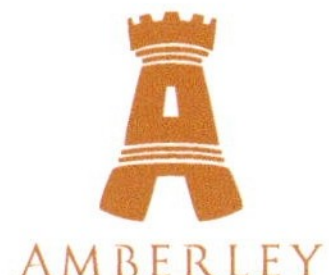

AMBERLEY

Acknowledgements

With grateful thanks to Ian and Jenny Jackson (City Arts Centre), Karrie Wright (Chichester Free School), St Richard's Roman Catholic Church, Claire Adams and Chichester City Council, Sarah (St Olav Christian Bookshop), Ian Tout and the Bishop of Chichester, Clara Herrera (Marriott House), West Sussex County Council, Jo Shapiro (Oxmarket Contemporary), Alex (The Buttery), Emma Shortt (Novium Museum/Guildhall), Katy Roberts (Waterstones), Lucinda Morrison (Chichester Festival Theatre), Gareth Edmunds (Chichester Library), Sarah Barnett (Almshouse Vintage) and Liv Nicholds (Pallant House Gallery).

Image Credits

Lidar and digital terrain models: contains public sector information licensed under the Open Government Licence v3.0; Brandy Hole Copse dyke: © Simon Burchell CC BY-SA 4.0; Pallant House: © Chris Ison; Chichester Free School images: © Chichester Free School; Luftwaffe aerial image of Graylingwell: National Archives and Records Administration, Washington, D.C.; Graylingwell water tower: © David Martin CC BY-SA 2.0. All other images, unless otherwise stated, are © Eddy Greenfield.

First published 2024

Amberley Publishing, The Hill, Stroud
Gloucestershire GL5 4EP

www.amberley-books.com

British Library Cataloguing in Publication Data.
A catalogue record for this book is available from the British Library.

ISBN 978 1 3981 2163 8 (print)
ISBN 978 1 3981 2164 5 (ebook)

Typesetting by SJmagic DESIGN SERVICES, India.
Printed in Great Britain.

Contents

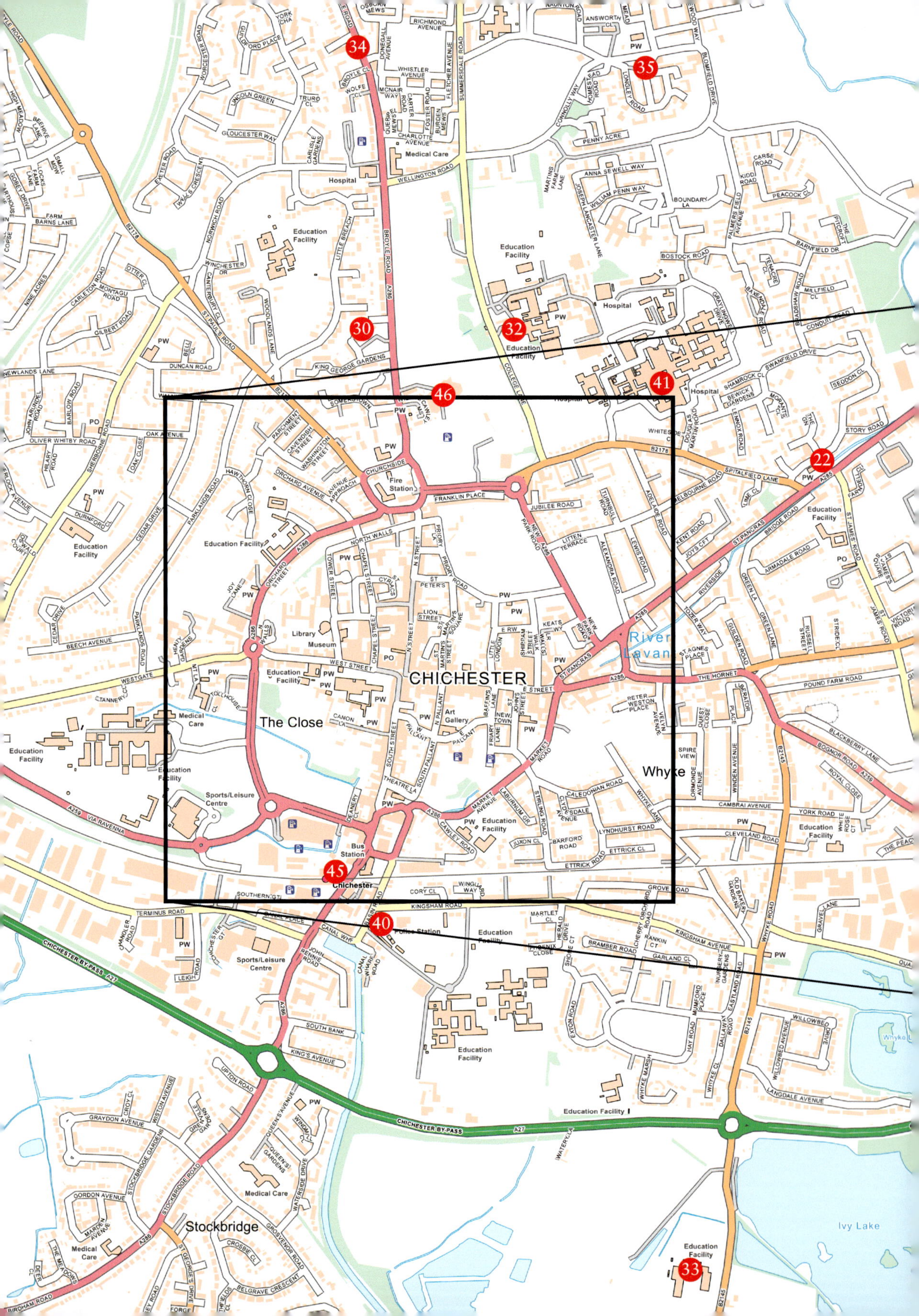

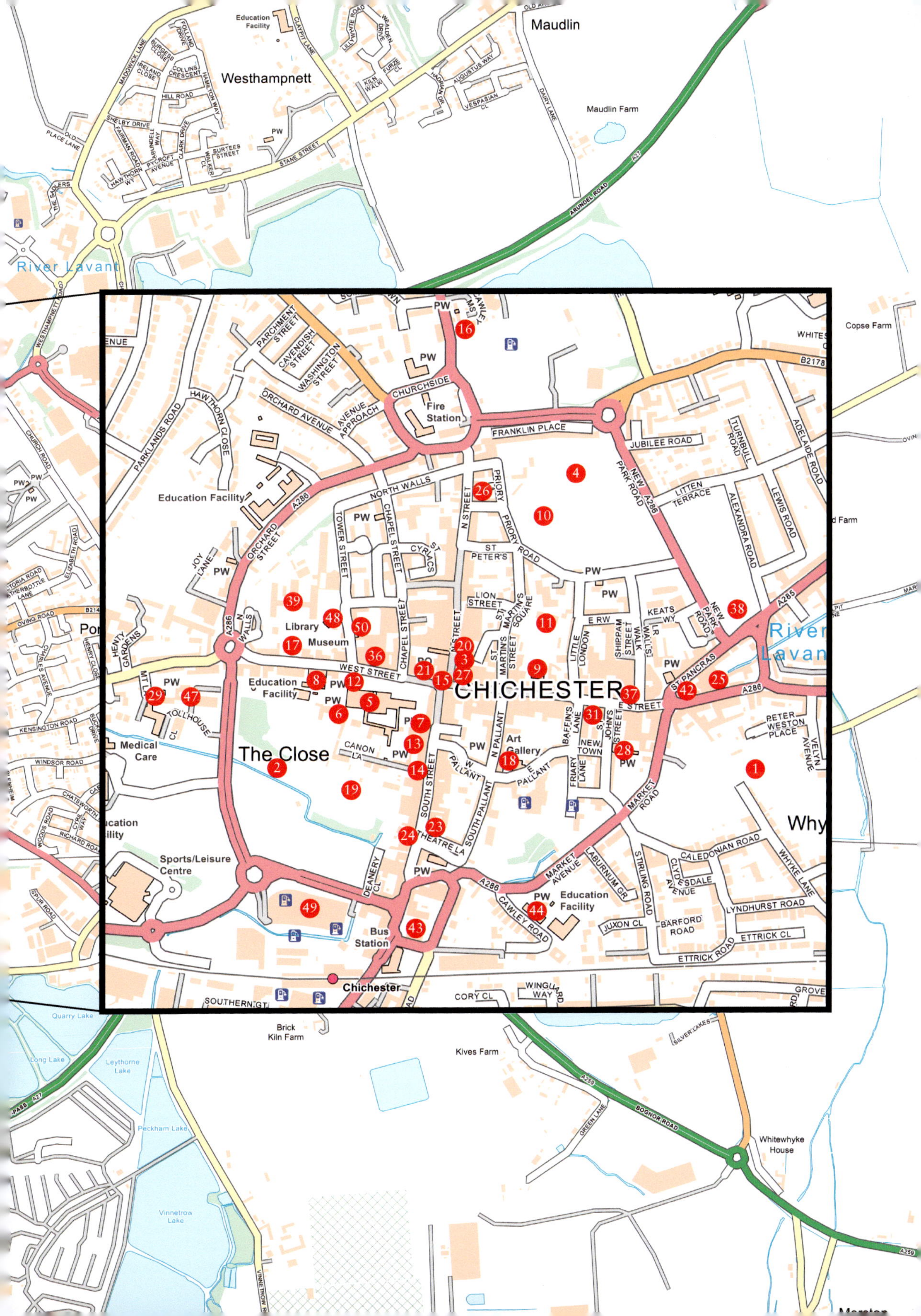

Key

1. The Amphitheatre (*c*. AD 70)
2. City Walls (*c*. AD 300)
3. St Olave's Church (*c*. 1050)
4. Chichester Castle (*c*. 1068)
5. Cathedral (*c*. 1088)
6. Bishop's Palace (1187)
7. Vicar's Hall and Undercroft (*c*. 1197)
8. Prebendal School (1232)
9. St Andrew-in-the-Oxmarket Church (*c*. 1248)
10. Guildhall (1282)
11. St Mary's Hospital (*c*. 1290)
12. Bell Tower (*c*. 1400)
13. Vicars Close (1475)
14. Canon Gate (1484)
15. Market Cross (1501)
16. Cawley Almshouses (1625)
17. Edes House (1696)
18. Pallant House (*c*. 1712)
19. The Deanery (1725)
20. Council House (1731)
21. Dolphin & Anchor (1768)
22. Leper's Cottage (*c*. 1781)
23. Old Theatre (1791)
24. The Fountain (1798)
25. Almshouse Arcade (1802)
26. Ship Hotel (1804)
27. Butter Market (1808)
28. St John the Evangelist's Church (1812)
29. St Bartholomew's Church (1824)
30. Royal West Sussex Hospital (1826)
31. Corn Exchange (1833)
32. University of Chichester (1849)
33. Convent of Our Lady of Mount Carmel (1870)
34. Roussillon Barracks (1875)
35. Graylingwell (1894)
36. Oliver Whitby School (1904)
37. Shippam's (1912)
38. War Memorial (1921)
39. County Hall (1933)
40. Police Station (1937)
41. St Richard's Hospital (1938)
42. Unicorn Inn (1938)
43. Chichester Crown Court (1940)
44. St Richard of Chichester Church (1958)
45. Railway Station (1961)
46. Chichester Festival Theatre (1962)
47. Marriott Lodge (1963)
48. Library (1965)
49. Avenue de Chartres Car Park (1991)
50. The Novium (2012)

Introduction

'It is the fair little cathedral city of one of the fairest counties in England, and everything that is enduring here is elegant and beautiful.'

Arthur Mee, *Sussex*, 1937

I doubt that many could disagree that there is a special charm about Chichester and trying to compose a list of just fifty buildings with which to explore the 2,000-year history of this city took some extraordinary effort.

The Chichester that we know today dates back to the settlement of Noviomagus Reginorum shortly after the Roman invasion of AD 43. However, archaeological evidence hints at an even earlier settlement in the area.

The Trundle, located just 4 miles north of Chichester, is sited on a Neolithic causewayed enclosure dating back to *c.* 3300 BC. Excavations have shown that the site remained in occupation throughout the Iron Age and possibly used into the early Romano-British era in the first century AD.

Approximately halfway between The Trundle and Chichester is the series of earthworks known as the Devil's Ditch. Testing carried out in 2010 dated the

The Trundle.

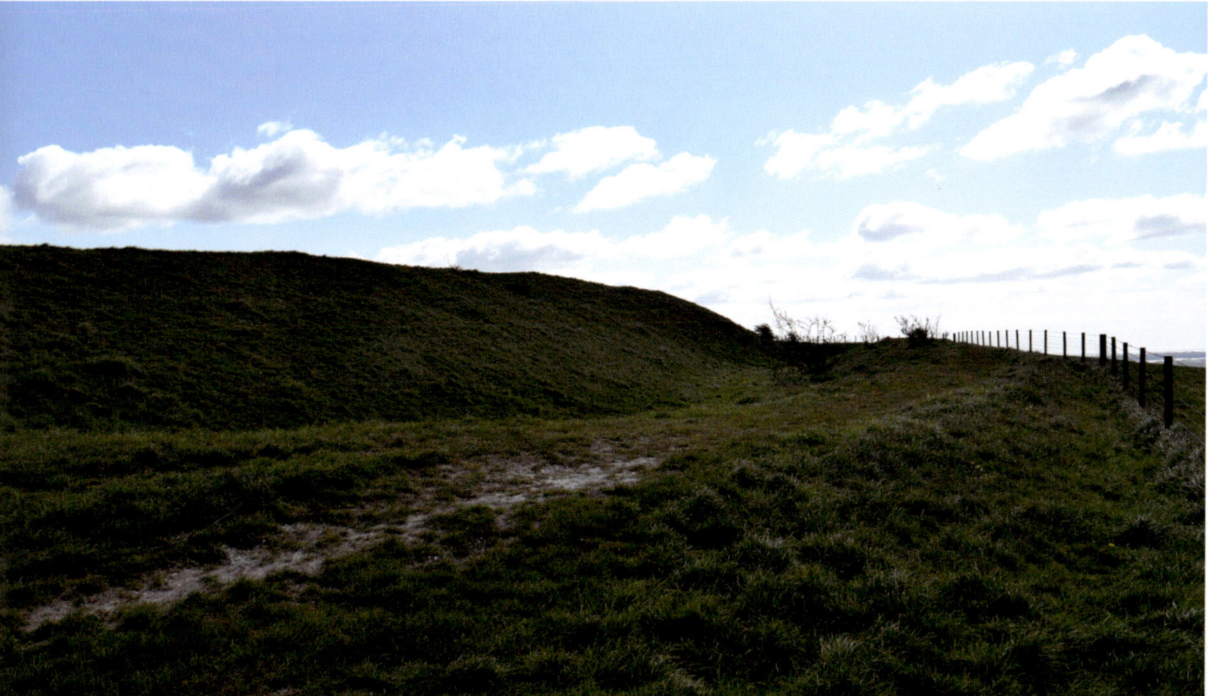

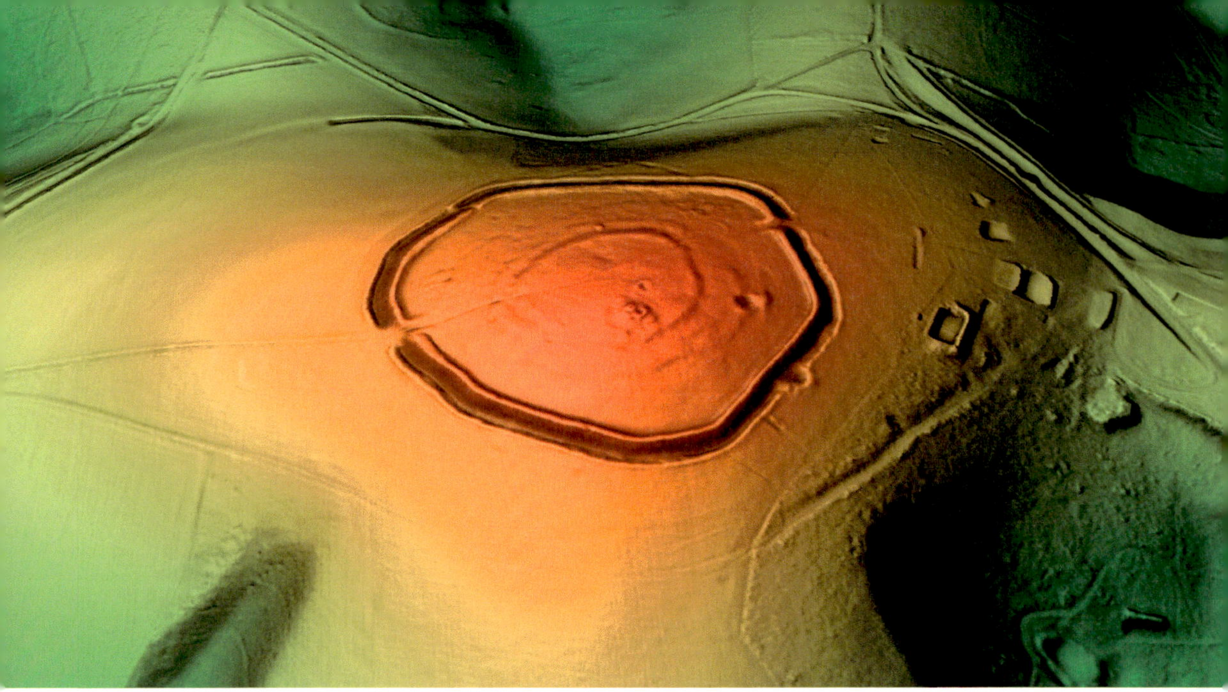

Above: Digital terrain model of The Trundle. (OGL/Rouven Meidlinger)

Below: Chichester from The Trundle.

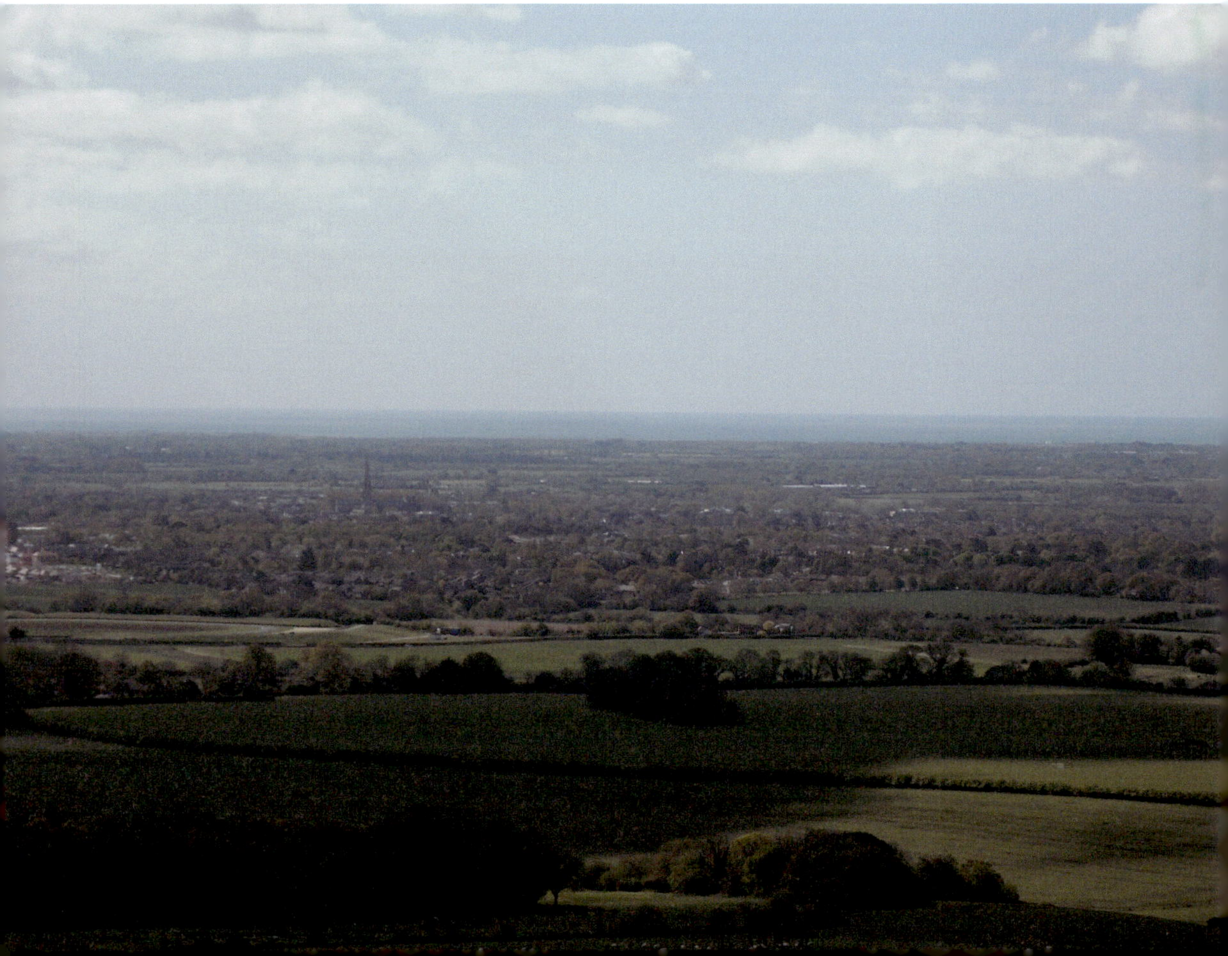

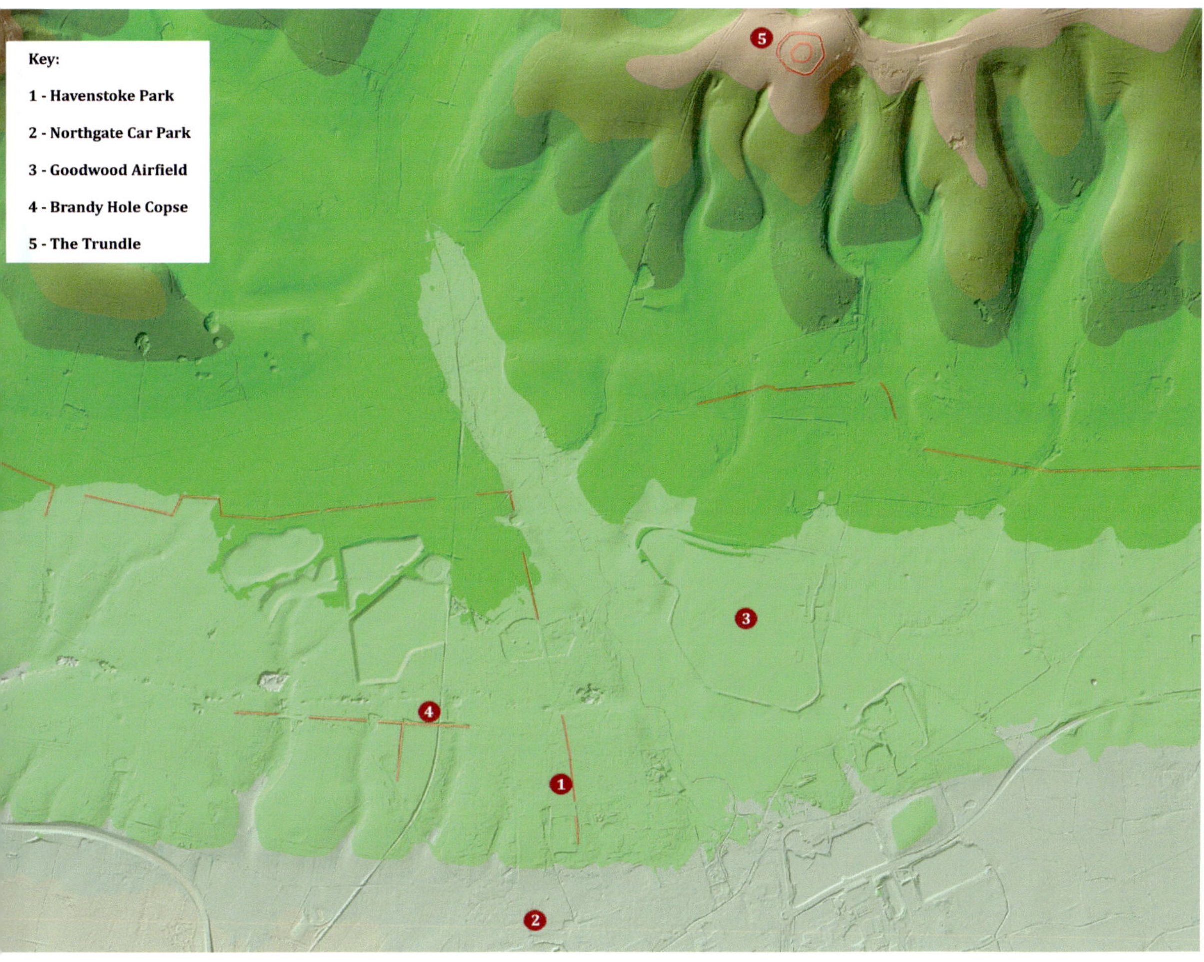

Surviving pre-Roman earthworks in the Chichester area.

earliest phase of the earthworks to *c.* 500–400 BC and was in place by no later than 80 BC. As at The Trundle, this ditch, and the accompanying earthworks known as the Chichester Dykes, appears to have been repurposed by the Romans in *c.* AD 50–60.

It has therefore been theorised that a Celtic client state of the Roman Empire existed in the local area (perhaps at The Trundle) before moving south to the present location of Chichester upon the foundation of the Roman garrison.

If this was the case, then the events leading up to the creation of Roman Chichester began ultimately with the arrival of the Atrebates from Gaul, led by King Diviciacus, at about the time the earthworks between Chichester and The Trundle were built.

Julius Caesar conquered the Atrebates in Gaul in 57 BC and appointed Commius as the new king of the tribe. Rendering aid in Caeser's two expeditions to Britain in 55 BC and 54 BC, Commius' position as a friend of Rome was cemented and the Atrebates were allowed to remain as a semi-autonomous vassal state of the Roman Empire.

However, Commius was later suspected of treachery and narrowly escaped assassination in the winter of 53 BC. Whether he truly had reneged on his former allies, or if the failed assassination prompted his defection, the Atrebates joined a revolt led by Vercingetorix in 52 BC, taking part in campaigns in modern-day France. Upon Vercingetorix's defeat, Commius allied himself with another Germanic tribe against Rome.

Escaping with his life, Commius returned to his homeland in northern France and made preparations for continued resistance operations. However, he was wounded in another battle and, once more escaping, sued for peace to Mark Antony in exchange for hostages and exile to Britain.

A section of the Chichester Dykes, Brandy Hole Copse. (Simon Burchell)

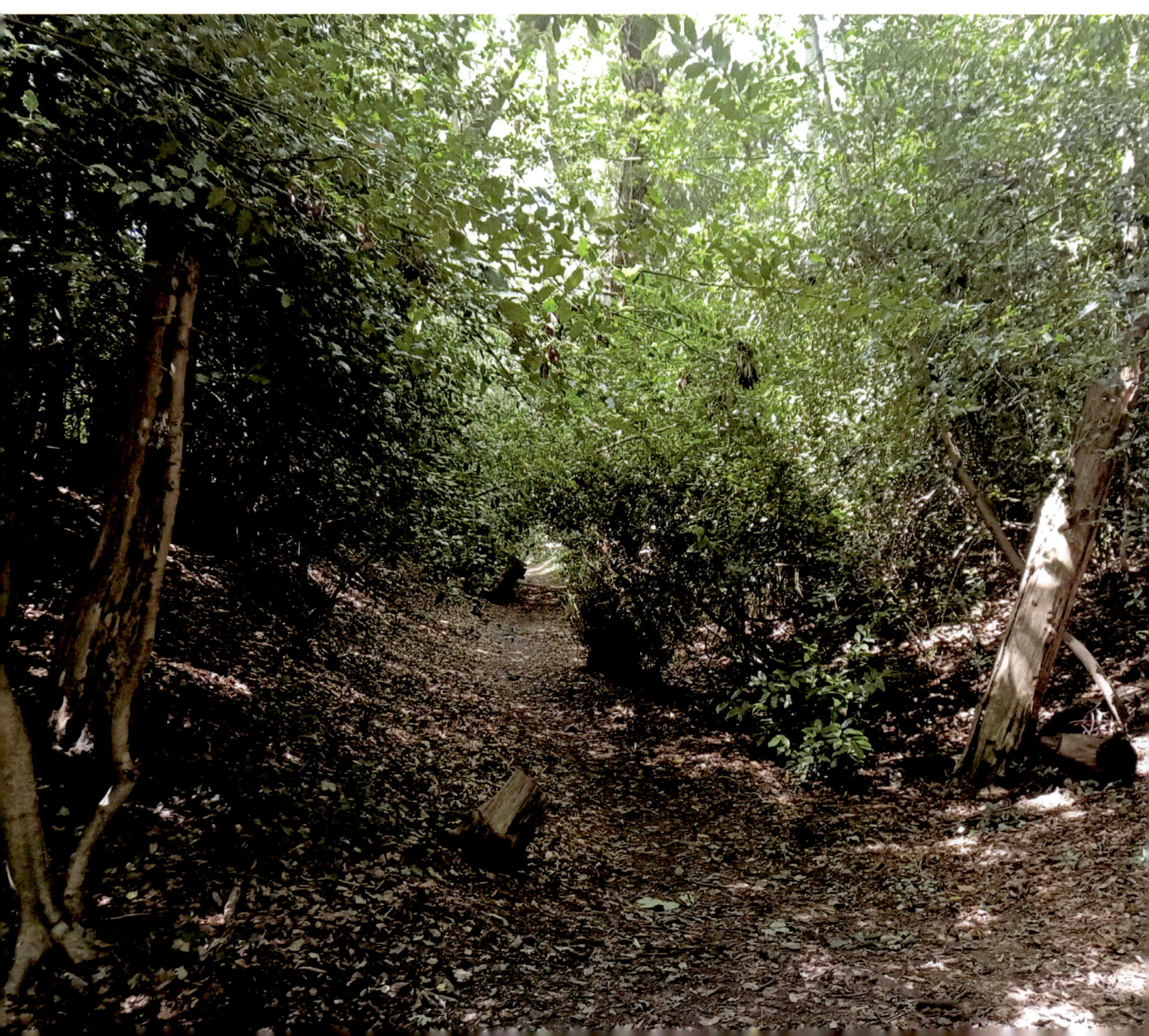

Here, in *c.* 30 BC, he had firmly established himself as King of the Atrebates, ruling over a kingdom encompassing modern-day West Sussex and parts of Surrey and Hampshire, once more entering into friendly terms with the Romans.

He was succeeded in *c.* 20 BC by his sons, Tincomarus, Eppillus and Verica. Verica took over the kingdom in *c.* AD 15, making his capital near Chichester, and continued to forge ever stronger links with Rome.

Verica's rule faced challenge from the Catuvellauni tribe in the east and was eventually deposed in a revolt in AD 42. By this time, the Atrebatic Kingdom had diminished to just the area contained by the Chichester Dykes and Devil's Ditch.

Having fled across the Channel, this series of events prompted Emperor Claudius to mount a full-scale invasion of Britain in AD 43 in an attempt to shore up the north-western flank of the Empire and restore Verica to the kingdom. The Roman force crossed from Boulogne and succeeded in pushing the Celtic tribes back to the Thames.

With the south coast secured, Togidubnus was installed as the new king as heir to the elderly Verica, and was rewarded with additional territories in the region, forming a trio of Roman client states in the south-east: the Atrebates, the Belgae, and the Regni, the latter with its capital at Noviomagus and palace at Fishbourne – the largest known Roman palace north of the Alps.

So begins the story of Chichester in the mid-first century AD.

The 50 Buildings

1. The Amphitheatre (c. AD 70)

One of just twelve known examples in the UK, this is not just Chichester's oldest public theatre, but likely the earliest surviving structure in the city, dating to *c*. AD 70–90, making it contemporary with Fishbourne Roman Palace.

Although easy to miss by the casual passer-by, surviving above ground as just a circular earth bank in the corner of Velyn Avenue Recreation Ground, the amphitheatre survives remarkably well, in archaeological terms, below the surface. Covering an area of 70 metres by 60 metres, the inner wall would originally have been faced in plastered timber and the gates constructed of flint and mortar.

Since Noviomagus was a provincial capital, it was unlikely that there were many, if any, gladiatorial combats due to the expense of these events, but other bloodthirsty 'entertainment' such as bull and bear baiting, cockfighting and perhaps public executions would have been common, in addition to circus and other sporting activities.

The structure does not appear, based on the archaeological evidence, to have been in use for any great length of time, perhaps for as little as 100 years, with its materials robbed for use in constructing and/or improving the city's defences.

Amphitheatre bank.

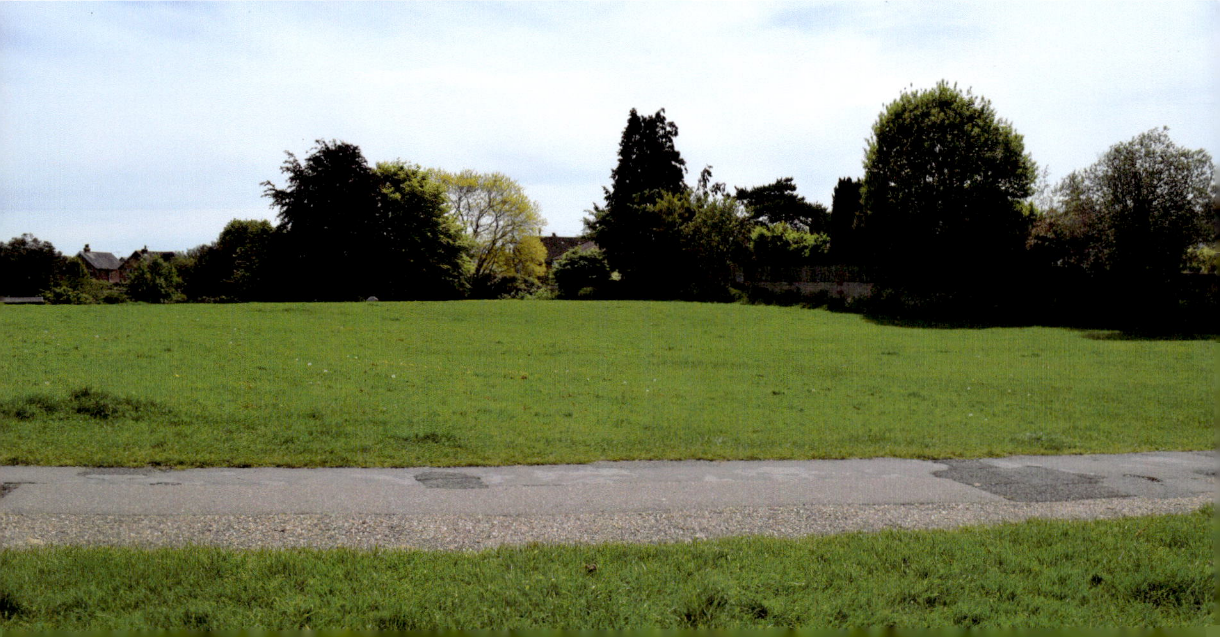

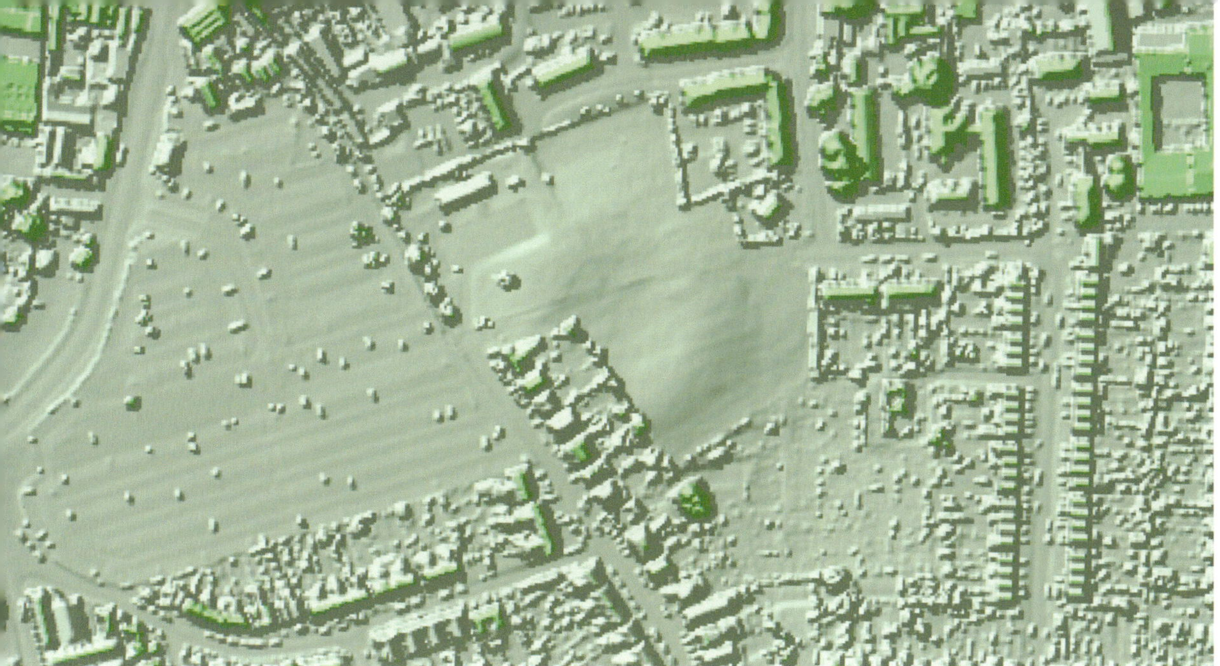

The extent of the surviving sections of the amphitheatre are evident in this Lidar image. (OGL)

In 2020, Chichester City Council put forward proposals to bring the amphitheatre back into use as a public performance area (though not of the bloodthirsty kind it was originally built for!) and an outdoor classroom by erecting sympathetic seating on the earth bank and improving the overall landscaping of the park.

2. City Walls (c. AD 300)

The ancient walls still encircle much of the city centre, although the four gates have long since disappeared, and later repairs and improvements in Saxon and medieval eras have built on the Roman foundations. Aside from these later changes and more recent restorations, the walls are still mostly Roman at their core and appear much as they would have done in the third century AD.

The construction of the walls occurred in three distinct phases, beginning with a double ditch and earth bank faced with a 2.5-metre-thick flint revetment in around AD 200. The bastions and a new ditch followed in the following century, and the final major phase was the twelfth century repair and reconstruction by the mayor and citizens of the city in 1378.

The walls successfully protected Noviomagus throughout the city's early history, but fell into decay. New life was breathed into the city firstly by Alfred the Great in the ninth century, and then by the Normans in the late eleventh century, when the city once more became a military garrison.

Breached by invading French forces in 1216, it was not until December 1642 that the walls saw any major combat and were put to use in defending the city. With the Royalists having taken control of Chichester early on in the war, a force of 6,000 Parliamentarians surrounded the city and laid siege, firing canon at near

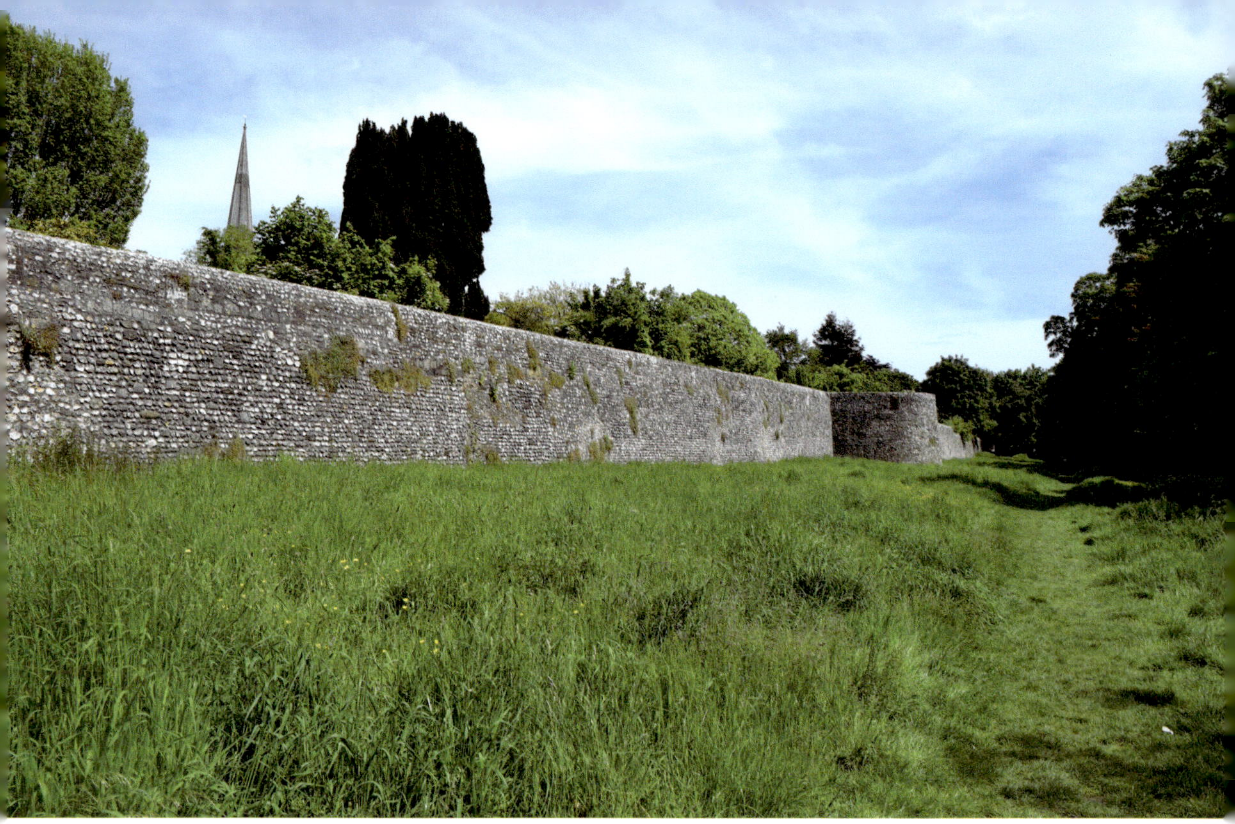

Above: Section of City Walls in the south-west quadrant.

Below: View along the walls from one of the bastions.

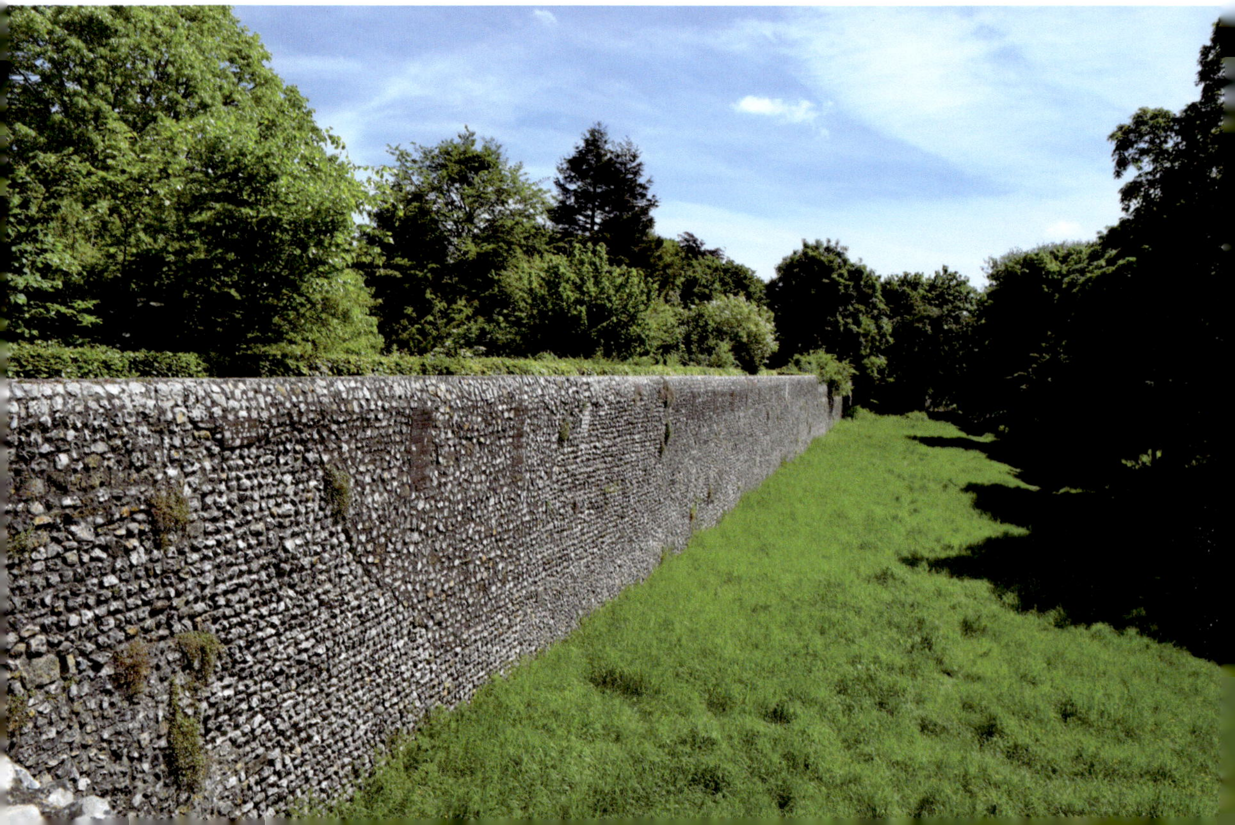

point-blank range through the Northgate and preparing to detonate a petard on the wall backing onto the Deanery garden before the Royalist occupiers finally surrendered after eight days. A number of orders were given in the following decade to slight the walls, but this was thankfully never carried out.

Today, the walls provide an opportunity for visitors to enjoy a peaceful and scenic elevated walk around the historic centre of Chichester.

3. St Olave's Church (c. 1050)

St Olave's Church is a remarkable survivor of this Saxon era of Chichester's history. Named for St Olave (or St Olaf), a Norwegian king who rendered assistance to King Æthelred during the Viking invasion of southern England in 1014, it was likely erected by Scandinavian merchants residing in Chichester. St Olaf was canonised in 1031, and the earliest church fabric (discovered in 1851) is clearly Saxon, and therefore the building must have been erected between 1031 and 1066; a plaque on the front of the building states *c.* 1050.

Below left: St Olave's from North Street.

Below right: Thirteenth-century murals prior to destruction in 1851. (*Sussex Archaeological Collections* Vol.5, p. 213)

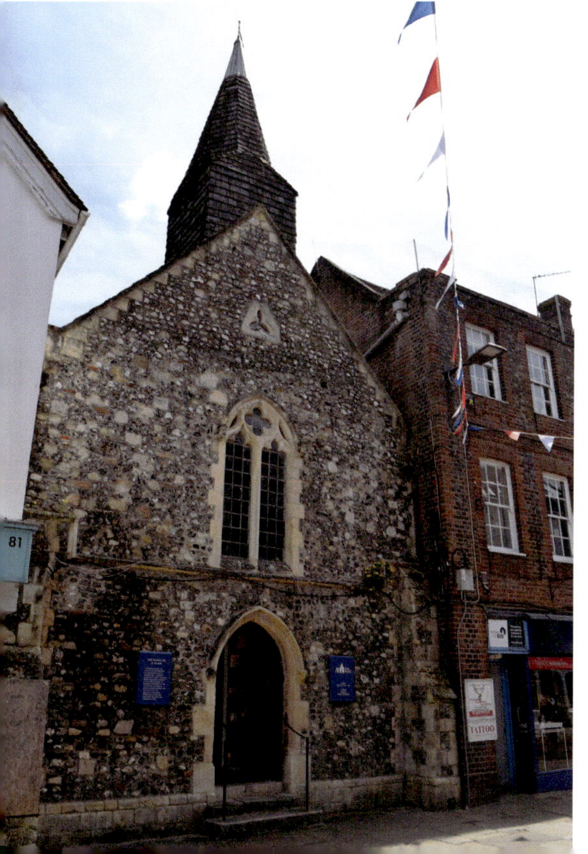

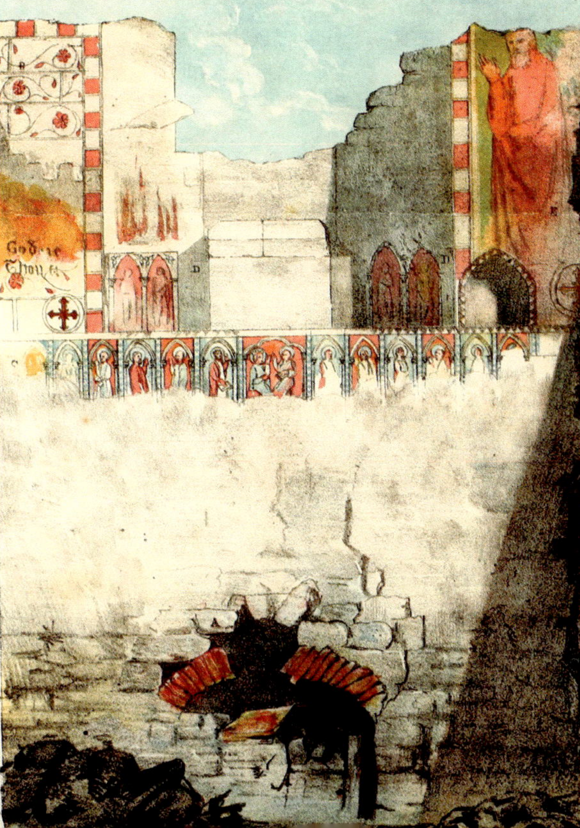

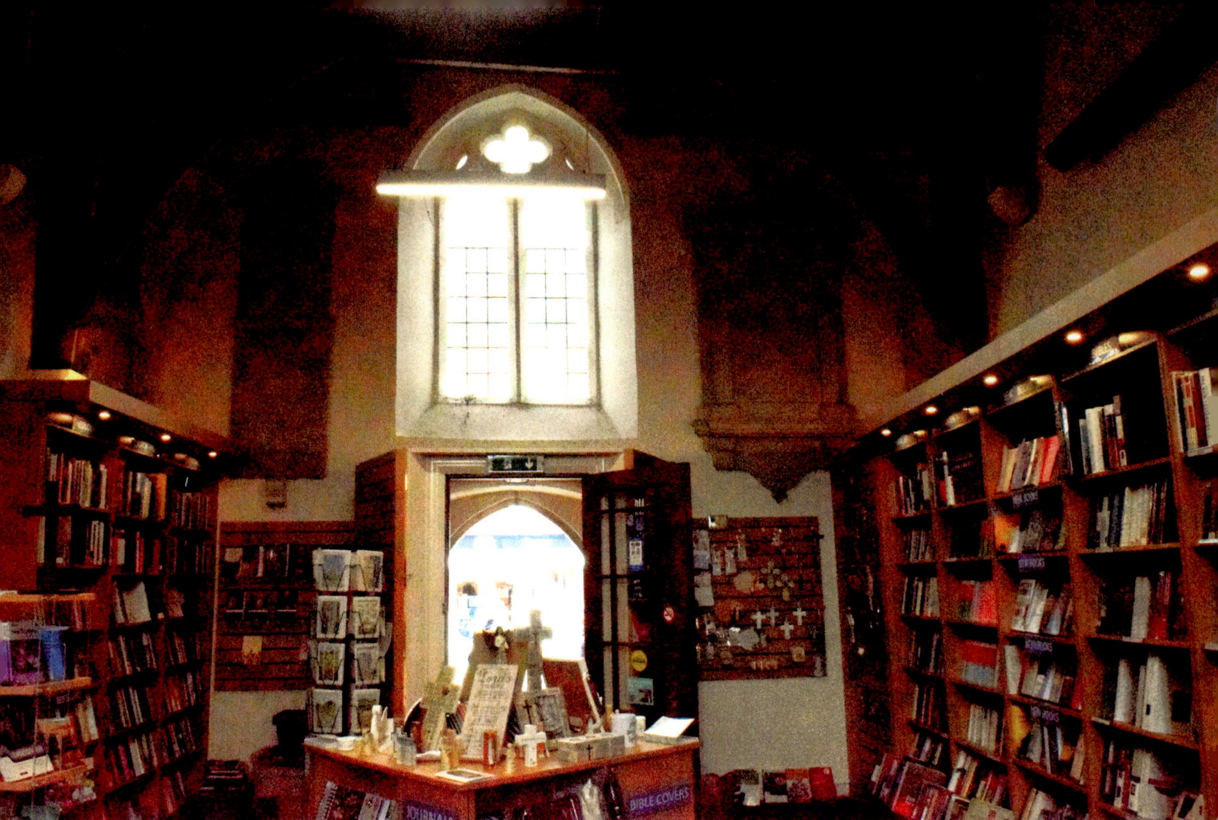

St Olave Christian Bookshop.

Originally just a small nave and chancel, making use of Roman material in its construction, the chancel was rebuilt and enlarged to its present size in the thirteenth century. Considerable alterations were made in the fourteenth century.

By 1602 the church had fallen into near ruin, but was not restored until 1851. These Victorian renovations were typically destructive and resulted in much damage to the internal fabric. In particular, thirteenth-century murals were uncovered on the east wall, but were lost when the wall was subsequently demolished.

Oddly, a pair of Roman urns were discovered during the restoration work embedded in the wall above the arch of the east window. It was speculated that they may have been funerary urns with ashes of martyrs, but there is no evidence to support this.

St Olave's was closed in 1956, when most of the fittings were removed, and was converted into a Christian bookshop. This shop still remains, albeit in a different guise (and different ownership) following a controversial move by the former owners in 2009 to align the shop with a more radical interpretation of the faith.

4. Chichester Castle (c. 1068)

Roger de Montgomery was awarded extensive lands following the Norman victory at the Battle of Hastings in 1066, including the whole of West Sussex. To cement the victory over the local population, he erected a wooden castle in Priory Park.

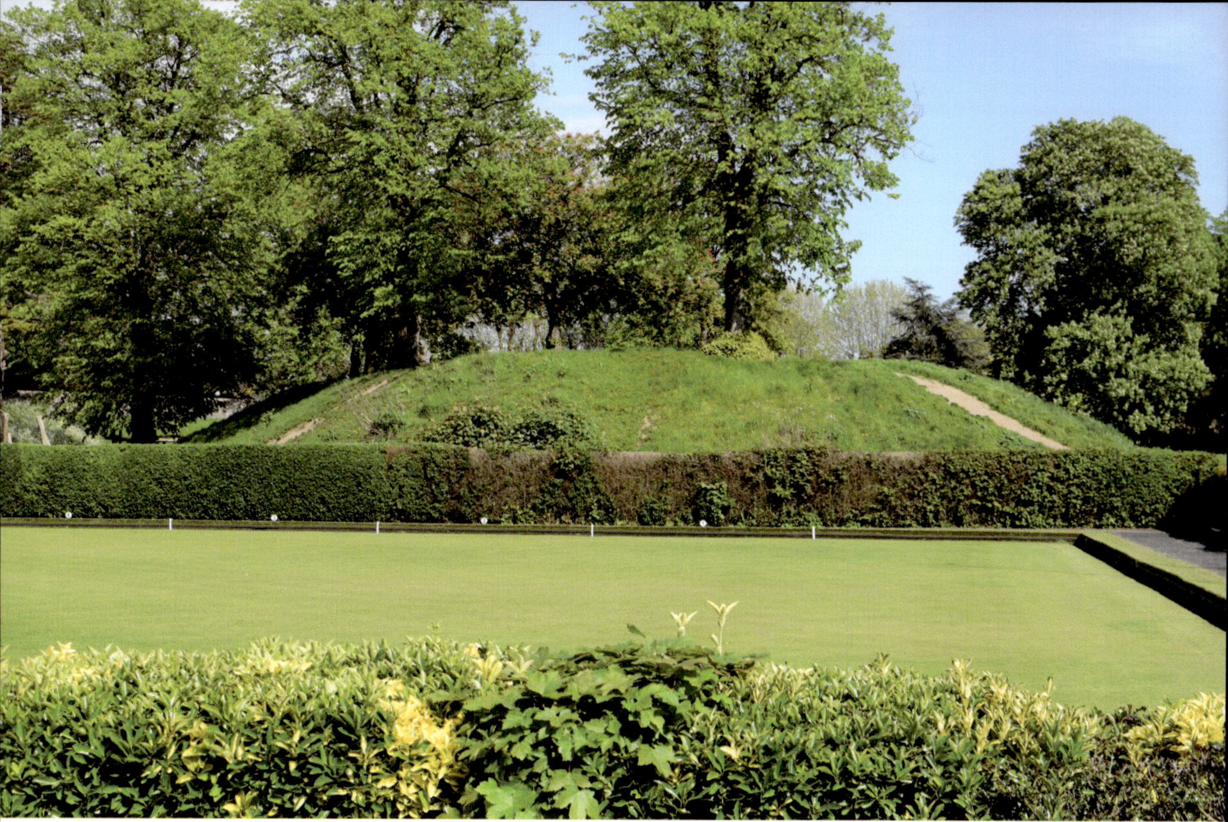

Above: Castle motte.

Below: Castle from the Guildhall.

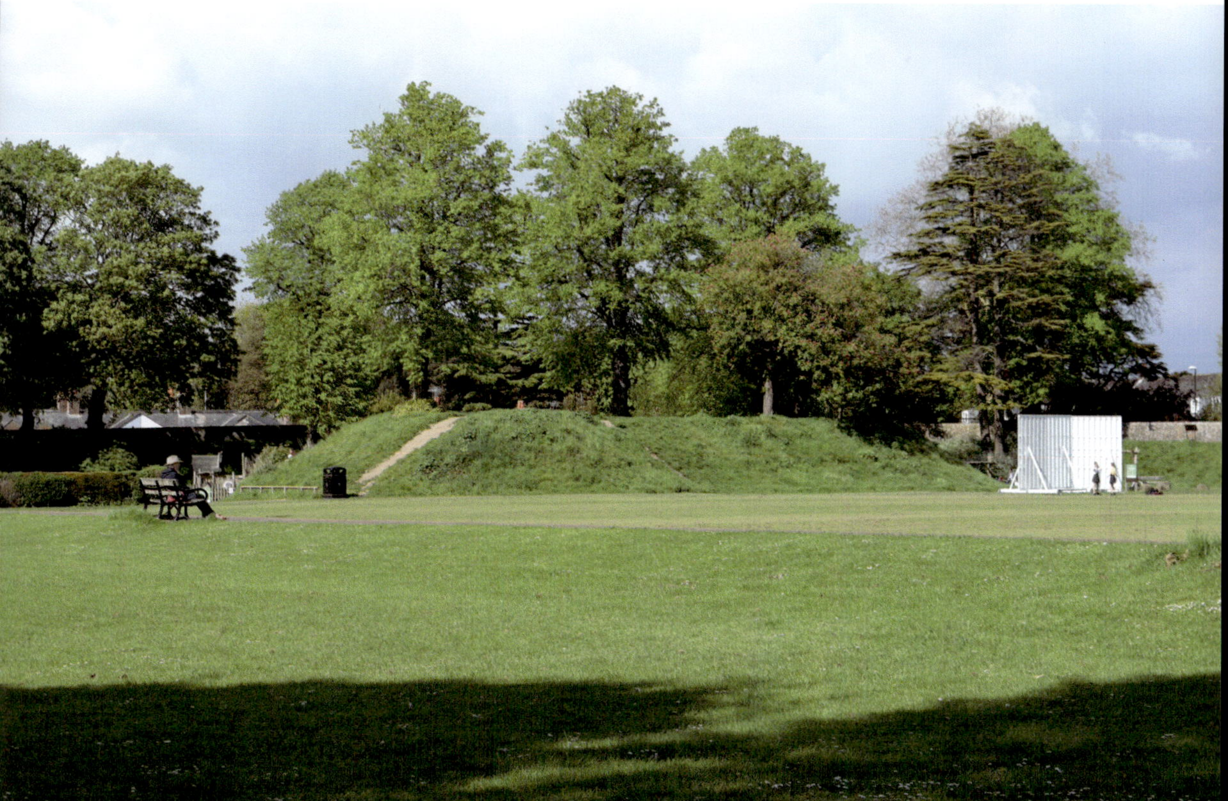

Hugh de Montgomery inherited Chichester until he was killed in battle in 1098. His older brother, Duke Robert, subsequently took over the castle. However, he joined a revolt against Henry I and had his estates stripped away; Chichester Castle eventually entered into the hands of Queen Adeliza upon her marriage to Henry I in 1121.

Over the following century, the castle had a chequered history. In 1193 the defences were put into a state of readiness in anticipation of a siege by Prince John, but this never materialised. However, the siege came the following year while King Richard was being held captive in France, and fell into the hands of King John. The latter's disastrous reign led to the First Baron's War in 1215, when dissenting noblemen attempted to force John from the throne and replace him with Prince Louis of France.

King John ordered the castle to be demolished in 1216 in anticipation of a French attack, but the orders were not received in time and the fort was seized by Prince Louis' forces soon after. It was not until the following year that the castle was retaken by the English and renewed orders for its destruction were given by the new King Henry III to Philip de Albini on 16 April 1217.

The demolition only appears to have been in so far as the castle's use as a defensive structure, since the Sheriff of Sussex ordered it converted into a prison on 9 April 1219, with the remainder of the land outside the castle granted to the Bishop of Chichester.

The site was originally intended to be used to found a hospital, but the plan was soon abandoned, and the land was instead granted to the Greyfriars to build a new friary at some time between 1222 and 1269.

When the castle was finally demolished between 1219 and the building of the friary, the motte upon which it stood was retained, and came into use once more during the English Civil War of the mid-seventeenth century, when it was improved by excavating the outer circumference and building up the height in the centre to provide a gun platform for cannon.

Today, the motte is only around a fifth of the size of the original, which would have been comparable in size to that at Arundel Castle. However, it survives as a Scheduled Ancient Monument in the corner of Priory Park, while recent archaeology continues to unearth more discoveries about the site.

5. Cathedral (c. 1088)

When William I ordered all cathedrals be removed to populous towns in 1075, land in the city was donated. This site was already occupied by St Peter's Church, delaying construction of the cathedral until *c.* 1088. The eastern end of the cathedral was the first to be completed and consecrated in 1108. Surviving a small fire in 1114, work progressed across the tenure of five bishops before being completed in 1184. A second fire struck in 1187, causing extensive damage. It took twelve years to repair the damage before Bishop Seffrid II reconsecrated the cathedral in 1199.

In 1210 two towers collapsed during a storm; the south-west tower was rebuilt in 1230–40, but the central one, rebuilt using the original rubble, ultimately led to issues six centuries later. The spire, built in stages between 1286 and 1337, reached a total height of around 300 feet.

Bishop Robert Sherburne commissioned two large paintings by the Tudor artist Lambert Bernardi, depicting the Kings of England and the Bishops of Selsey and Chichester. Bernardi and his two sons also painted the cathedral ceilings, which survived intact until whitewashed in 1817. Later rediscovered in the twentieth century, the Lady Chapel ceiling art is once more on display.

Over a century later, extensive damage was caused to the fabric of the cathedral by the Puritans in December 1642. However, they also carried out perhaps one of the most important actions that saved the cathedral for another two centuries by removing the bells in the central tower to the separate bell tower in 1644, owing to concerns over the building's strength. The north-west tower had also by this time collapsed and been left in ruin, but no action was taken until it was rebuilt in 1901.

Chichester Cathedral.

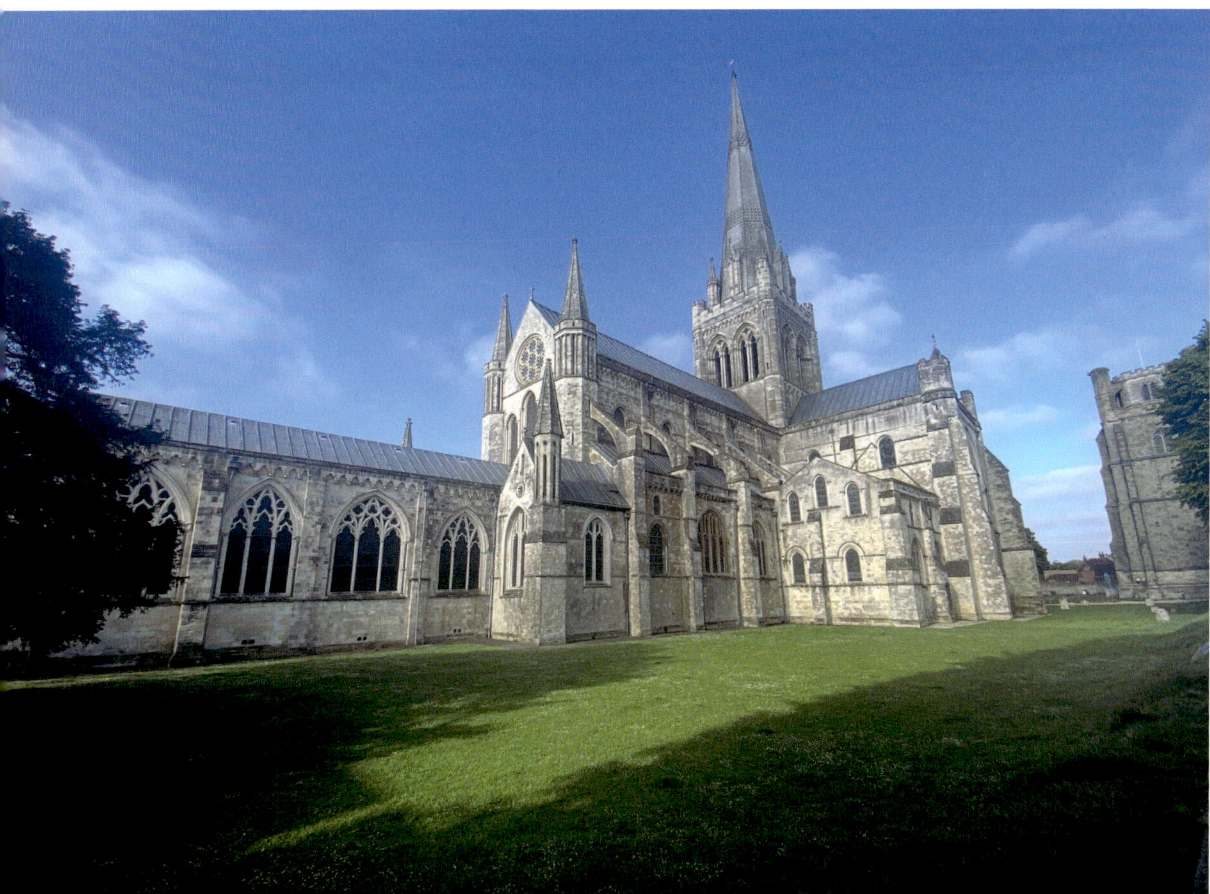

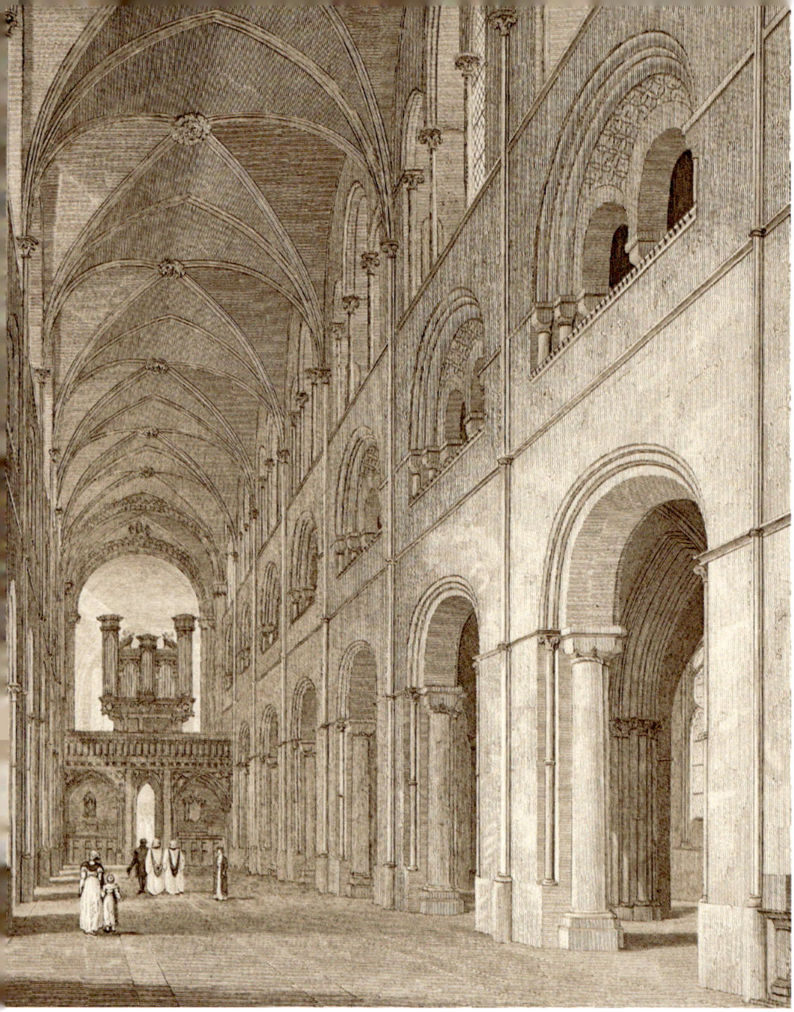

Left: Cathedral nave, *c.* 1861. (*Architectural History of Chichester Cathedral*)

Below: Cathedral from the Bishop's Palace Gardens.

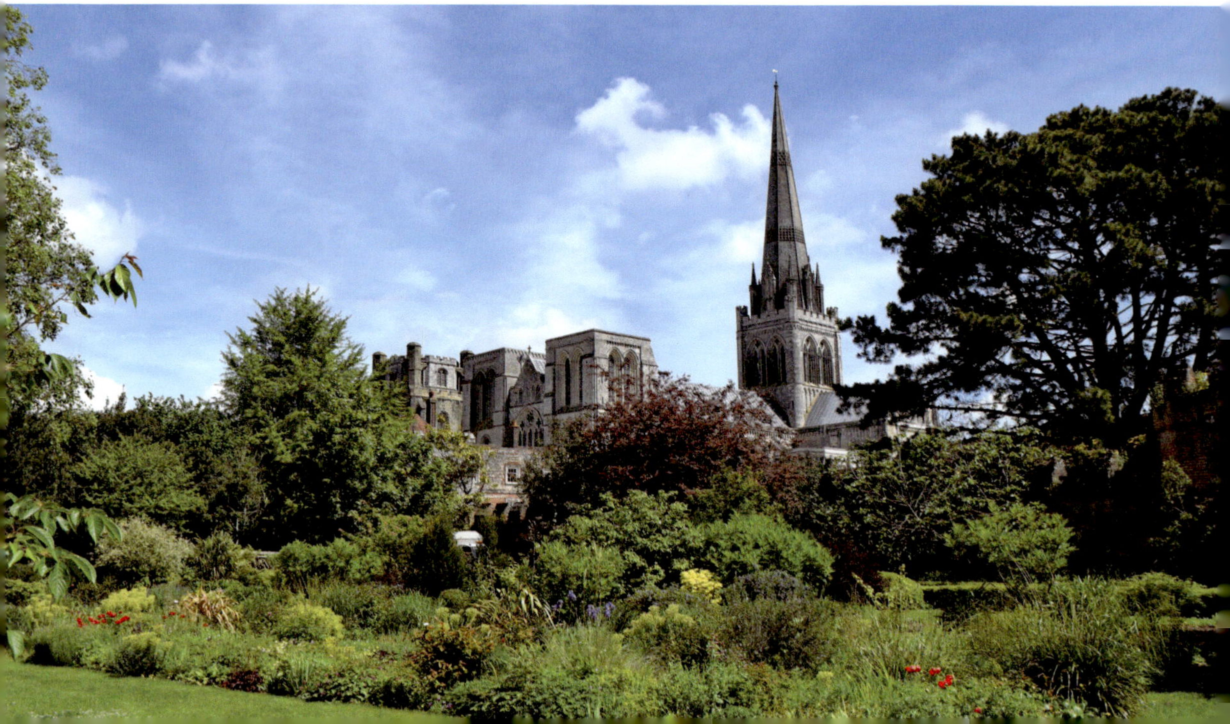

During works to remove the fifteenth-century Arundel Screen in 1860, builders discovered that the piers supporting the troublesome central tower were too weak and the walls bulging outward. At 13:30 on 21 February 1861 the spire telescoped neatly into the choir beneath. Remarkably little damage was sustained due to the way in which it collapsed in on itself. A fundraising effort was immediately launched to rebuild the spire, and the 277-foot structure was completed on 28 June 1866.

As the twentieth century arrived, a number of changes were made once more, beginning with the restoration of the Chapel of St George and conversion into the memorial chapel of the Royal Sussex Regiment – the regimental colours, dating from several different eras, hang from the ceiling and the names of 8,000 men killed in the First World War are inscribed on wooden panels mounted to almost every wall.

Perhaps the last major change came in 1961, when the Arundel Screen, removed 100 years earlier and kept in storage, was reinstated to its original position. Today, the cathedral is as much known for its artwork as for its history, and regular exhibitions or displays take place throughout the year.

6. Bishop's Palace (1187)

Situated at the end of Canon Lane is the ancient Bishop's Palace. This is but one of several official residences of the Bishops of Chichester that had been acquired over the centuries, with others formerly located at Cakeham near West Wittering, Aldingbourne, Laythorne, Amberley Castle and a private house in London.

The palace at Chichester was supposedly built on the site of an ancient nunnery dedicated to St Peter and was destroyed in the great fire that gutted the cathedral in 1187. It was rebuilt that same year but has undergone many changes since. Some of the original twelfth-century building can be seen in the south wall of the Great Kitchen, but the earliest surviving portion is the bishop's chapel at the eastern end, dating to the very early thirteenth century. Remodelled by Bishop John Langton in the early fourteenth century (who also added the north-east wing) and restored in the early twentieth century, the chapel is largely unchanged from its original form, including the thirteenth-century wall painting of the Virgin and Child.

In this earlier phase of the palace's history, the gatehouse at the western end of Canon Lane was built *c.* 1327, with the Bishop's Prison attached to it until it was demolished in 1608–09. Connecting the gatehouse with the Great Kitchen of the palace is the long range of buildings that have had a variety of uses over the years, and undergone so many changes that it is not evident as to what the original purpose was.

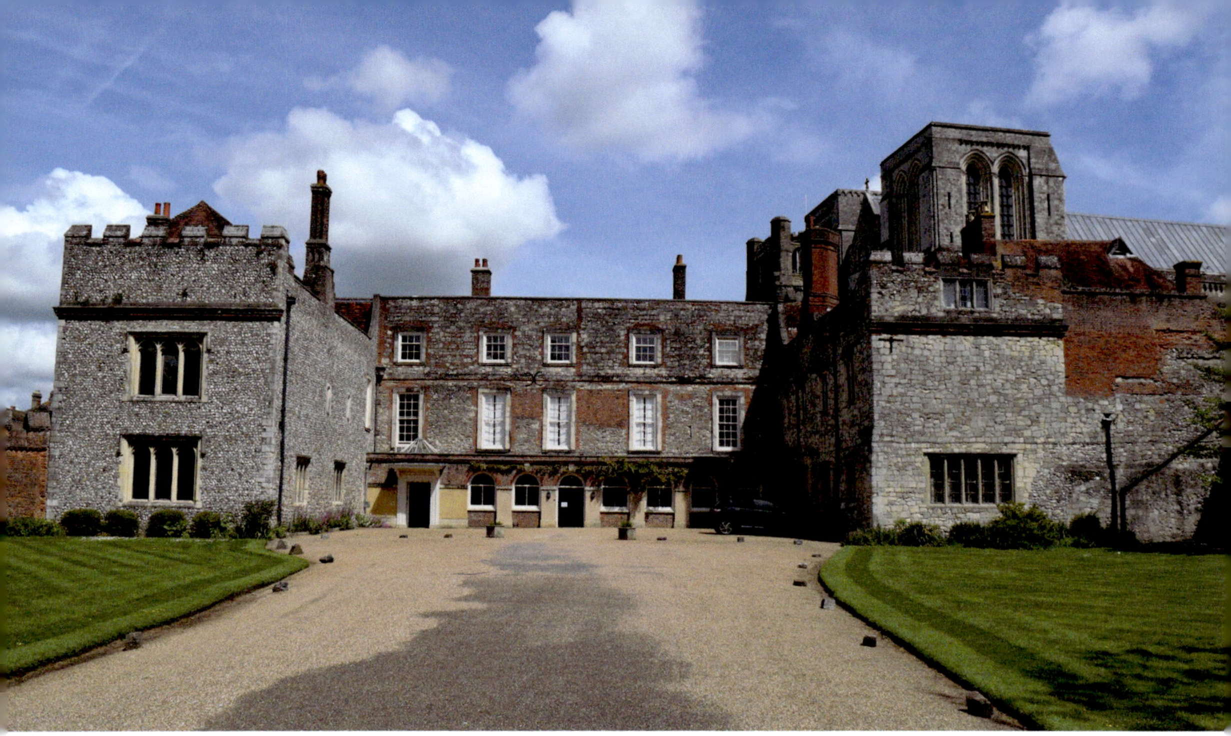

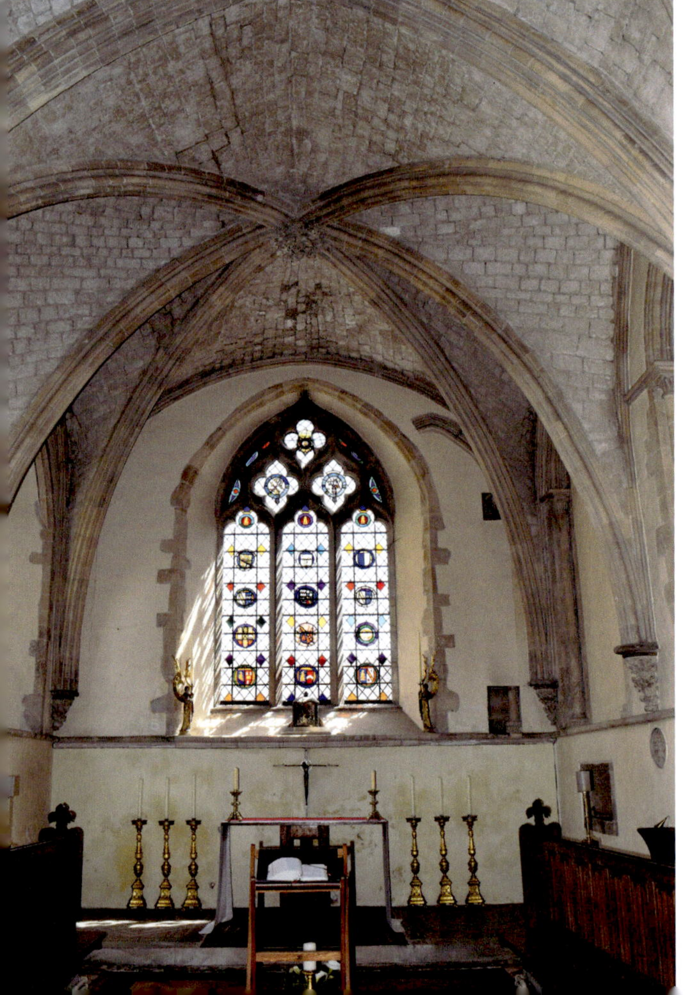

Above: Front elevation. (By kind permission of the Bishop of Chichester)

Left: Palace chapel. (By kind permission of the Bishop of Chichester)

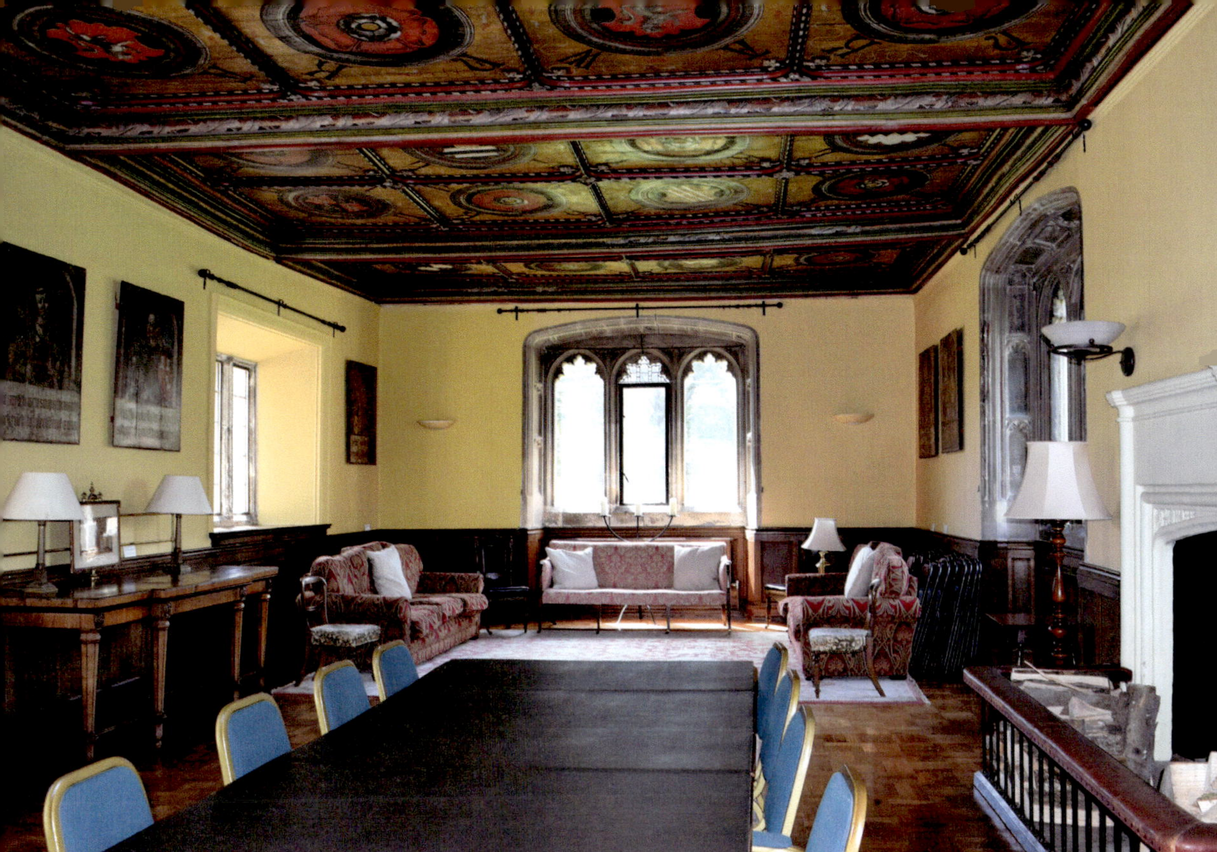

Sherburne Room. (By kind permission of the Bishop of Chichester)

The south-west and south-east wings are from the fifteenth century, but the painted ceiling of the dining room was the work of Bernardi and commissioned by Bishop Sherburne. Sherburne may also have been responsible for the north-west wing, giving the palace a more symmetrical shape, but another possibility is that it is a post-Reformation addition to house for the female servants. Both of the northern wings were destroyed by canon fire during the siege of 1642, although some traces of red brick can still be seen.

By the eighteenth century, the Bishop's Palace was in an extremely poor state until it was restored by Bishop Waddington in 1727, with further internal alterations carried out under Bishop Buckner in 1800.

The building is not normally open to the public, but rooms can be hired and the chapel is opened up on occasion for special visit days.

7. Vicar's Hall and Undercroft (c. 1197)

Built and consecrated in 1397, the Vicar's Hall provided space for the vicar's choral of the cathedral – a body of clergymen providing prayers and masses for wealthy patrons. The site, previously part of the more ancient Guildhall, was acquired from the Crown by Bishop Mitford, and the foundation stone of the new

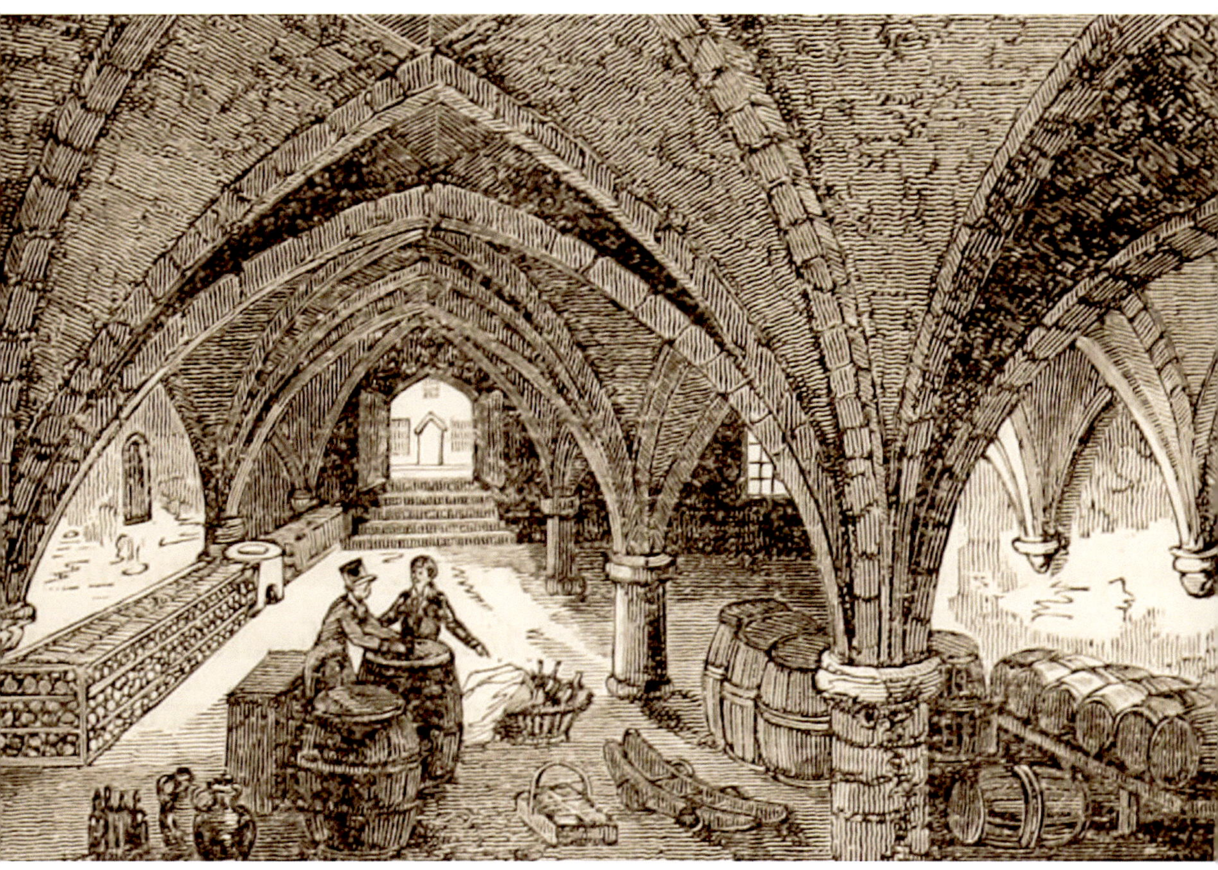

Original merchant's undercroft. (*The Chichester Guide*, p. 21)

hall laid by the dean and sprinkled with holy water. Used later as a school and then as the cathedral library, it is now an events venue available for hire.

The Undercroft (also erroneously referred to as The Crypt) predates the Vicar's Hall above it by at least two centuries and is contemporary with the former Guildhall, serving as the cellars for the latter. Despite its later ecclesiastical associations, this underground space was never used as a tomb or place for worship, but instead was simply a merchants' storeroom.

Built of Quarr stone from the Isle of Wight, the cavernous space sits around 4 feet below street level and is connected with other undercrofts beneath South Street via short tunnels.

In 1661, the vicar's choral leased the undercroft to the White Horse Inn, then located directly opposite in South Street, for use as a wine cellar, in exchange for an annual rental payment of one pint of sack or twelve pence to the vicars each Lady Day (25 March). By 1686, however, it had become a pig sty, and in more recent times has been a horticultural supply store, antiques shop and, since 1957, a restaurant. It is presently occupied by The Buttery in the Crypt.

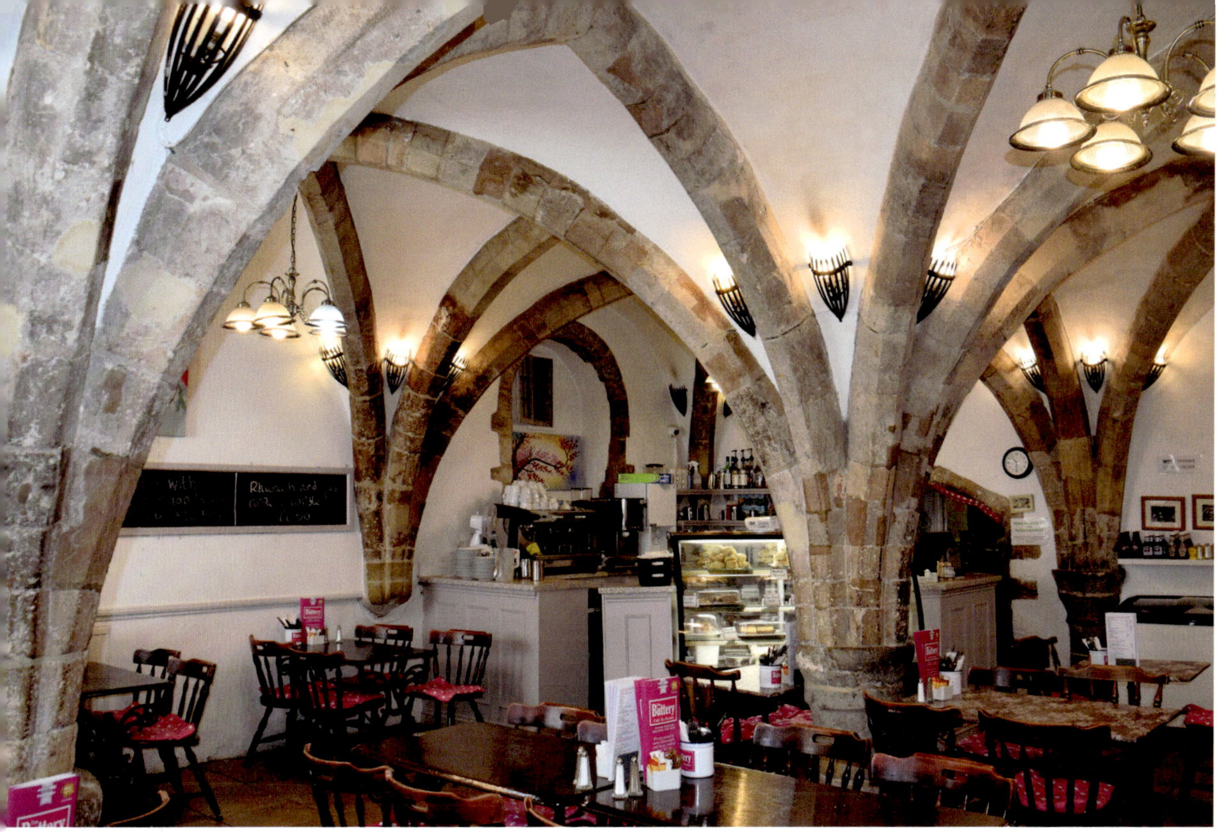

Above: The undercroft in 2024.

Below: The Buttery.

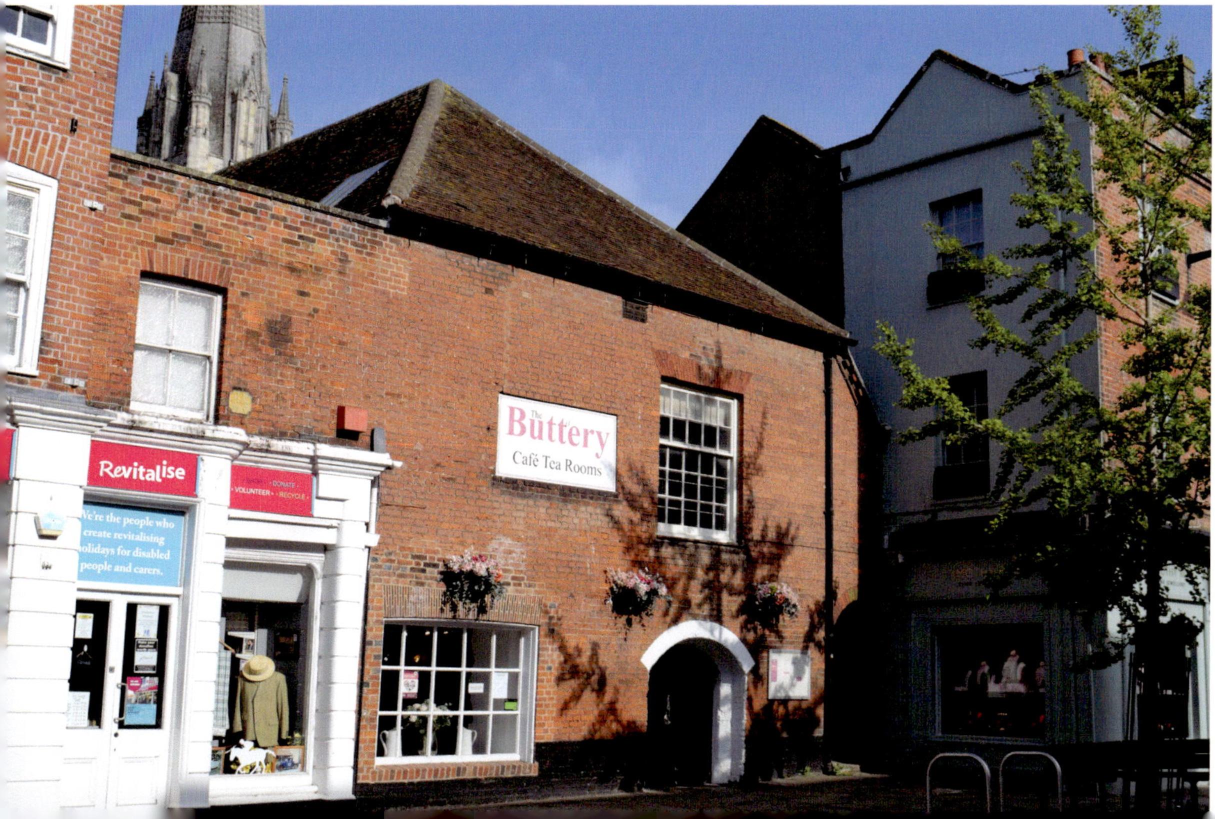

8. Prebendal School (1232)

The oldest school in Sussex has provided education in Chichester since the early thirteenth century, although the school known today is the work of Bishop Story, who re-founded it for local boys in 1497. The school still provides residential education for the cathedral choristers.

It is possible that a school has existed here since the foundation of the cathedral, and was originally the Chichester Grammar School. These earliest days are not well recorded, but the first schoolmaster was appointed in 1232; before then, the Cathedral Chancellor acted as the headmaster.

Money appears to have been an issue, culminating in Thomas Gyldesburgh, an eighty-year-old headmaster, being imprisoned for debt in 1462. It was not until Bishop Story re-established the school that the establishment had a secure financial footing in the form of the living of Highleigh Manor in Sidlesham. The rents from this estate were such that in the late eighteenth century, Dr David Davis was able to purchase three adjacent houses to expand the school, as well as undertake various repairs and restorations.

Aside from the summer of 1665 when Chichester was ravaged by the Great Plague, the Prebendal School has remained open throughout its entire history. The school came into difficulties in the 1920s, when pupil numbers dropped so low that the old buildings could not be maintained, and the remaining choristers were removed to other premises around the city. A fundraising effort by the dean in 1931 led to the reopening of the school buildings and its re-establishment as a

Prebendal School's eastern range.

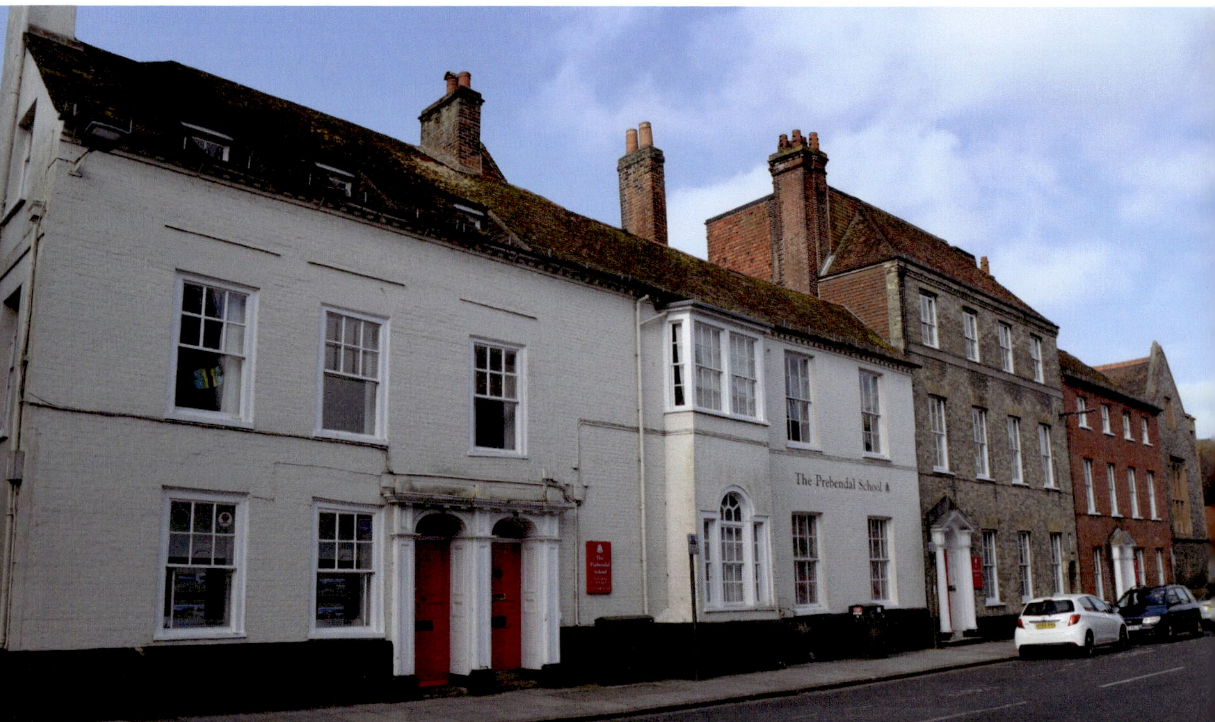

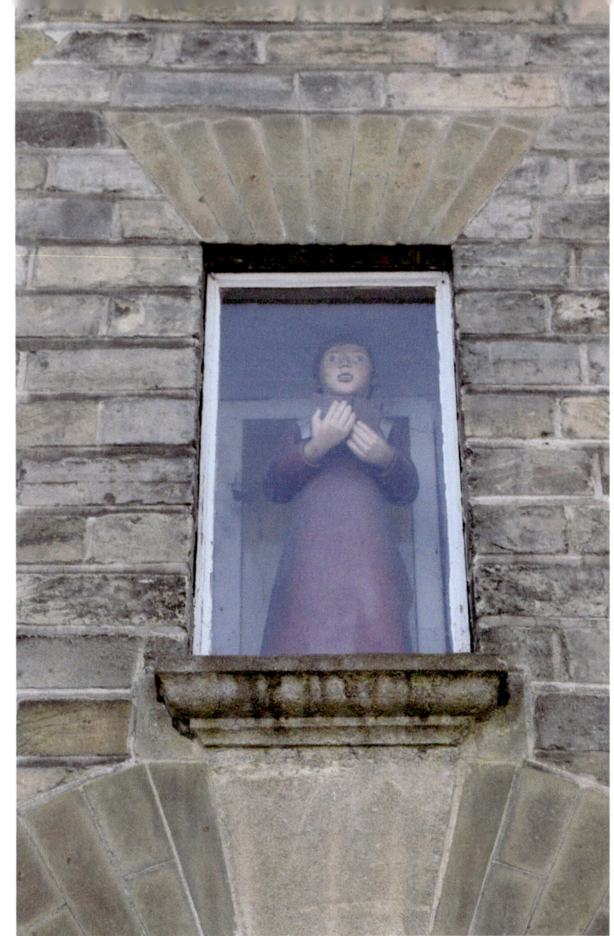

Right: Figure of a Red Coat Boy.

Below: Western range.

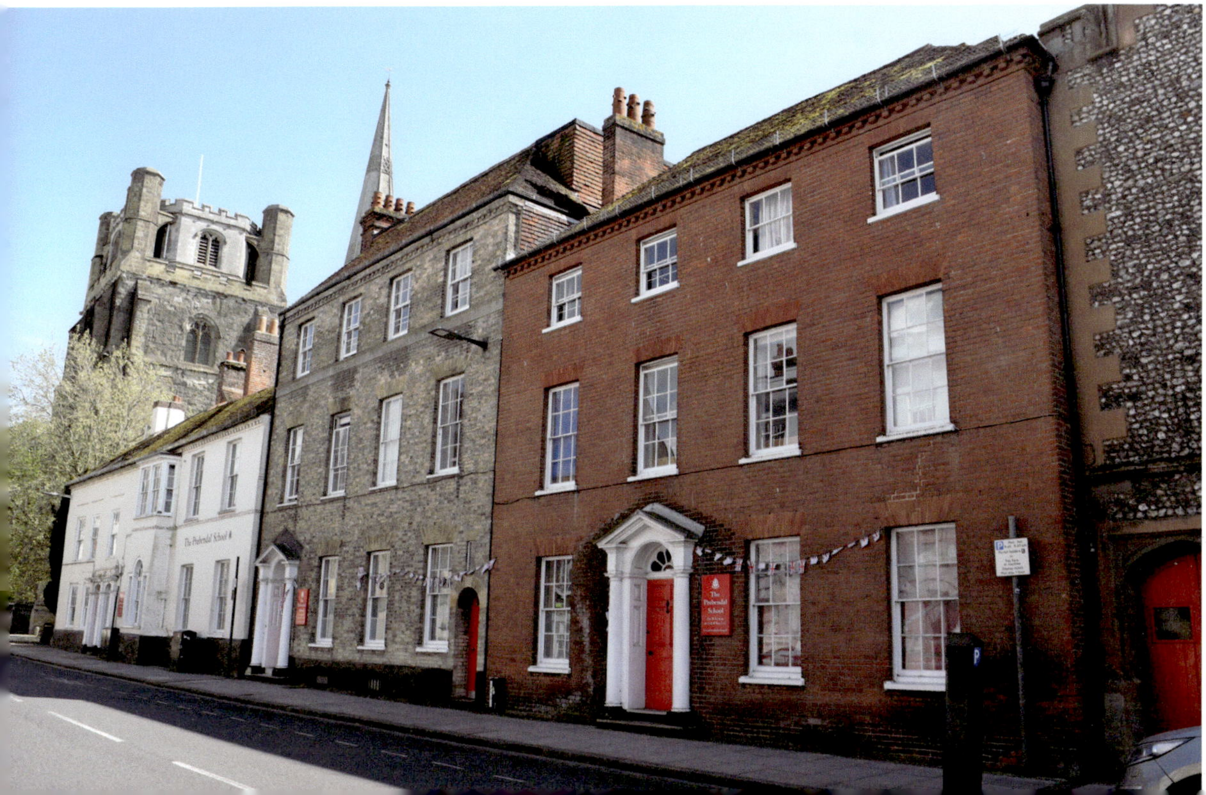

prep school. It later went on to be one of the first co-educational schools in the UK, when girls were admitted for the first time in 1972.

Among the notable alumni are Archbishop William Juxon (chaplain to Charles I, and present his execution in 1649), William Cawley (one of the signatories of the king's death warrant), and John Seldon (the first lawyer appointed at the king's trial). Oliver Whitby, who went on to found another of the city's famous schools, was also a pupil.

9. St Andrew-in-the-Oxmarket Church (c. 1248)

Dating to the reign of Henry III, the former church now houses a popular art gallery in the heart of the city centre.

Originally surrounded by a small churchyard and tucked away from the major thoroughfares, St Andrew's became notorious in the Tudor era for being the scene of frequent fistfights and other unbecoming behaviour. Aside from this violent reputation, this part of the city also suffered the worst in the several plagues that hit in the late sixteenth and early seventeenth centuries between 1563 and 1608.

Oxmarket Contemporary.

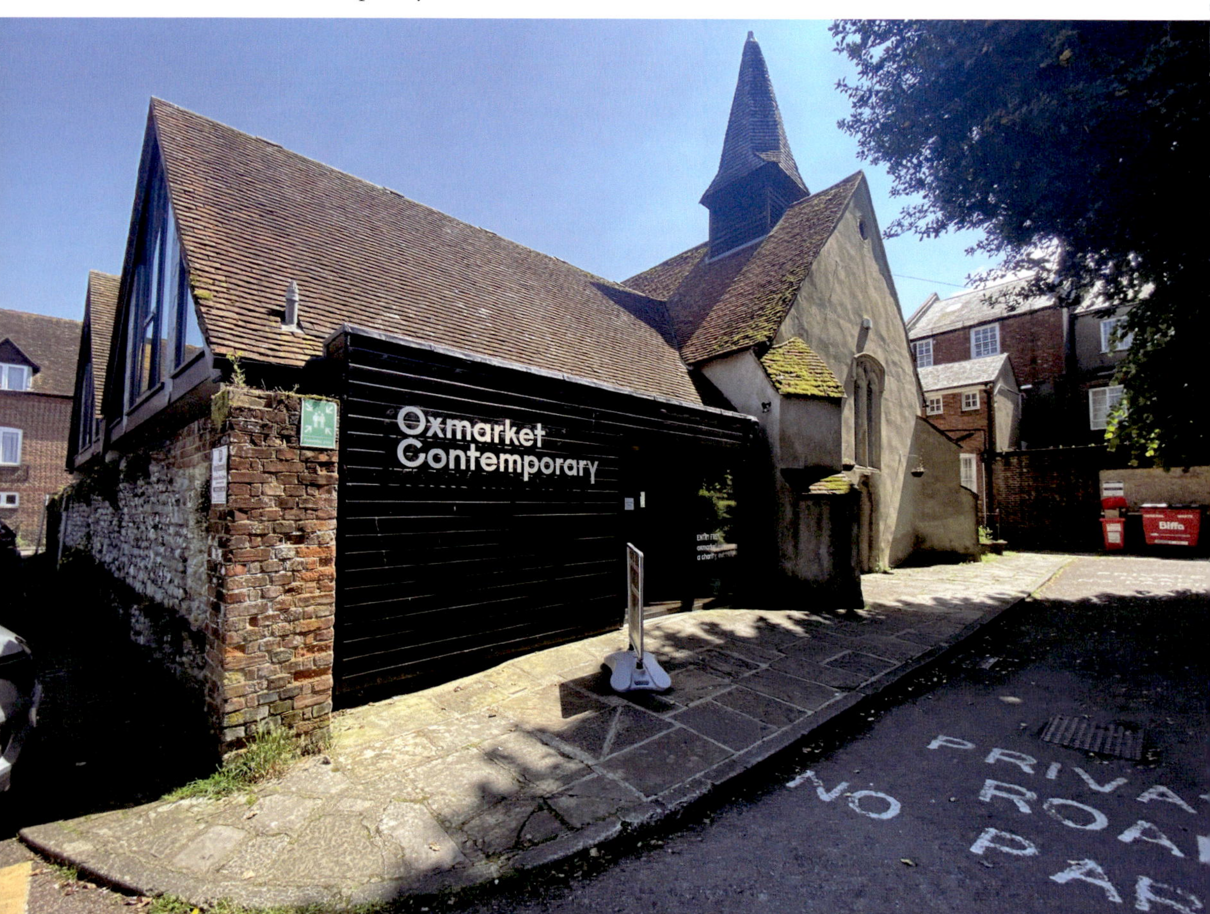

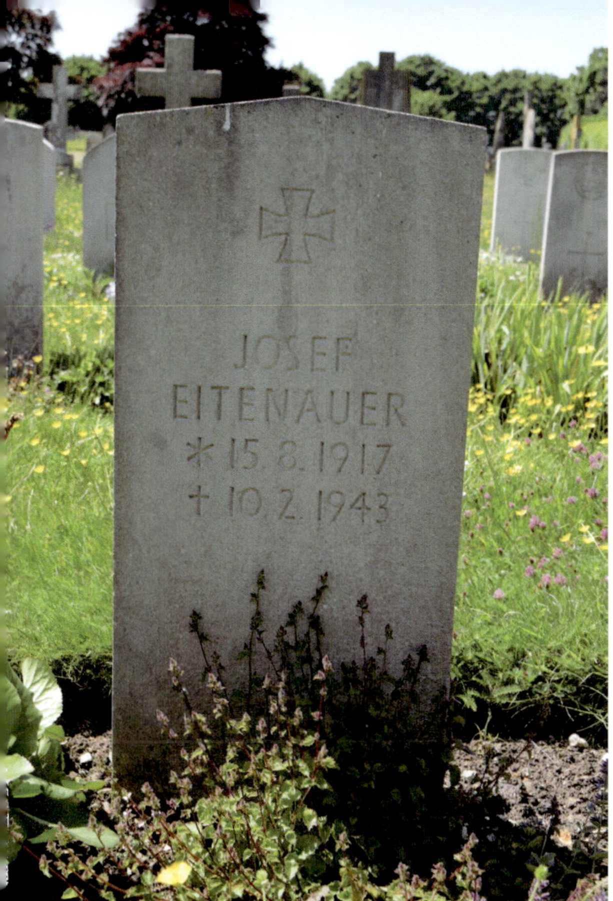
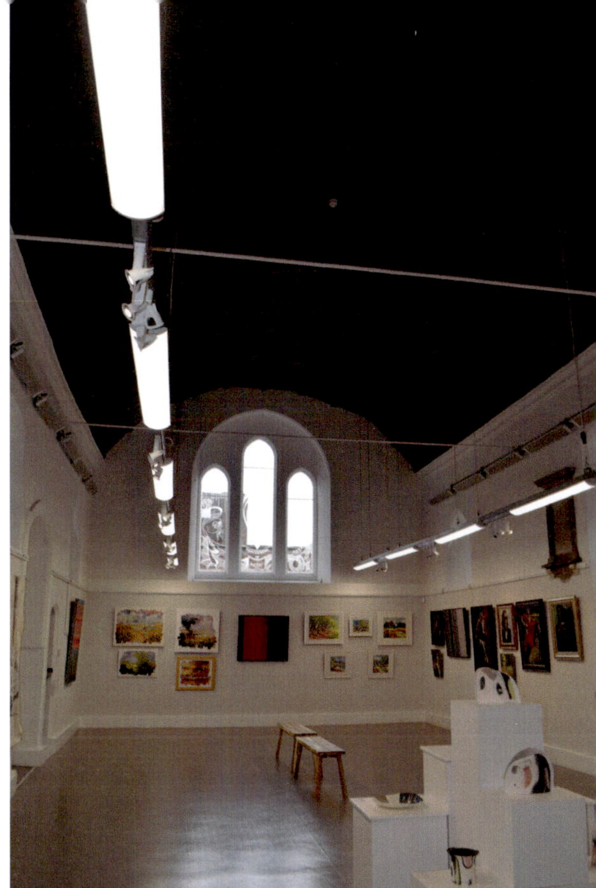

Above left: Grave of Josef Eitenauer, Portfield Cemetery.

Above right: Interior of the former church.

The decline of the church began at around 15.30 on 10 February 1943, when one of four high-explosive bombs dropped by a single Dornier Do217-E4 fell in the garden of St Mary's Hospital (now Little London car park). In total, this short raid killed eighteen people and injured another thirty-five, with 241 buildings destroyed or damaged, including St Andrew's Church, which suffered badly from the blast and was never reopened. The four-man crew of the bomber also did not survive the raid, being shot down soon afterwards by anti-aircraft fire near Tangmere; Unteroffizier Josef Eitenauer, the radio operator and gunner, is buried in Chichester Portfield Cemetery.

As a result of the damage, the church was deconsecrated in the 1950s and sat dormant for a number of years. The Archdeacon of Chichester proposed turning the building into an art gallery in the 1960s, but it took another decade before restoration works commenced in 1971, becoming the Chichester Centre of Arts once it reopened in 1976.

This volunteer-run institute has been a hub for artists, designers and craftspeople since, undergoing several rebrands variously as the Oxmarket Centre of Arts in 2001, then the Oxmarket Gallery and now Oxmarket Contemporary.

Extended in 1989, a number of changes have taken place, including the paving over of the churchyard to form a car park and the removal of the memorial to John Cawley (buried in the church in 1621) to Chichester Cathedral.

10. Guildhall (1282)

Despite being called the Guildhall, it actually formed the chapel of the Greyfriars' friary and had nothing to do with the Merchant's Guild.

Dissolved in 1538, the land and buildings were handed to the mayor and have been in municipal hands since. The other buildings and grounds were leased out until sold to Admiral Frankland in 1790, who demolished the friary buildings (except the Guildhall) for a new house on the site.

During the early months of the Civil War in 1642, a public meeting in the Guildhall on 15 November attempted to bring both sides together. However, the Royalists used this as a ruse and assembled a large force outside. As the meeting concluded the men inside were met by the sight of drawn swords and the Northgate cannon under Royalist control. Unarmed and unable to resist, the other guns around the city fell to the Royalist coup.

The Guildhall also became the city's law courts, undergoing a number of alterations to accommodate this until the 1850s. These included a lock-up and

Guildhall north elevation.

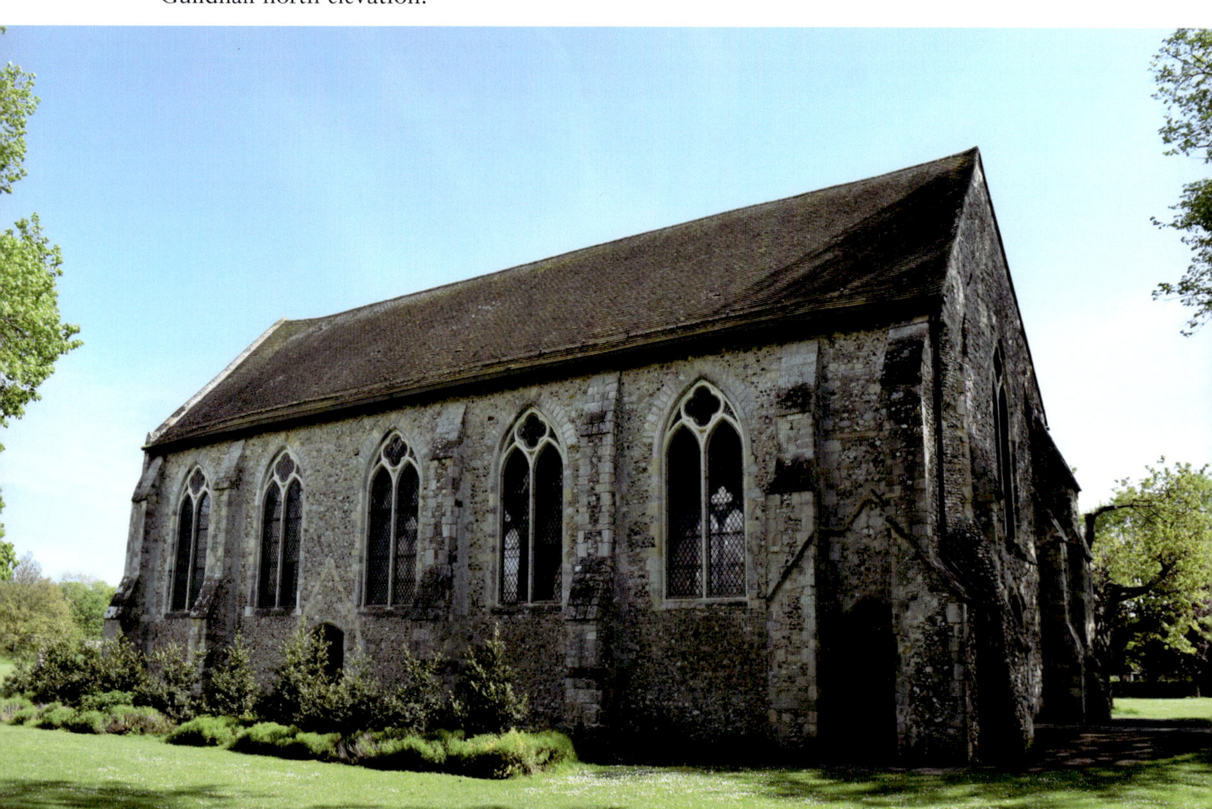

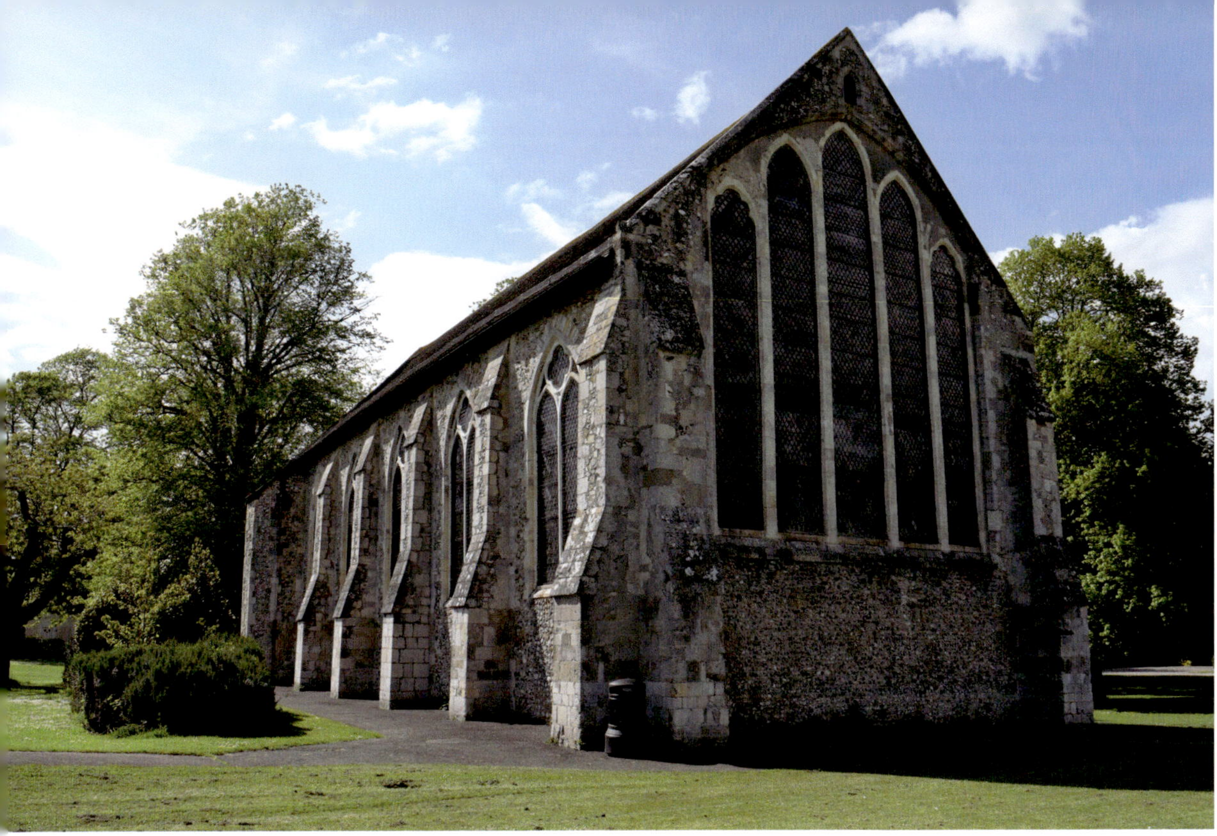

Above: East window.

Below: Guildhall courts, 1784. (*Sussex Archaeological Collections* Vol. 51)

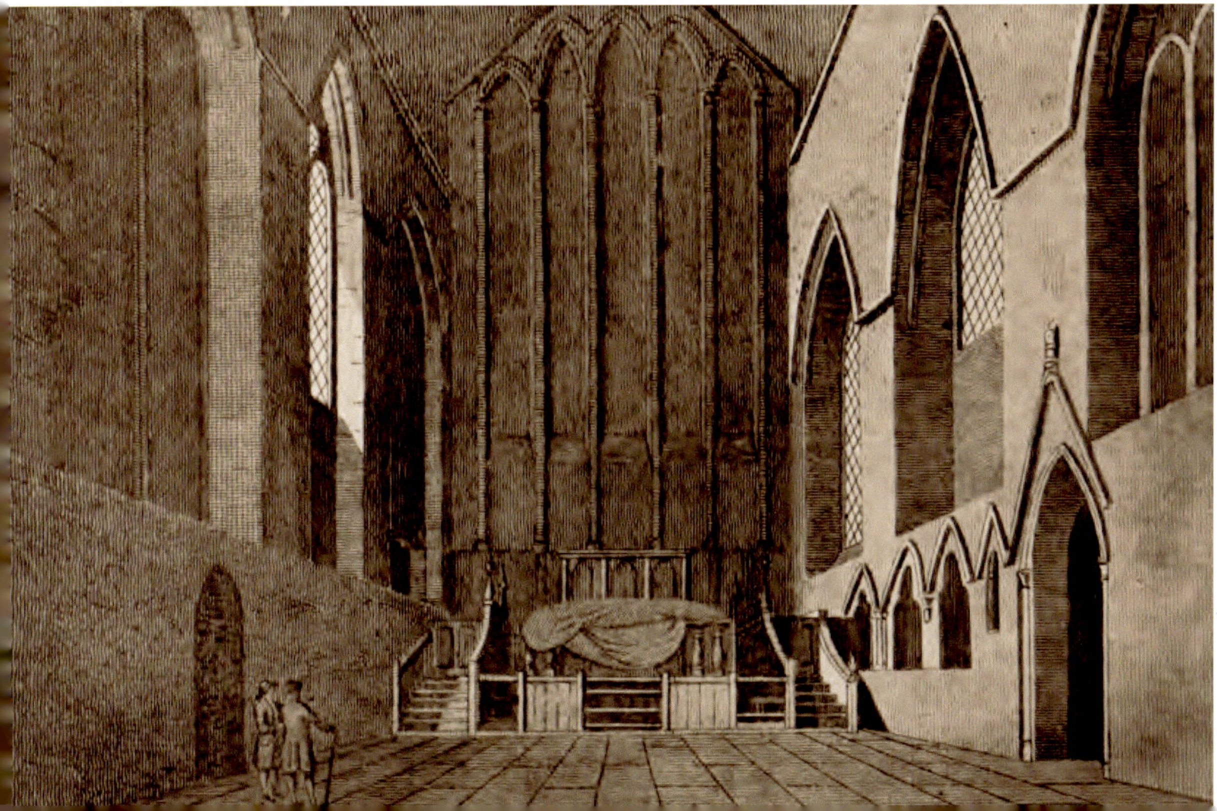

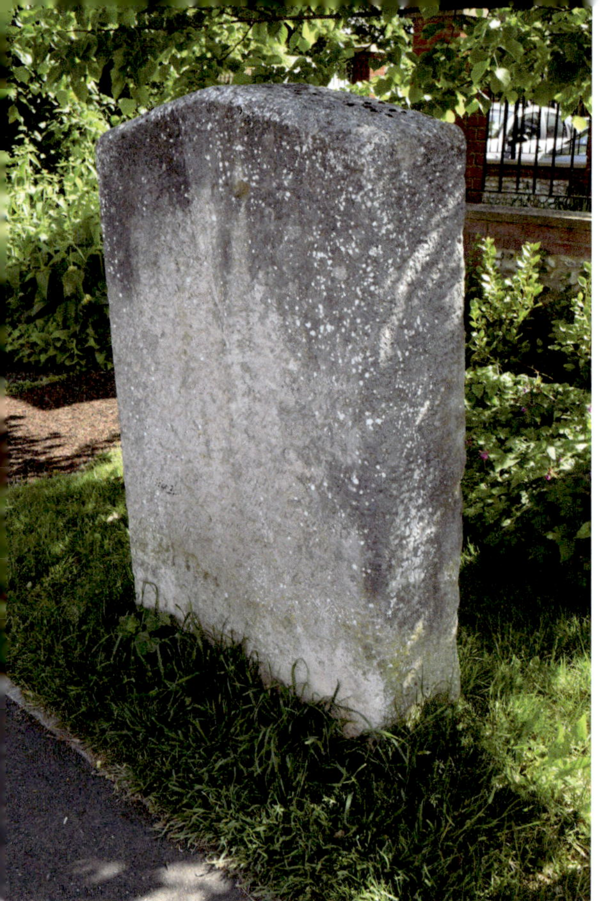

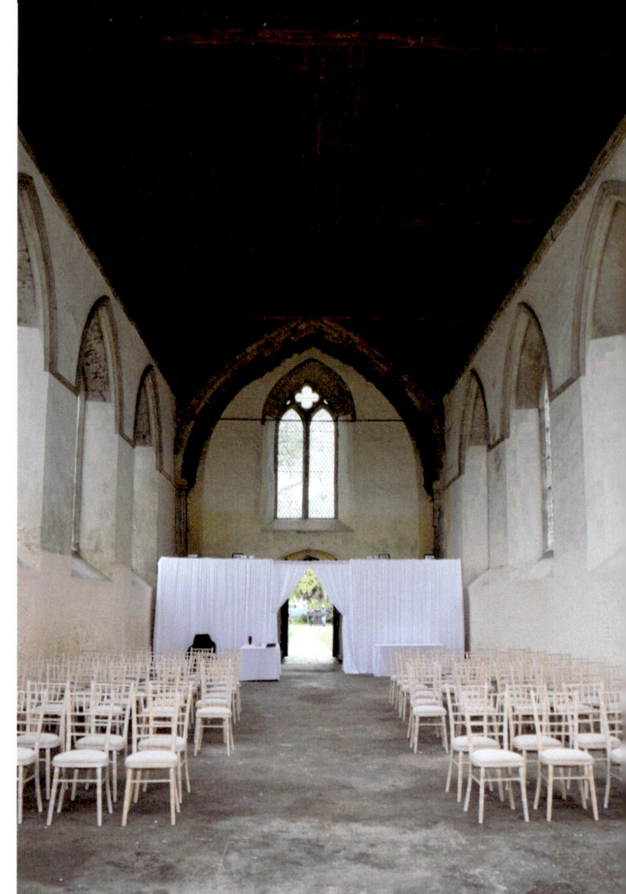

Above left: Smugglers' Stone.

Above right: Guildhall interior.

a jury room added onto the south side and punching a new entrance through the tomb niche.

Although Chichester did not become a favoured place for trials, a number of significant cases were brought before its courts, including that of the two Catholic martyrs, Ralph Crockett and Edward James, in 1588. Brought before the justices on 30 September, along with John Oven and Francis Edwardes, all four priests were condemned to death by hanging, drawing, and quartering, and taken to the place of execution on Broyle Heath the next morning. Here, Oven took the Oath of Supremacy (swearing allegiance to the monarch as the supreme head of the Church) and granted a reprieve. Crockett declined to renounce his faith and was executed, followed by James. Having witnessed the gory spectacle, Edwardes also opted to take the Oath and was spared. Crockett and James were later beatified by Pope Pius VI in 1929, but what became of the other two priests is not known.

A couple of centuries later, seven members of the Hawkhurst Gang of smugglers found themselves in the dock in January 1749. The seven men had tortured and murdered two men, and were hanged together on Broyle Heath on the afternoon of 19 January. Their bodies were later cut down and hanged in gibbets throughout the county, including two at the execution site. A stone marks the location.

Perhaps the most famous person to appear in the dock at the Guildhall was William Blake, summoned on the charge of sedition and assault of a soldier. The trial in January 1804 quickly acquitted him of any wrongdoing.

The courts ceased in the 1850s, when the building became a drill hall and armoury for the Sussex Rifle Volunteers, as well as for use in elections until 1888. By 1908 this grand building had become no more than a storage shed for sports equipment. In 1947 it became the first location of Chichester Museum, and in more recent years, having undergone major repairs between 2007 and 2009, it gained a licence to host civil ceremonies in 2015, witnessing its first ever marriage that same year.

Today, the Guildhall is principally used as a wedding venue, but is open to the public on select days throughout the year.

11. St Mary's Hospital (c. 1290)

The original hospital, founded between 1158 and 1170, stood close to the Market Cross. In 1253 it moved to the present site in St Martin's Square after that site was vacated by the Greyfriars.

The existing buildings were evidently demolished to make way for the new hospital. As a religious establishment the hospital ran like a monastery, with the healthcare provided by brothers and sisters bound by an oath of poverty, chastity and obedience, living together, eating in silence, and taking part in regular daily services.

Beds were arranged along the two side walls and provided a free bed for the night for the sick and poor in need of shelter. In 1528, Dean William Fleshmonger reorganised the hospital into an almshouse to provide for five poor and infirm residents of the city, and no longer provided respite for travellers.

Following the Civil War, a survey in 1656 found financial irregularities. The church leadership was removed and prominent men of the city were appointed in their place, as well as increasing the number of residents to ten. Although appearing to benefit the residents, this system ended with the Restoration in 1660, with the dean and chapter of the cathedral once more becoming the trustees.

Around this time, small apartments divided up the previously open-plan building, with the four chimneys added in 1680 to supply heating. In 1905, the four cottages in St Martin's Square that now form part of the property were purchased and adapted into almshouses for men. Later, women and married couples were admitted, and in the post-war years, kitchens and bathrooms were provided for the residents.

The hospital was severely damaged by the same bomb blast that also damaged St Andrew's Church in 1943. The roof of the hospital lost most of its tiles, as well

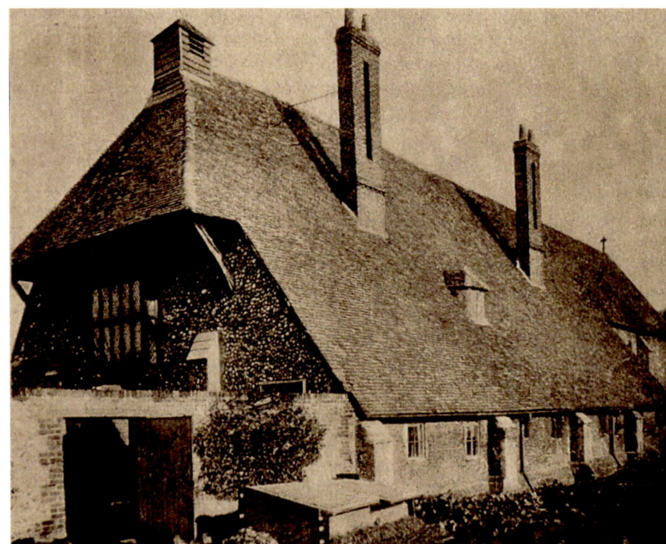

Left: St Mary's Hospital, *c*. 1894. (*An Old English Hospital*, p. 1)

Below: Hospital interior. (*An Old English Hospital*, p. 7)

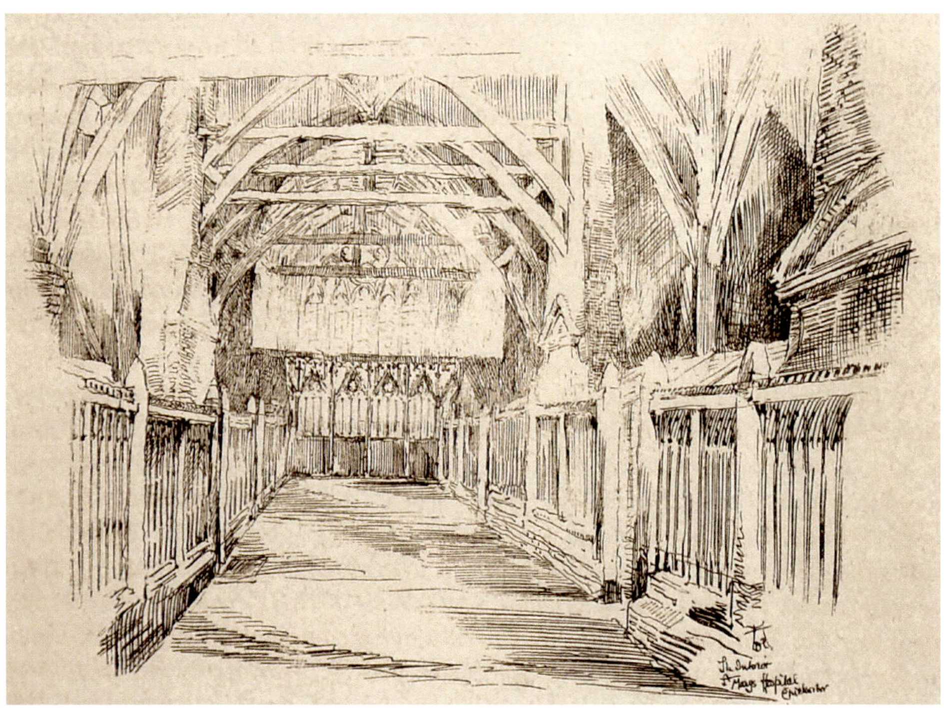

as distorting the wooden structure of the building. The great east window was destroyed, and a hostel for elderly residents was demolished. Luckily, this had been empty at the time, but two members of staff and two residents of the main building received slight injuries. The east window was repaired in 1950 by Christopher Webb, who was also responsible for many of the windows in the cathedral's nave.

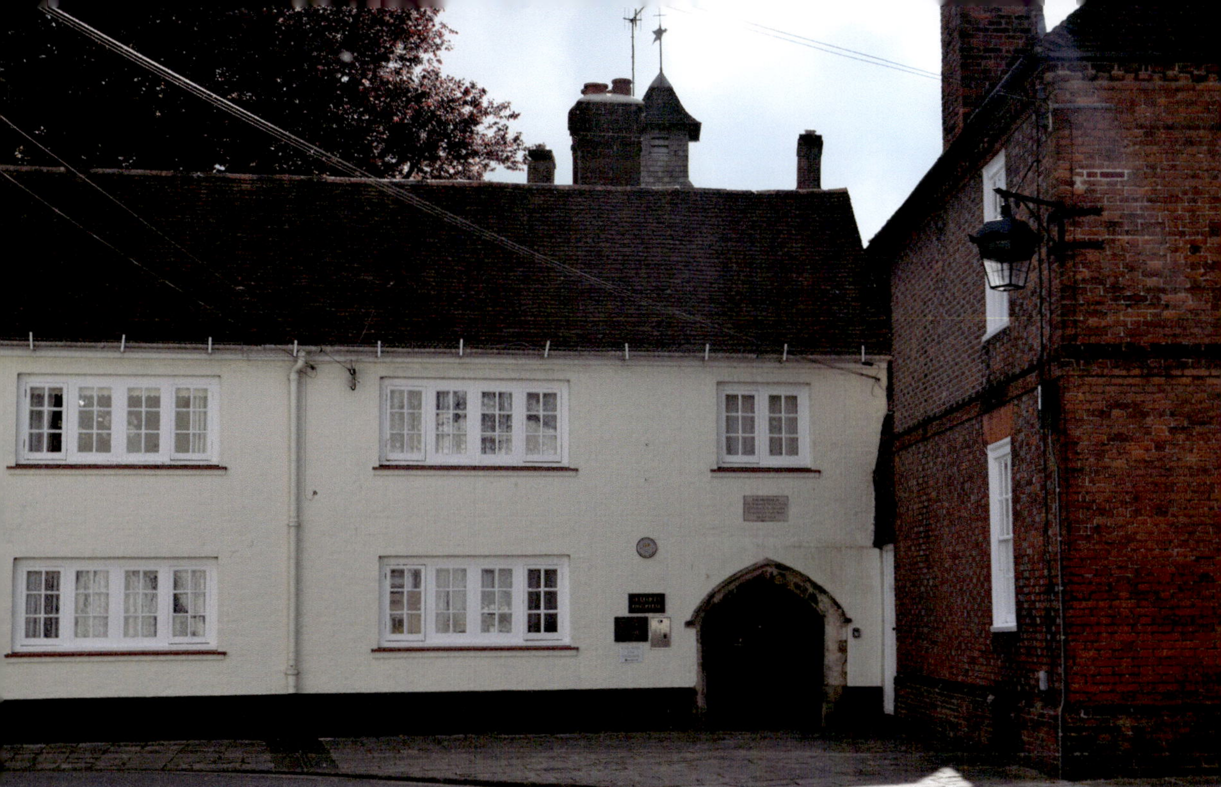

Main entrance, St Martin's Square.

In early 2018, independent trustees were appointed to sit alongside those of the cathedral, and in January 2021 merged with Martha Dear's charity, acquiring a number of other buildings in the city.

The hospital is a unique survivor, with the only known similar building being a smaller example in the German city of Lubeck.

The hospital is closed to the public but offers monthly tours by prior arrangement.

12. Bell Tower (c. 1400)

Believed to be the work of William Wynford, who also designed the cathedral cloisters, this campanile built of large sandstone blocks is unique as the sole surviving medieval cathedral bell tower in England. Formerly known as Ryman's Tower, this name is derived from the legend that the stones used in the tower's construction came from William Ryman of Appledram, who had intended to build a castle but was prevented from doing so by Edward II's refusal to grant him a licence. This is unlikely since it would predate the tower by around a century.

Evidence of the construction is still visible in the many 'putlog' holes in the walls of the lower tier of the tower, formed by the insertion of wooden scaffolding beams as the stones were laid. It was built to receive the cathedral's bells that

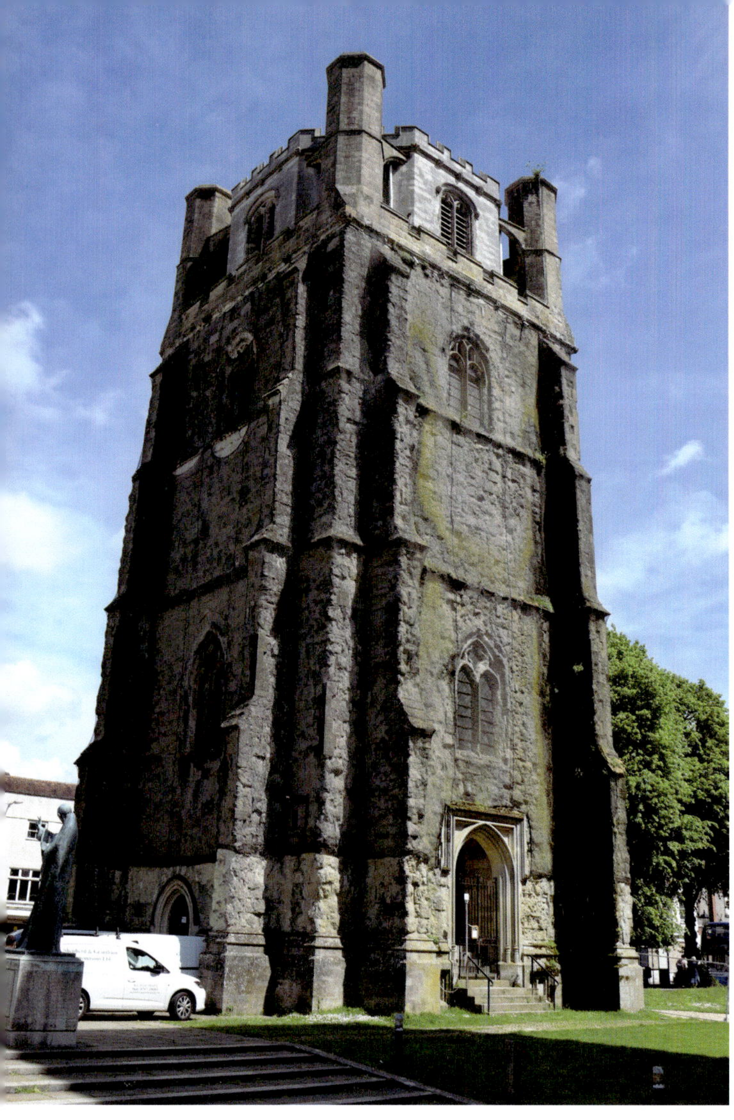

The bell tower.

originally hung in the central tower, with further bells added in later centuries; today it holds eight bells dated between 1583 and 1729.

The tower was restored between 1902 and 1908 with the exterior stonework chemically treated to help reduce weathering, and with the replacement (either wholly or in part) of the four pinnacles. Modern gargoyles were also added around the top.

During the Second World War, the tower provided an observation post for the several anti-aircraft gun sites in the city. Whether or not the cathedral authorities were happy with their tower being used in such a way is not known, but they did succeed in prohibiting the soldiers from bringing their weapons into the building.

This building is still in regular use by the cathedral's bell ringers. It is, however, in urgent need of repair, having been added to the Heritage at Risk Register in 2016 due to the degrading external stonework and cracks in the buttresses caused by structural movement.

13. Vicars Close (1475)

Beginning in 1251, the practice of granting prebends to non-resident canons became increasingly popular, requiring the appointing of additional vicars to act as the canons' representatives in conducting services, eventually leading to the building of twenty residential units in Vicars Close off Canon Lane, forming a square bounded by two facing rows of lodgings on the east and west sides (the former being the buildings on South Street) and the Vicar's Hall to the north.

Until 1831, the close was entirely shut off to the outside world and only accessible via the Chain Gate, built into an end wall just north of Canon Gate. In 1825 the buildings that backed onto South Street were 'turned around' internally, with new frontages onto the street, and converted into shops. The whole area was then opened up in 1831 by the removal of the Chain Gate and the erection of a large wall down the centre of the former gardens to split the remaining buildings on the west from the new shops on the east. Later alterations knocked through the earlier lodgings to make larger accommodation, and now form the four houses seen today.

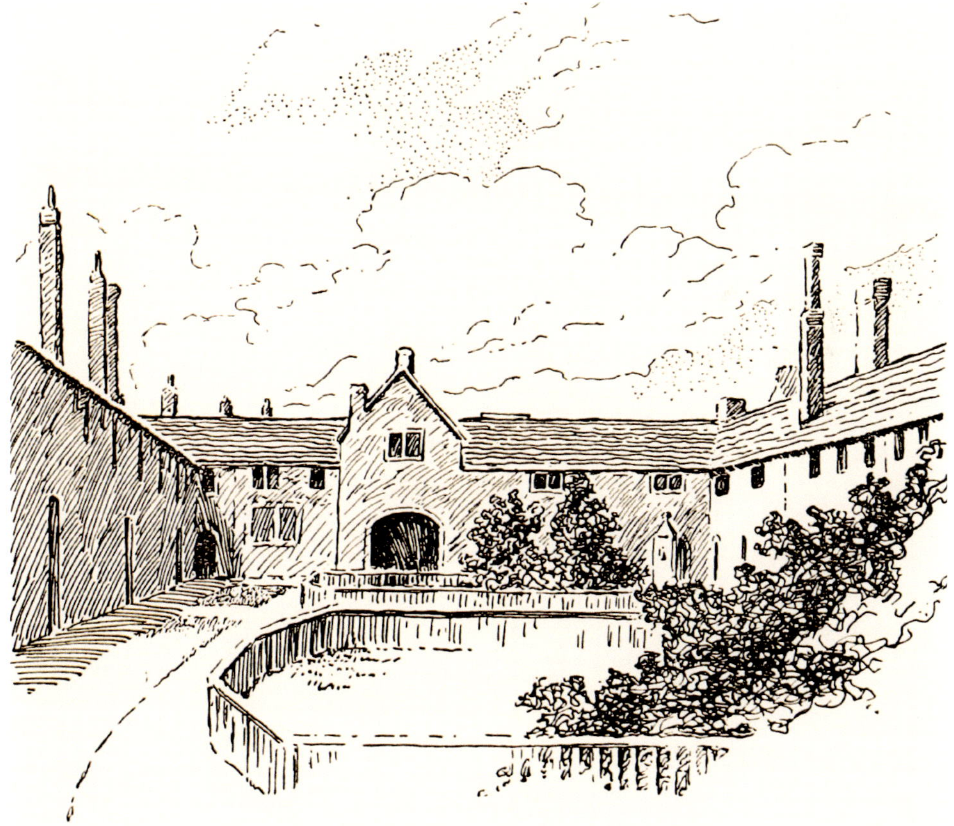

Original layout of Vicars Close. (*Sussex Archaeological Collections* Vol. 56)

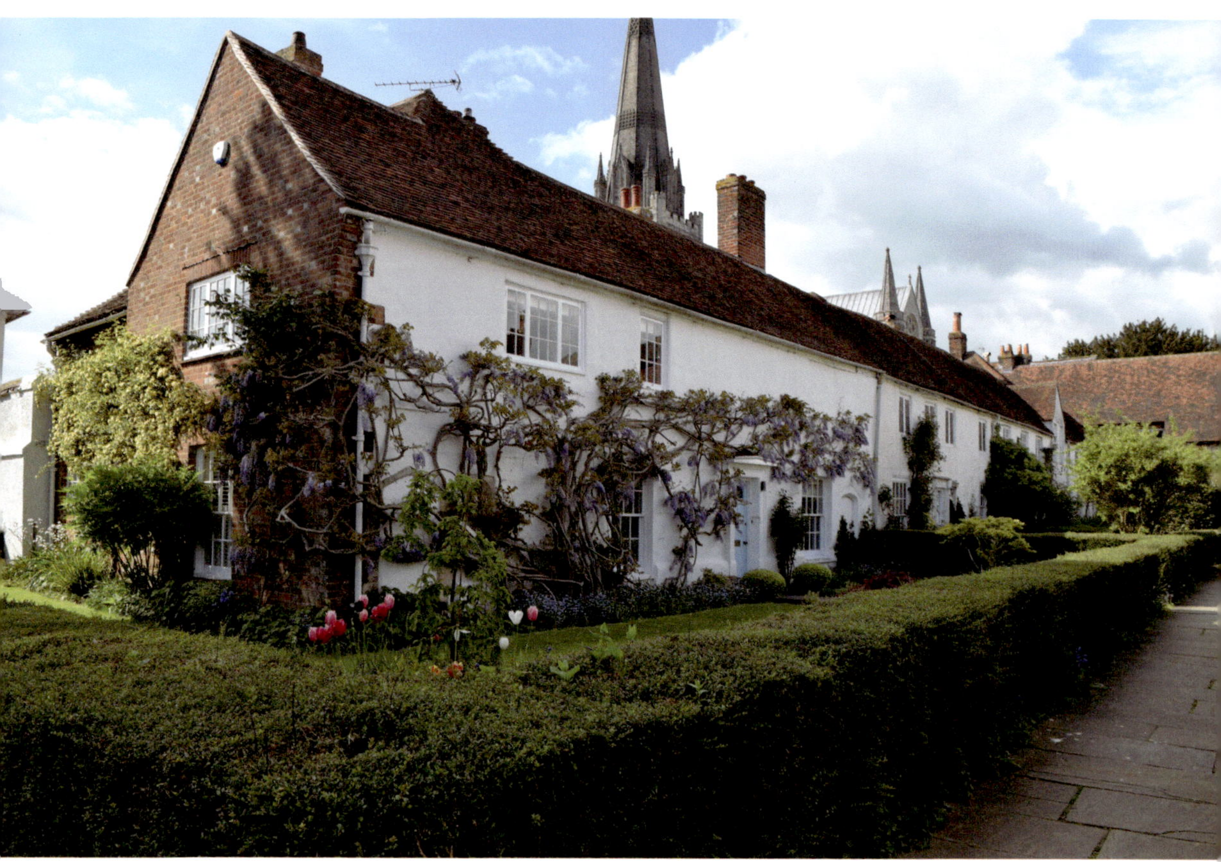

Vicars Close.

Vicars Close was, however, also the scene of horrific violence in 1555. Just as two Catholics were to be martyred over three decades later, two Protestant martyrs gave their lives for their faith in Chichester. Upon the accession to the throne of Queen Mary in 1553, Roman Catholicism again became the state religion, outlawing English language editions of the Bible.

Being present at a private sermon read from such a version in Brighton, Thomas Iveson – a carpenter from Godstone – found himself fighting for his life. Arrested with nine other men and taken to London for trial before Bishop Edmund Bonner on charges of heresy, he refused to denounce his faith and instead outlined the issues he had with the Catholic interpretation of the faith. This led to a guilty verdict, and he was sent down to Chichester and burned at the stake in Vicars Close on 24 July 1555.

The second person martyred here was Richard Hook, a disabled resident of Alfriston. The details of his alleged crime and trial are unknown, but he was tried by the Bishop of Chichester, George Day, and burned at the stake in the same spot three months after Iveson.

Bishop Day was an avowed Catholic and had been imprisoned for his faith in 1550, before being released by Queen Mary and having his bishopric restored. Among his first acts was to preside at the queen's coronation and was among the most ardent of persecutors of Protestants, presiding over the executions of both Iveson and Hook, but was also known to have condemned others to the same fate.

14. Canon Gate (1484)

Somewhat of a mystery, the origin of Canon Gate is disputed as either being contemporary to Richard III or, due to the presence of the arms of Archdeacon Edward More on one of the carvings, no earlier than the sixteenth century, though this could, of course, be a later addition to the building.

Aside from guarding the entrance to Canon Lane, the gatehouse's purpose was as the home of the Custos Palatii, or Keeper of the Palace, who's salary was paid out of the Broyle Estate.

Later, it became home of the Pye Poudre (or Pie Powder) Court in connection with the annual Sloe Fair. This was a special tribunal court presided over by the mayor and bailiffs on the occasion of the fair, and had unlimited jurisdiction over any and all civil and criminal actions taking place at the fair. The presence of the court here also meant that the official proclamation for the opening of the fair was given under the gate by the bishop's steward.

Canon Gate, South Street.

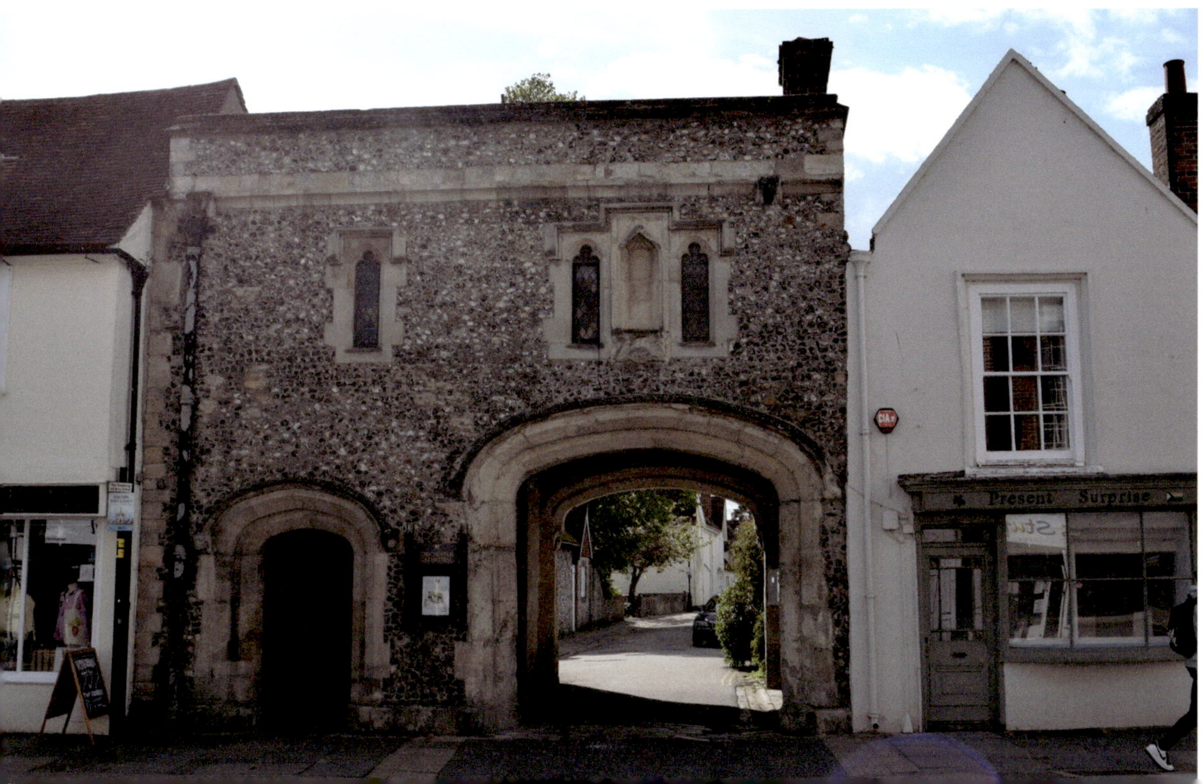

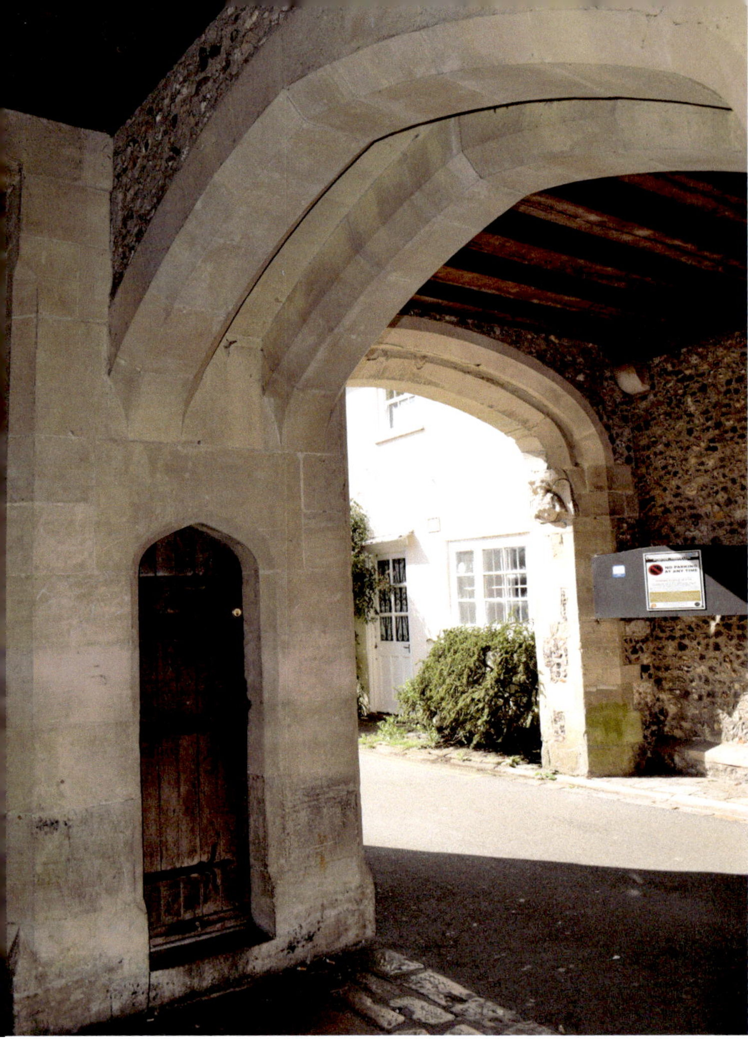

Entrance to the upper floor.

Canon Gate later fell into disrepair and, for a time in the 1820s, was used as a stable. It was later restored by Mr. Ewan Christian in 1894, who reconstructed the upper storey. The former chamber of the Pye Pouder Court has since been converted into a luxury two-bedroom holiday apartment.

15. Market Cross (1501)

The taxes and levies on medieval market traders presented a barrier to the poorest. Seeing a need to relieve this burden, Bishop Edward Story purchased the land and commissioned the Market Cross to be erected to give residents somewhere to trade free of any tolls or duties in perpetuity.

Described variously as a 'poem in stone' or a 'jewel in stone,' the cross is ornately decorated with angels, coats of arms, grotesques and foliage. Above the centre of each arch is a niche that once contained effigies of various bishops of Chichester until they were destroyed by Parliamentarian soldiers in 1642.

The east-facing niche was remodelled upon the Restoration of the Monarchy to receive a bronze bust of Charles I, cast by the famed French sculptor Hubert Le Suer. The original sculpture was removed in the 1970s to Pallant House and latterly at the Tate Britain. In 2019 it returned to Chichester and is now on display in The Novium. A fibreglass replica was installed at the Market Cross in 1978.

The Parliamentarians also removed the pinnacle atop the Market Cross, which found its way to a small plot of grass in Barnham, with a plaque to commemorate the Falklands War of 1982.

The next major change came in 1724 with the addition of a belfry and clock. Considered unsightly, the clock was removed twenty-two years later, when the Duke of Richmond paid for a complete restoration of the cross.

The cross ceased to serve its purpose in 1808, when the Butter Market was built in North Street. The City Council proposed to demolish the cross, but it was instead fenced off by metal railings to prevent traders from using it to evade the tolls charged at the Butter Market. The railings were removed, and the arches opened up again in 1872.

The present clock was installed in 1904, but the structure was badly defaced during a 'restoration' in 1928, which obscured many of the carvings and required restorative repairs in the 1950s and again in the late 1970s.

Below left: Bust of Charles I, facing East Street.

Below right: The Market Cross.

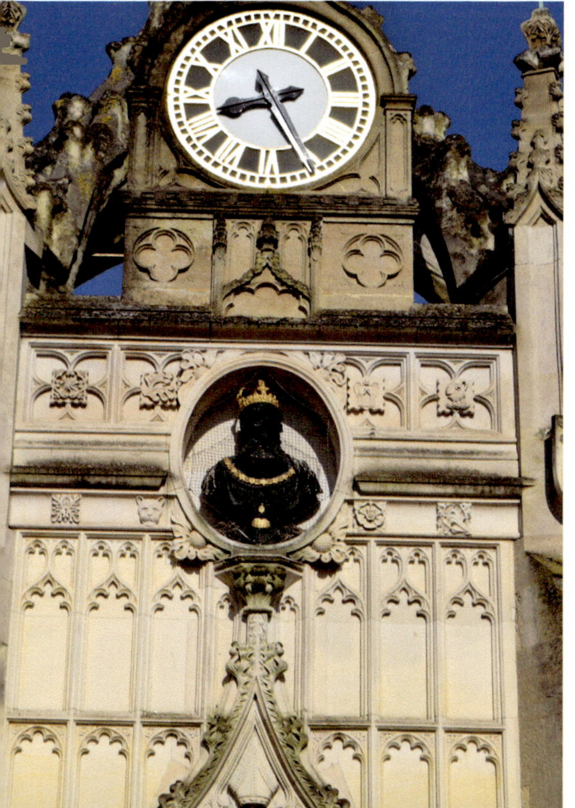

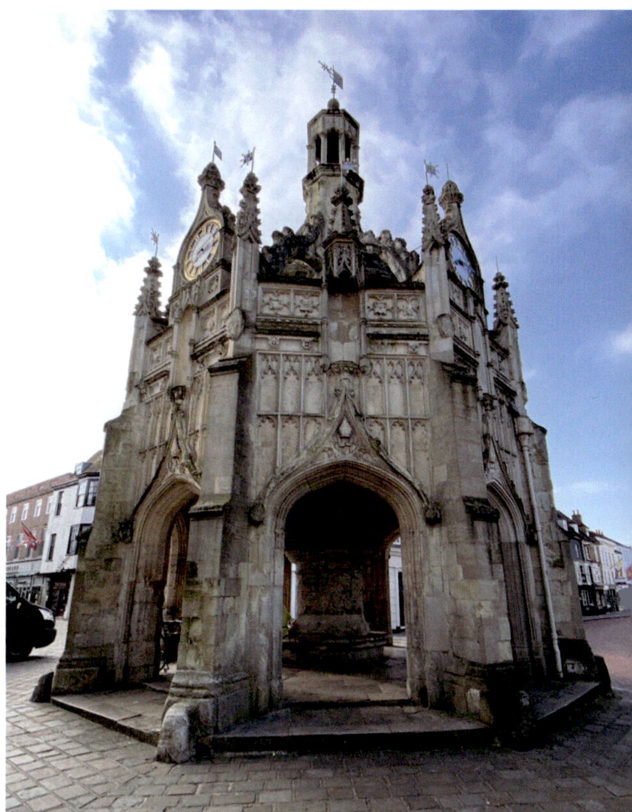

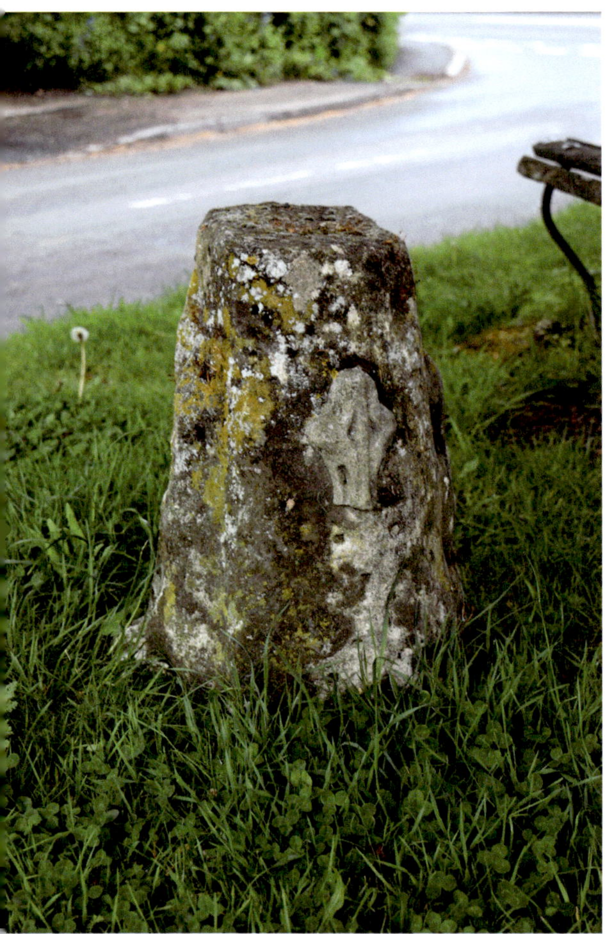

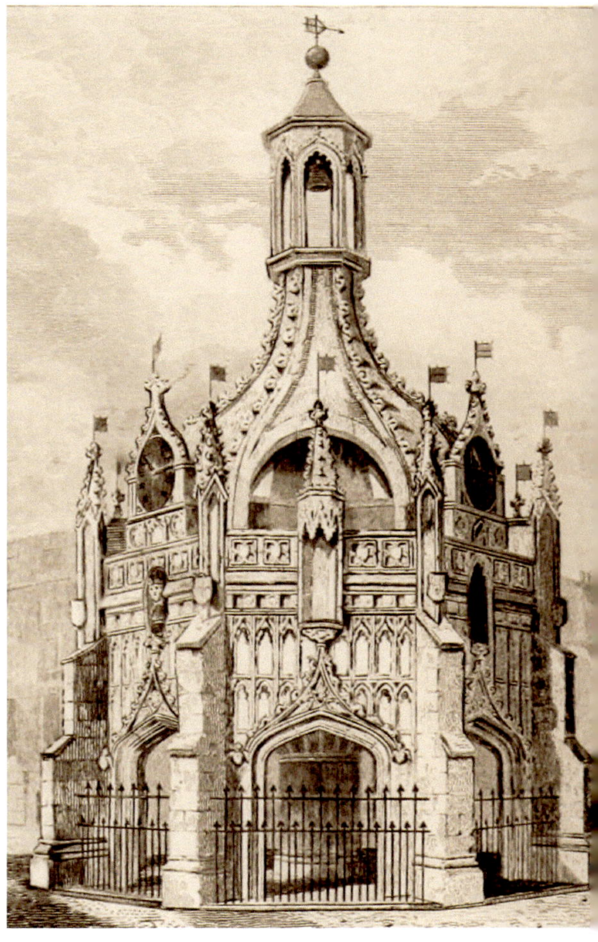

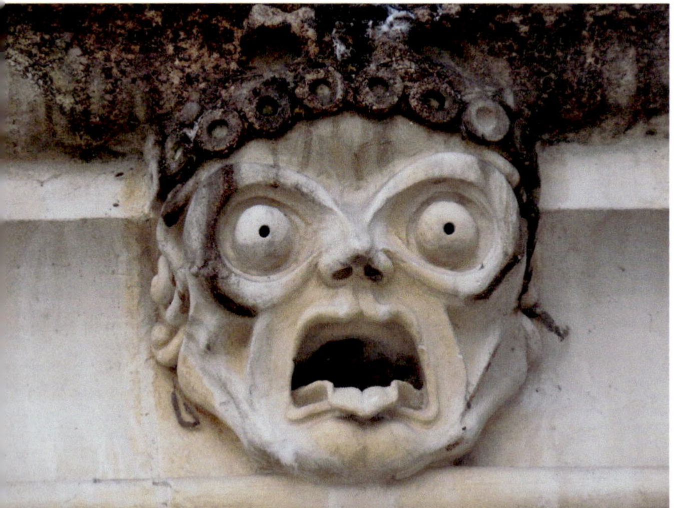

Above left: Former pinnacle at Barnham.

Above right: Market Cross in 1831; note the railings. (*The Chichester Guide*)

Left: One of the numerous carvings on the Market Cross.

Aside from being a place to trade, the Market Cross has long been the centre of many events and festivities, especially on New Year's Eve when it used to be the tradition for a crowd to march around it three times, led by the town band, singing 'Auld Land Syne' at the stroke of midnight. For many years, the town crier has also proclaimed news of importance from the cross. Interestingly, it also became one of the first places to host civil weddings in Chichester, when, for a few brief years during the Commonwealth, couples could choose to wed there rather than in church.

16. Cawley Almshouses (1625)

Before becoming a leading Puritan and later regicide of Charles I, William Cawley enjoyed a prosperous life as a brewer and provided an almshouse just outside the Northgate in 1625 to care for twelve elderly and disabled tradesmen of Chichester, also known as the Hospital of St Bartholomew.

The building played a key role in the Siege of Chichester in 1642, when, on 24 December, Sir William Waller ordered his cannon up to the almshouses from

Cawley Almshouses.

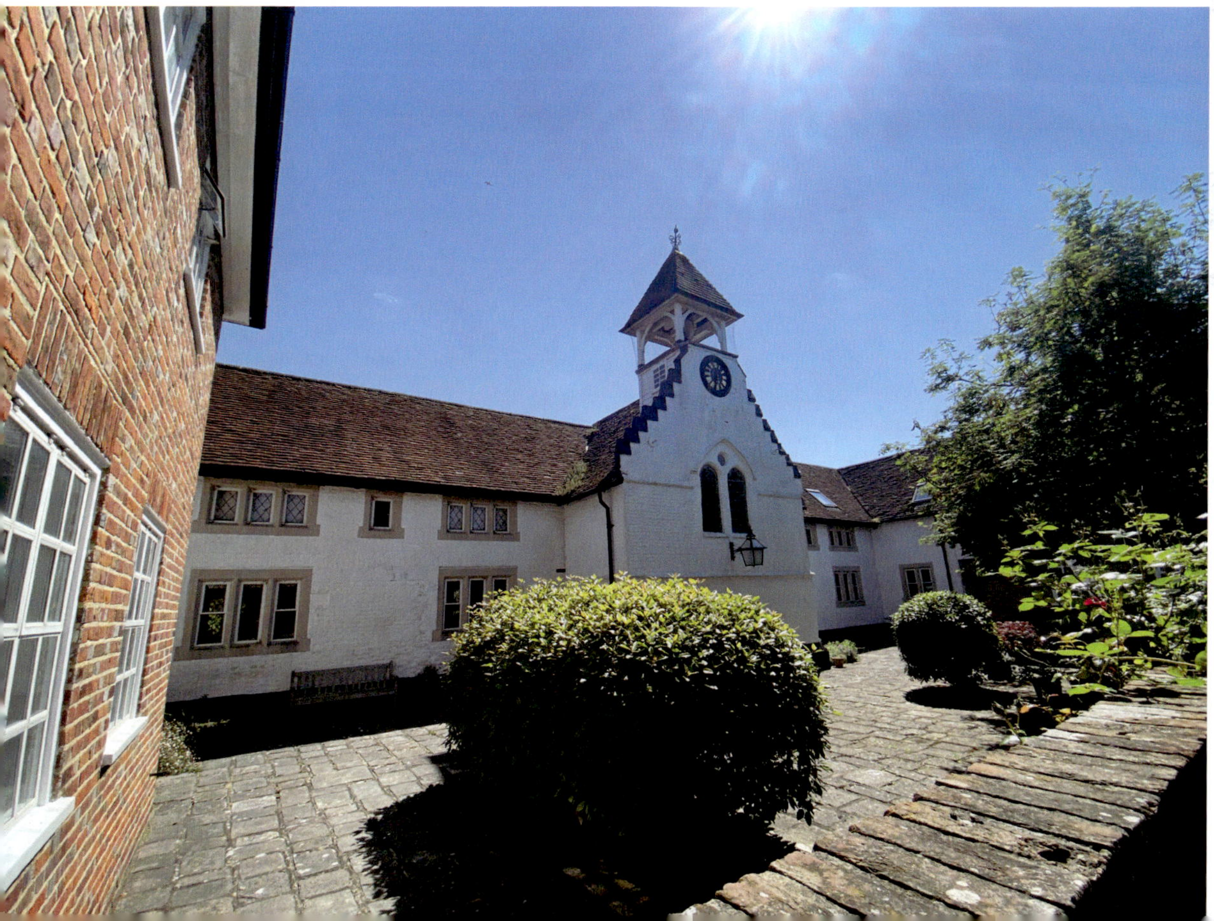

where they could fire directly through the North Gate and into the city centre. On the final day of the siege the Royalists agreed to parley for surrender, and six offered themselves as hostages to guarantee the safety of six Parliamentarian officers entering the city to negotiate. The six men were held captive in Cawley Almshouses for three hours until the negotiations concluded, and the city handed over to Waller.

In 1681, the almshouses were converted into the city's workhouse, but this was not made official until 1753. In this same year, new wings were added, the cellars and pantries paved over, the garden enclosed with a wall, and a room converted into a prison cell.

Further additions were made over the years to follow, and by its peak in 1875 it covered 1.2 acres. A font was introduced to the chapel in 1897, when the bishop granted a licence to conduct baptisms.

Today, the original 1625 building survives, but the later additions were all demolished in 2001.

A mystery surrounds a vault concealed beneath the chapel. This space was first discovered in 1816 when the chapel paving was being repaired. The workmen opened the vault and discovered the fragments of two wooden coffins (with bones) and a third made of lead, with the perfectly preserved skeleton inside, said to be the remains of William Cawley. Covered over and forgotten about, it was rediscovered in 1882, by which time Cawley's tomb in Switzerland had also been discovered. Having died in exile upon the Restoration in 1660, some believe that his son secretly removed Cawley's remains back to Chichester and had them sealed up inside the mysterious vault.

17. Edes House (1696)

The first 'modern' house in Chichester, built of brick and stone and a tiled roof, Edes House is named for the first owner, John Edes. John, a local maltster and nephew of one of the Residentiary Canons of Chichester died before the house was completed, and so his wife, Hannah, took over the project.

The house originally had an extensive garden at the rear, complete with coach houses, stables and various outhouses, but the name Edes House is very modern. It was known as Westgate House until 1905, then as West Street House until 1911. For most of the twentieth century, the name changed to Wren's House (1911–67) or Wren House (1967–93), in the false belief that Christopher Wren had designed the house. It finally became Edes House in 1993.

West Sussex County Council took possession of the building in 1916, using it as their main offices until County Hall was built in the rear garden in 1936. It then became the headquarters of the county library service until 1967, when the new library was built in Tower Street. Undergoing extensive renovation in 1967, it was then converted into both the county record office and diocesan record office until the new West Sussex Record Office was built in Orchard Street in 1989.

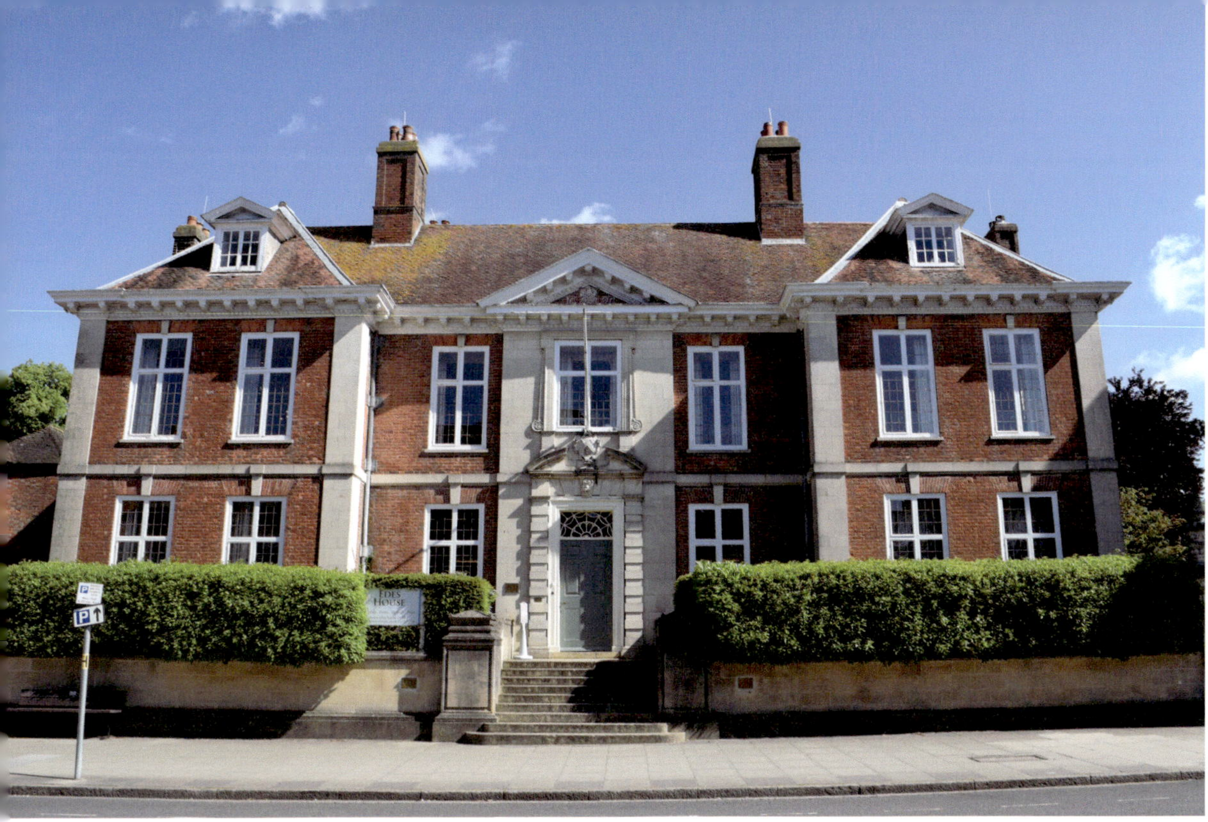

Above: Edes House.

Below: Rear elevation.

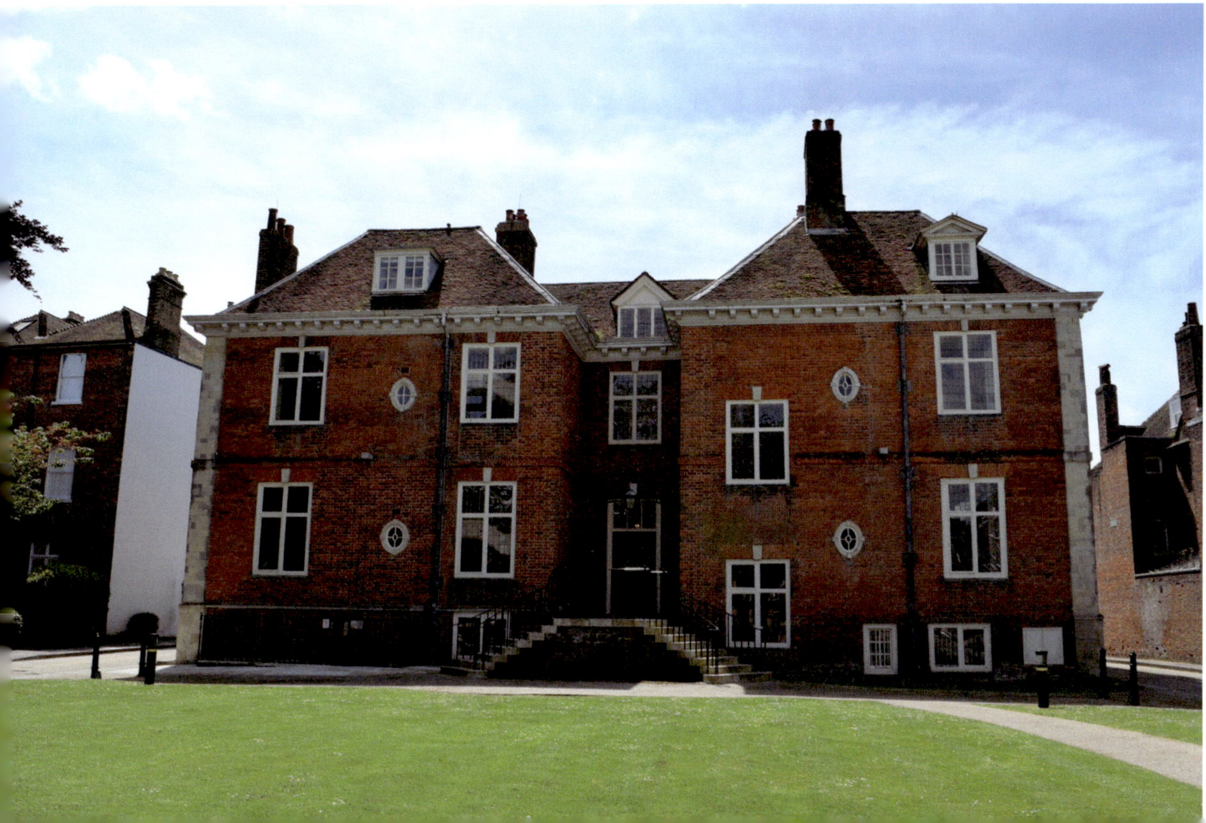

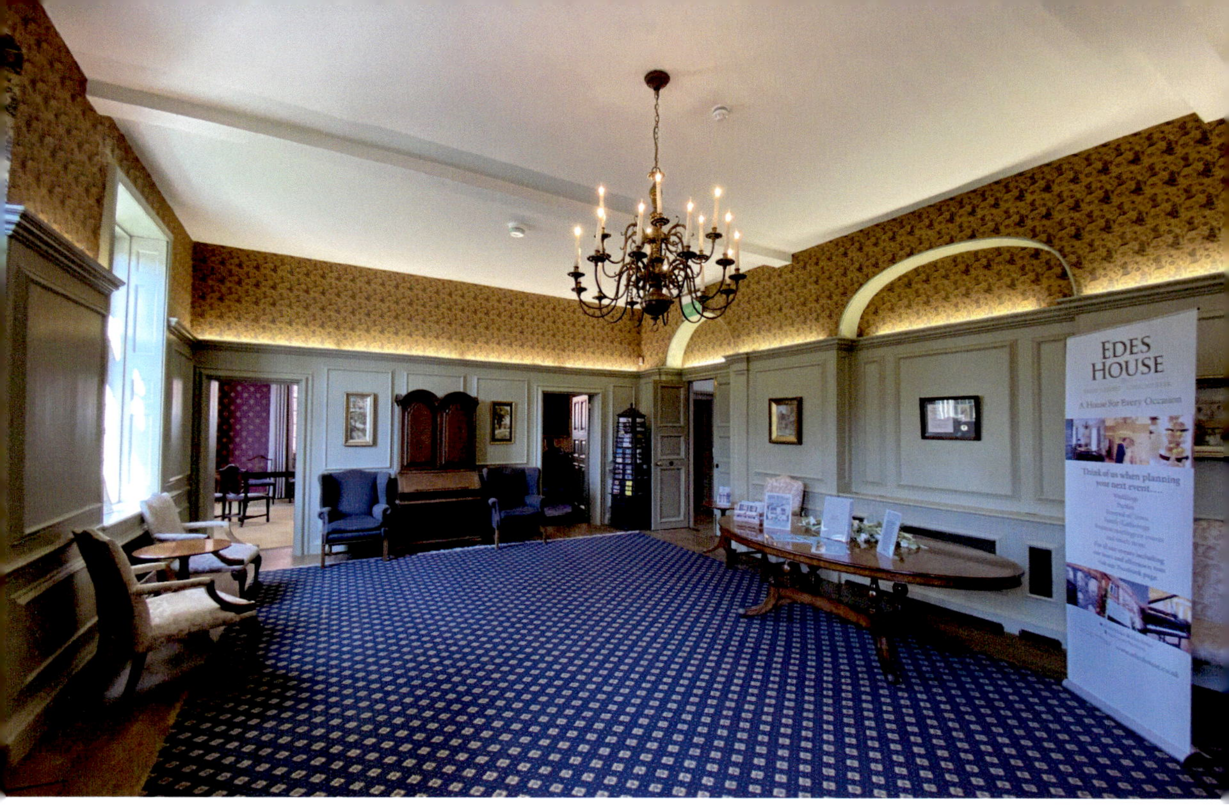

Above: Entrance foyer.

Below: The Warnham Room.

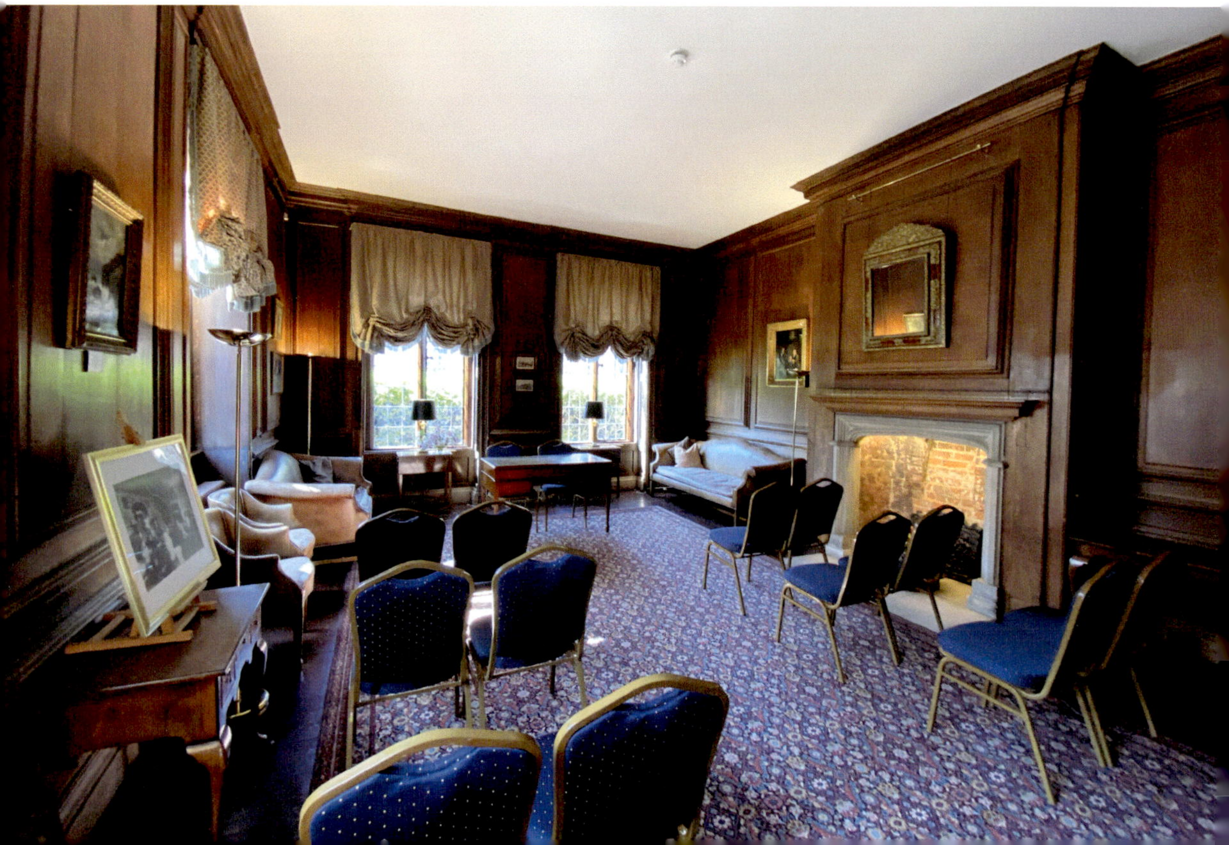

Further restorations returned the house to its Georgian character and domestic setting, although it continues to be a working council building hired out for corporate and community functions and for weddings. Tours take place at various times of the year by prior arrangement.

18. Pallant House (c. 1712)

Following the architectural trend of Edes House is Pallant House (known locally as Dodo House for the carved birds on the entrance gate), built in the early eighteenth century on the site of a former malthouse for Henry Packham and his wife, Elizabeth, who had inherited a sizeable fortune from her brother. The marriage did not last, and the couple divorced five years after the house was built. The lawsuit dragged on for several years, mostly regarding responsibility for the cost of the house, until it was finally settled in 1720. Once built, Henry received permission to demolish a wooden market cross that stood at the crossroads of the Pallants, just outside Henry's front door.

The house became council offices from 1919 until 1979, when Walter Hussey, the cathedral dean, offered to donate his entire private collection of modern art to the city on condition that it be displayed in Pallant House. This resulted in an extensive restoration to convert the offices into an art gallery, which opened to the public in 1982. Another large donation came in the 1990s from Professor Sir Colin St John Wilson and his wife. Unable to accommodate the growing collection, the gallery closed in 2003 to facilitate the building of an extension to the north.

Pallant House. (Chris Ison)

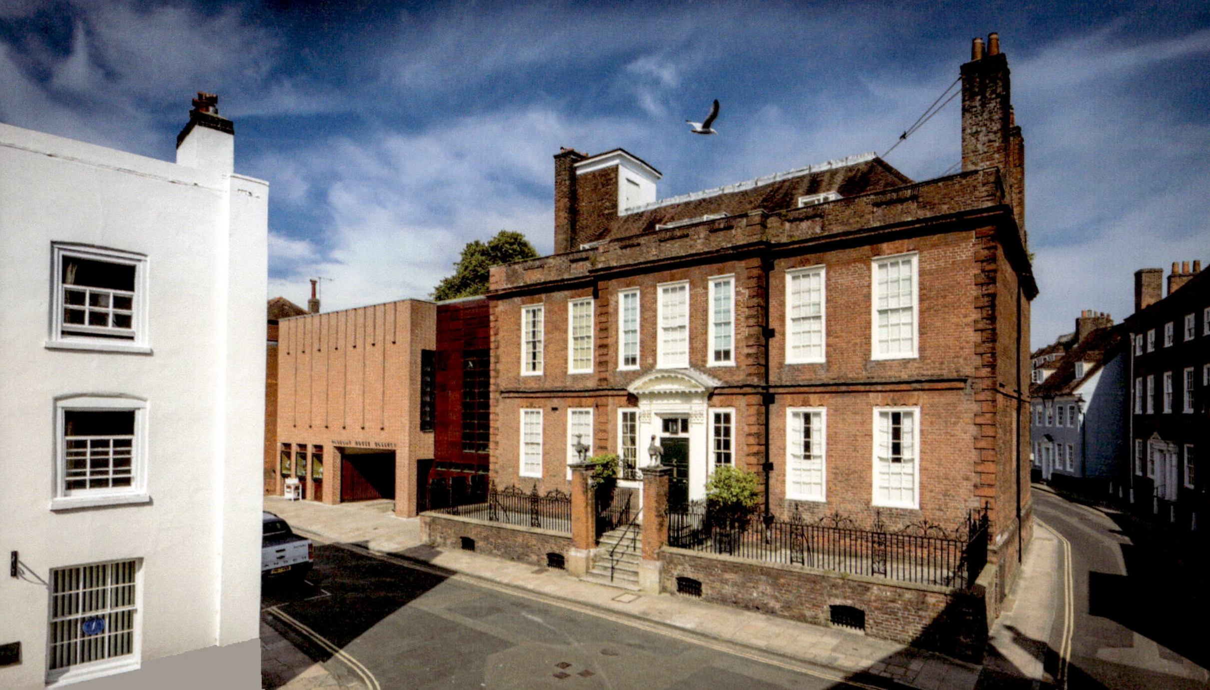

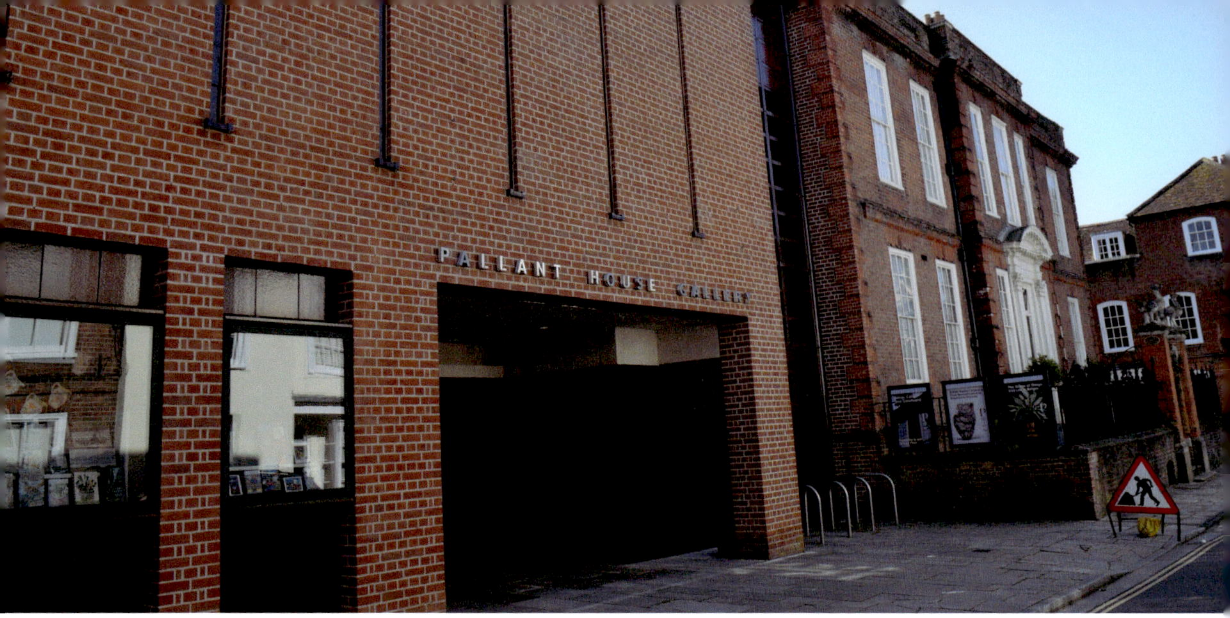

Gallery extension.

Reopened in 2006, Pallant House has become one of the foremost venues for modern British art. Most recently, the gallery has purchased the original coach house at the rear of the main building in 2017, which is being turned into a new Collections Centre.

19. The Deanery (1725)

A fine example of Georgian architecture, the present building replaced an earlier deanery on the same site.

The Deanery.

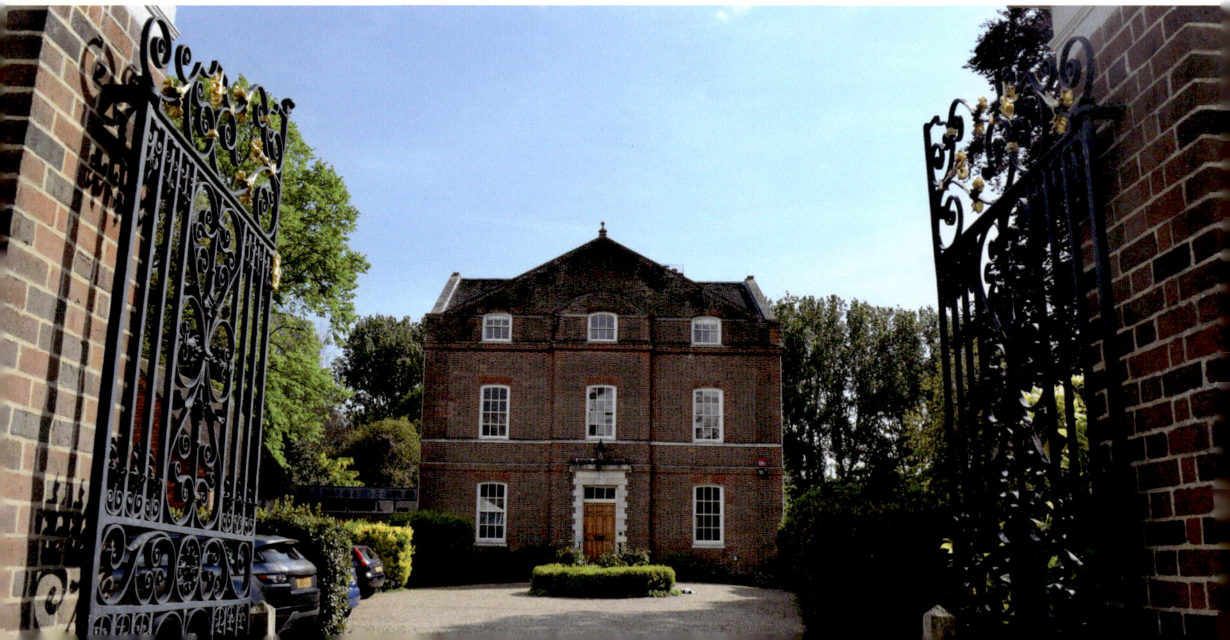

The original Deanery sustained substantial damage from Waller's cannon fire during the siege of 1642, and narrowly avoided further damage when a simultaneous attack on the East and West Gates was to coincide with the demolition of the Deanery garden gate with an explosive charge. At a late stage in the planning for the attack, a trumpet from inside the city heralded a ceasefire and, ultimately, the surrender of the city the following morning.

Following the cessation of hostilities, the Deanery underwent some repairs and restoration, but it never managed to regain its former grandeur. In 1725, Dean Thomas Sherlock demolished the building and started again from scratch.

20. Council House (1731)

Replacing a small room above a medieval timber market house, the Council House took up a central spot in North Street when it opened in 1731. Aside from the magnificent interior and imposing architecture, perhaps the most important feature can be found embedded in the front wall behind a sheet of clear plastic: the Minerva Stone. Found by labourers during the digging of foundations in April 1723, the large stone tablet belonged to a Roman temple on the site dedicated to Neptune and Minerva; it was unfortunately damaged when discovered. It is significant not only for being perhaps the earliest Roman inscription found in

The Council House.

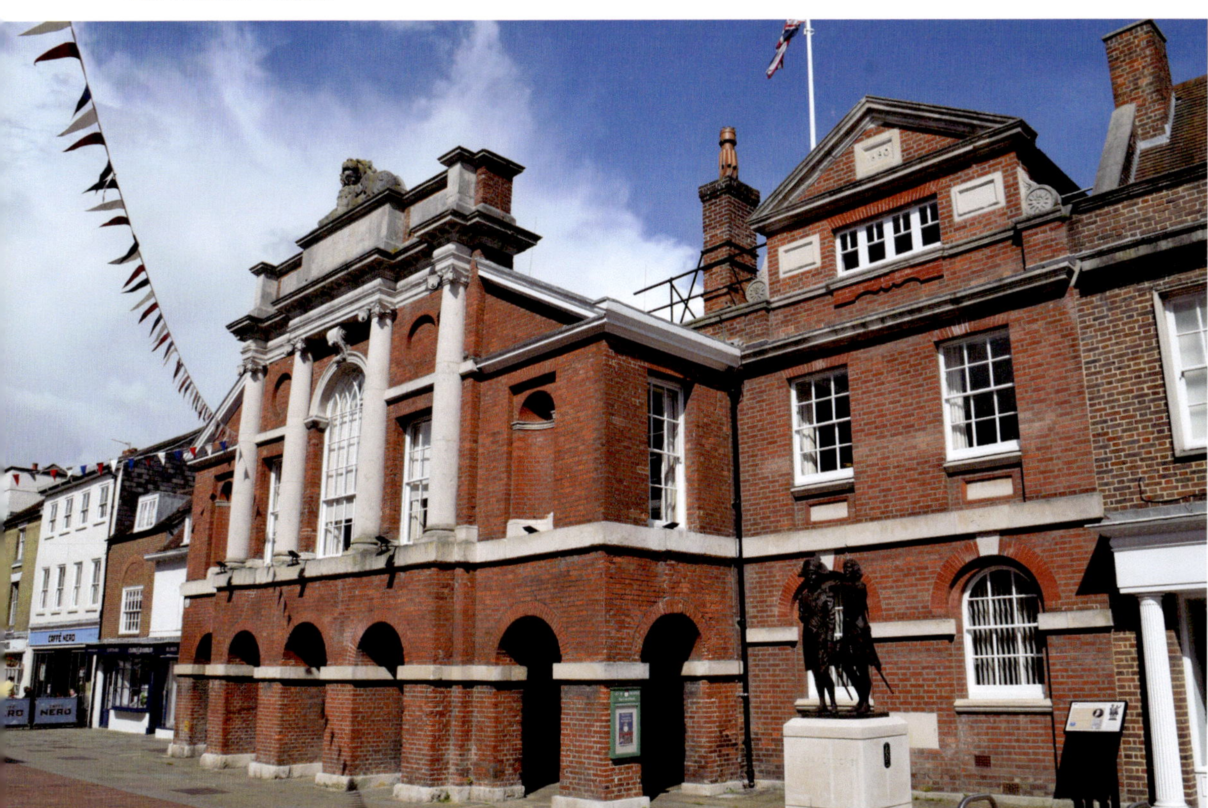

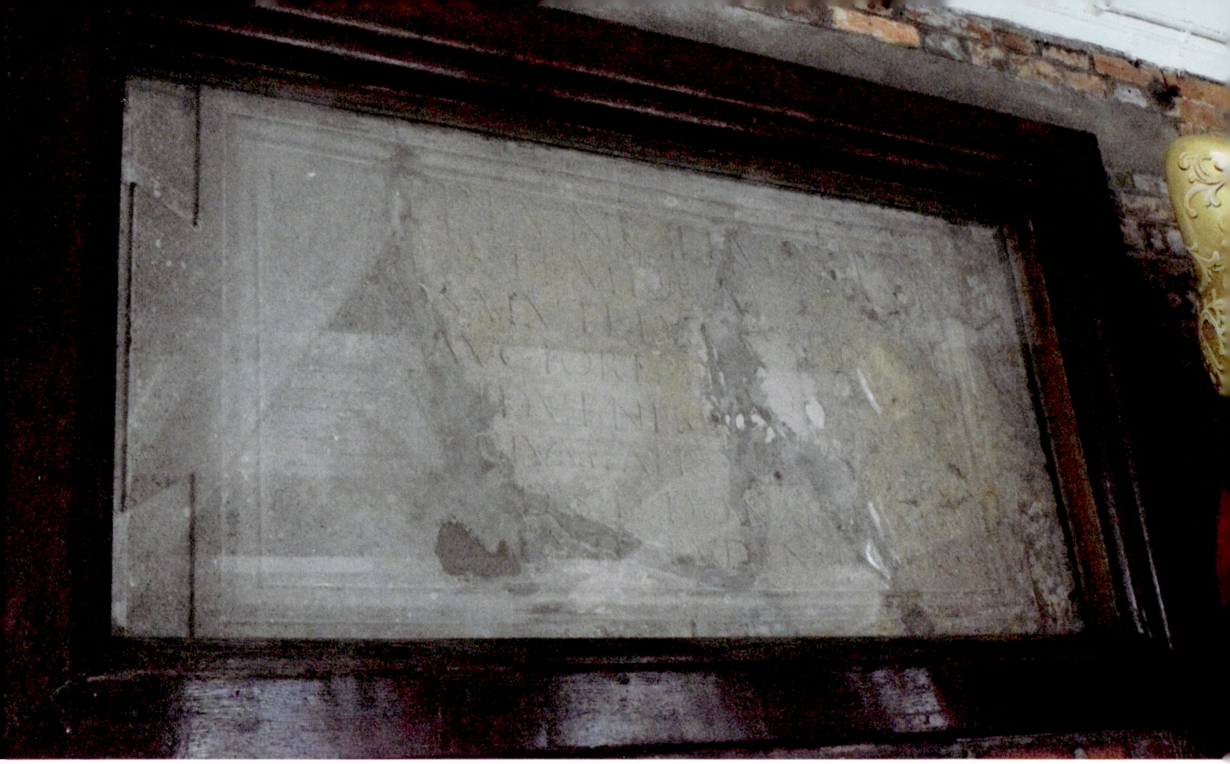

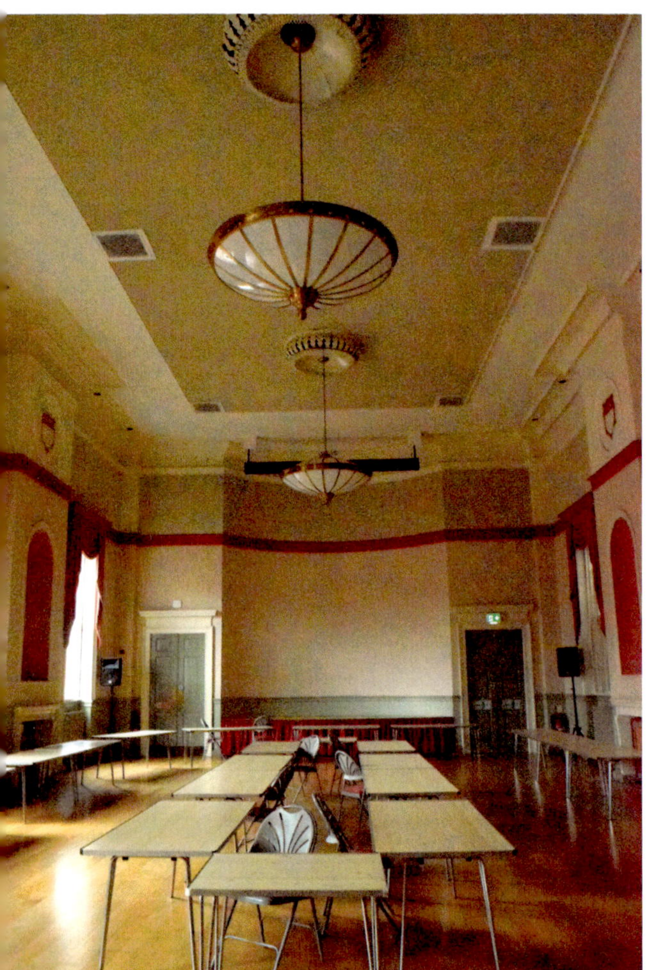

Above: Minerva Stone.

Left: Assembly Room.

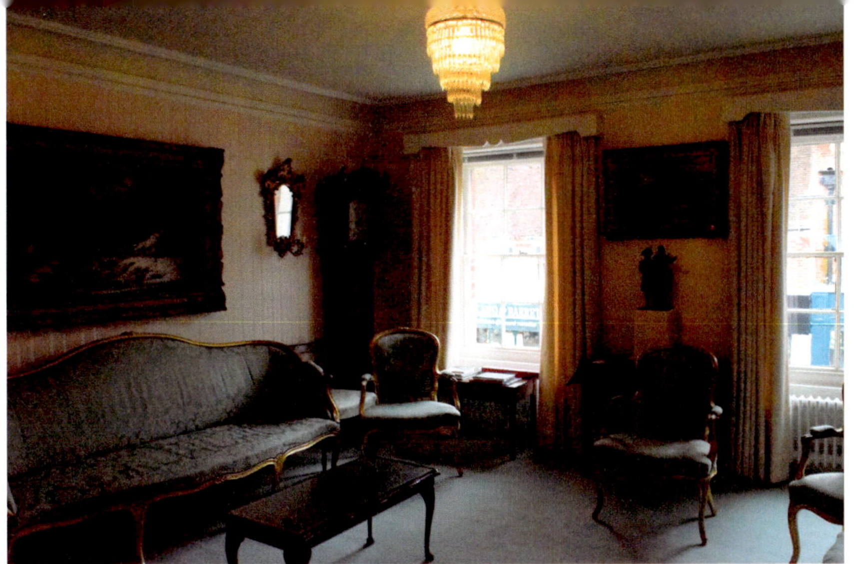

Mayor's Parlour.

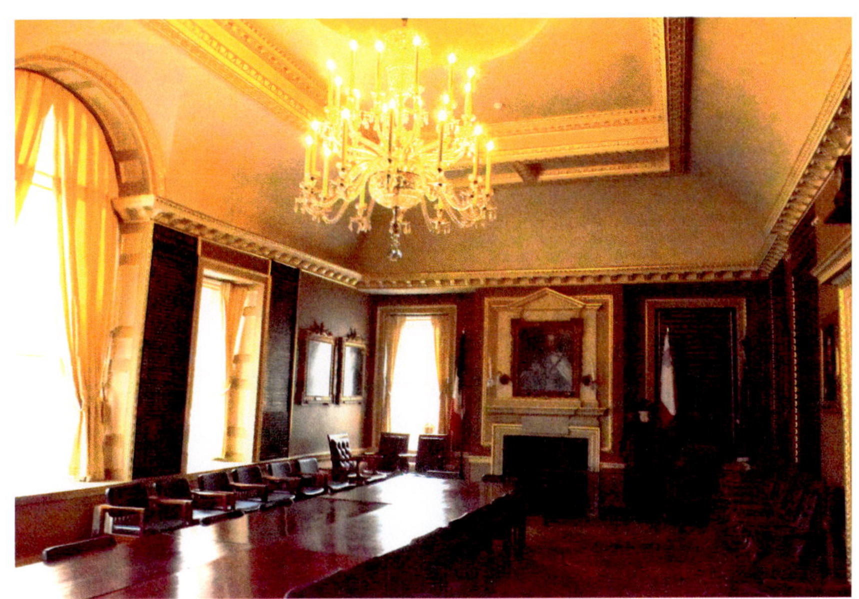

Council Chamber.

England, but also as a contemporary written record of Togidubnus, the local Romano-British king.

To the rear of the Council House is the Assembly Room, designed by renowned architect James Wyatt in 1783. With no expense or opulence spared, it is perhaps unsurprising that admission to the Assembly Room was restricted only to, in the words of Richard Daly, 'people of fashion and of the higher classes'. At the same time, the anteroom behind the chamber was added and is used to display the City Council regalia.

In *c.* 1881, the Old Court Rooms were added onto the building to house the magistrates' court, with the Mayor's Parlour and Town Clerk's Office added above, and a storeroom at the very rear of the building; most recently, new offices, a bar and kitchen in-filled a space on the south side of the building.

The magnificent Council Chamber underwent restoration in 1976, and features a large glass chandelier dating to *c*. 1790. Today, it is used mainly for council and mayoral business, but is also hired out exclusively for weddings and civil partnerships.

The Assembly Room, also available for hire, is regularly in use for concerts and markets and has hosted some famous – and infamous – guests, including Franz Liszt, William Joyce (better known as Lord Haw Haw) and Diana and Oswald Mosley.

21. Dolphin & Anchor (1768)

Occupying most of the frontage between North Street and Chapel Street, this impressive building originated as two rival establishments: The Dolphin (first mentioned in 1649) and The Anchor (first mentioned in 1716). The rivalry spread beyond commercial interests and into local politics, with The Dolphin being firmly Liberal and The Anchor being Tory. Both were rebuilt in the current form in 1768, and finally merged in 1910 as The Dolphin & Anchor Hotel, complete with a pair of 23.5 carat gold leaf statues atop the building.

The Dolphin, always the larger of the two, had always been a popular venue for functions and stopovers, once hosting Dr Samuel Johnson, as well as countless dances and parties up until it closed in 1996. The former ballroom now forms the

Former Dolphin & Anchor Hotel.

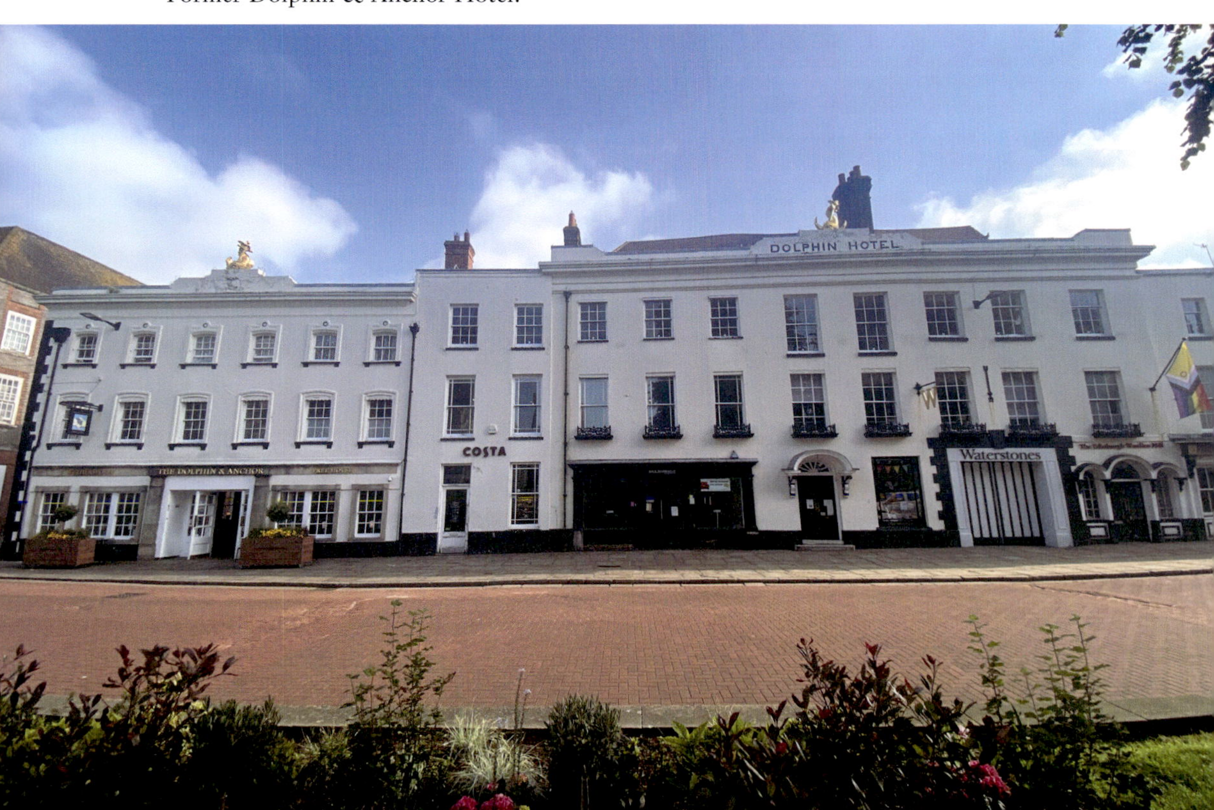

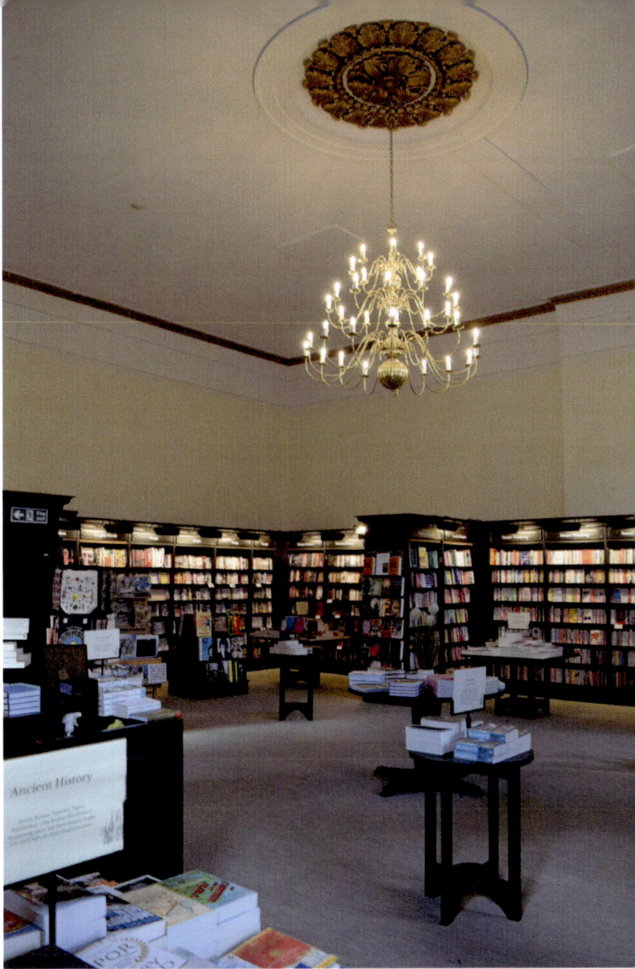

Former ballroom.

first floor of Waterstones, and in 1976 hosted a number of one-act plays produced by the Festival Theatre. The ground floor of Waterstones occupies the former coach entrance, complete with original barn doors.

The hotel experienced some tragedies in the early nineteenth century, beginning with the accidental death of the hotel's chaise-driver, Reuban Benham, who drove into the river at Midhurst in a storm one night in 1808, a fact that was later retold by his great-grandson, H. G. Wells. A few years later, the new landlord, Charles Triggs, dropped dead suddenly just twelve hours into his new job following a welcoming party in his honour.

Sold off in 1996 and split into retail units, the current Dolphin & Anchor pub opened at the far western end in 1997.

22. Leper's Cottage (c. 1781)

Little survives of the original twelfth century Hospital of St James and St Mary Magdalene other than a section of wall rebuilt into the north side of the late eighteenth-century Leper's Cottage.

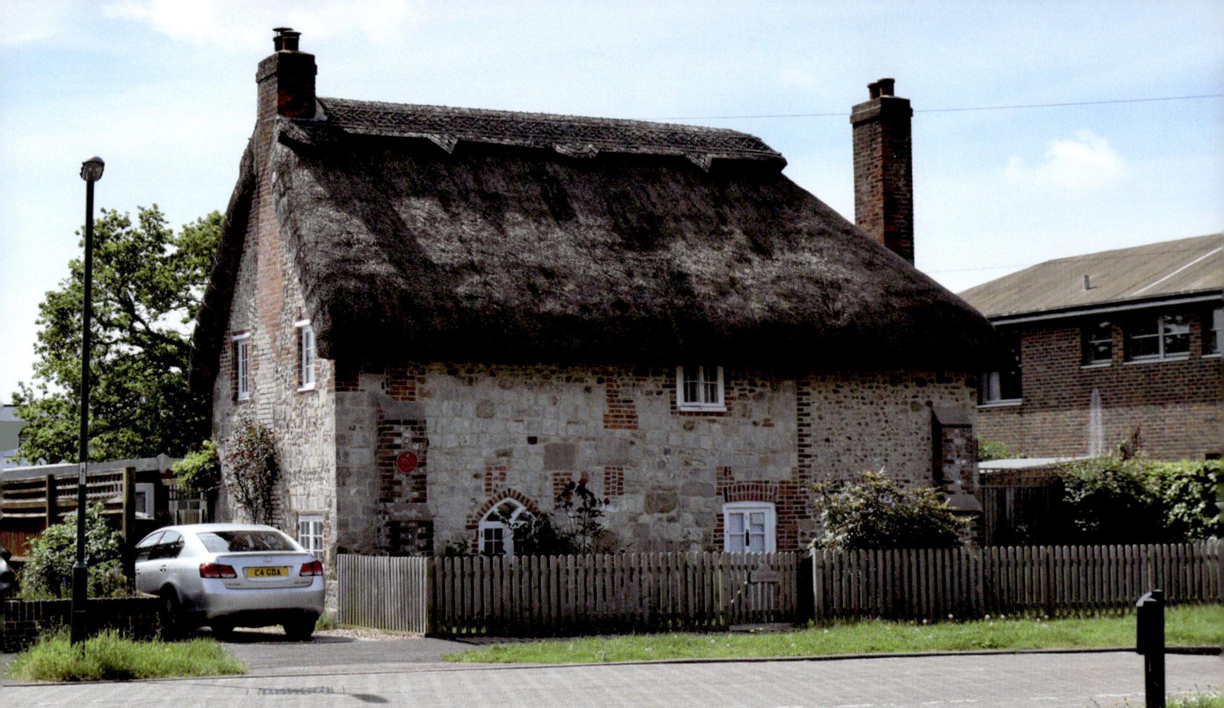

Leper's Cottage.

Founded in *c*. 1118 to treat leper victims, it remained in this role for three centuries. With the disease so poorly understood, the hospital was built almost a kilometre north-east of the Eastgate of the city, well away from the healthy population.

Originally caring for up to eight patients, it was the only one of its kind in Sussex. As this disease gradually subsided, the buildings presented an ideal opportunity to offer care for other illnesses.

It continued to undergo many changes in function for several centuries. Firstly, the hospital dissolved in 1442 (the last leper patient passed through its doors in 1418) and was re-founded as an almshouse. This, in turn, was dissolved in 1621, after admitting female residents for the first time in 1540. The later history of the site is murky, but probably became a smallpox hospital operating until 1755. By the latter half of the century, it no longer provided any care for the sick or elderly and instead became a sinecure for members of the cathedral.

The original buildings, already a ruin by the 1780s, burnt down in 1781. A new cottage was then built on the site shortly afterwards. Archaeological surveys discovered the hospital's cemetery in 1947, during the construction of the Swanfield Drive estate.

23. Old Theatre (1791)

The first purpose-built theatre in Chichester. Occupying the site of an older malthouse and granary, the 3rd Duke of Richmond donated money to convert

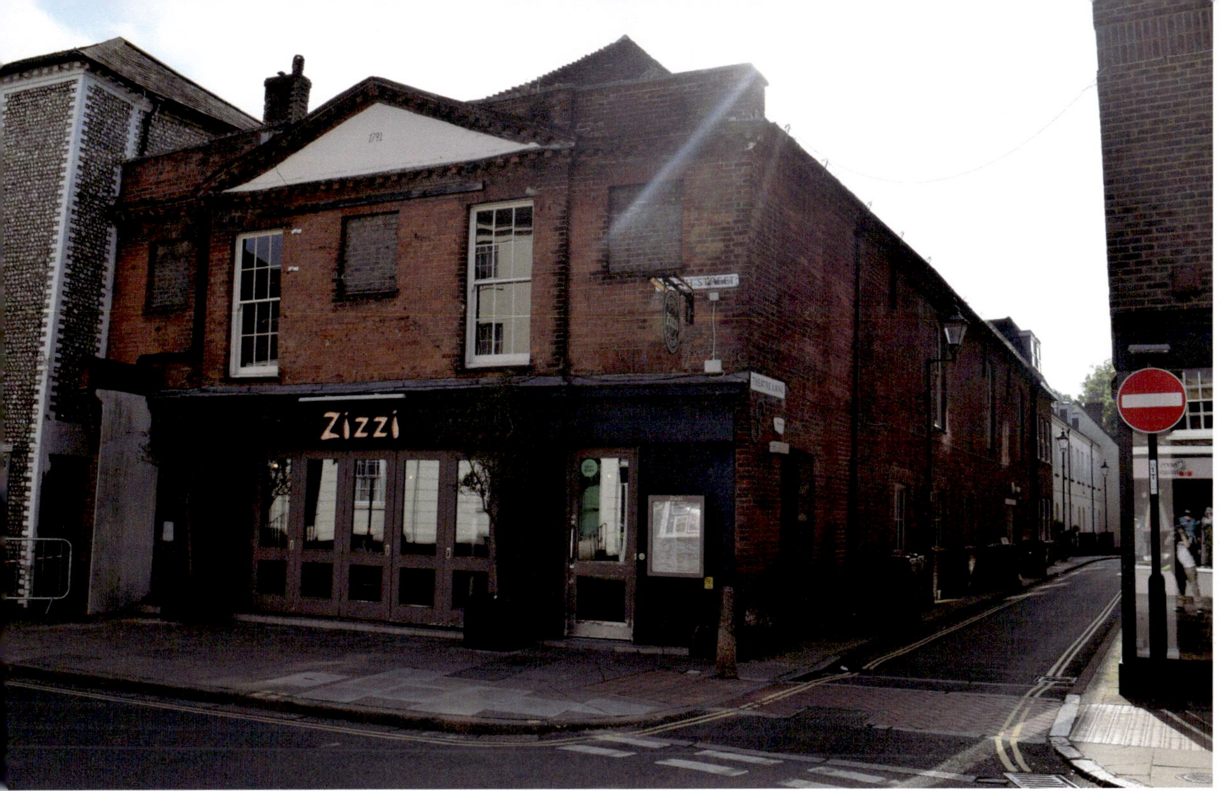

Old Theatre, South Street.

the old storehouse into a theatre in 1764, after his personal theatre at his London residence burnt down.

The current building, purpose-built as a theatre, dates to 1791 and was designed by Thomas Andrews, a local builder. Just as with the Assembly Room, only those of higher classes and military officers could attend the shows, which formed part of a local circuit with other cities in Hampshire. Despite undergoing renovation and upgrades in the 1820s, the theatre only lasted for less than thirty years. Sold off in 1850, the building saw many different uses, including as a brewhouse, gym, library, furniture shop and a box office for Chichester Festival Theatre. It now houses an Italian restaurant, with a modern shop front attached onto the otherwise original shell.

24. The Fountain (1798)

Almost certainly the oldest surviving public house in Chichester, and always known as The Fountain except for a brief spell as the Cathedral Tavern in the 1980s, this pub originally abutted the South Gate, as is still evidenced by the abrupt termination of the corbelling; the City Walls are still visible from the pub's restaurant area.

Perhaps its greatest claim to fame is that in the 1830s the landlord, George Neal was the grandfather of H. G. Wells.

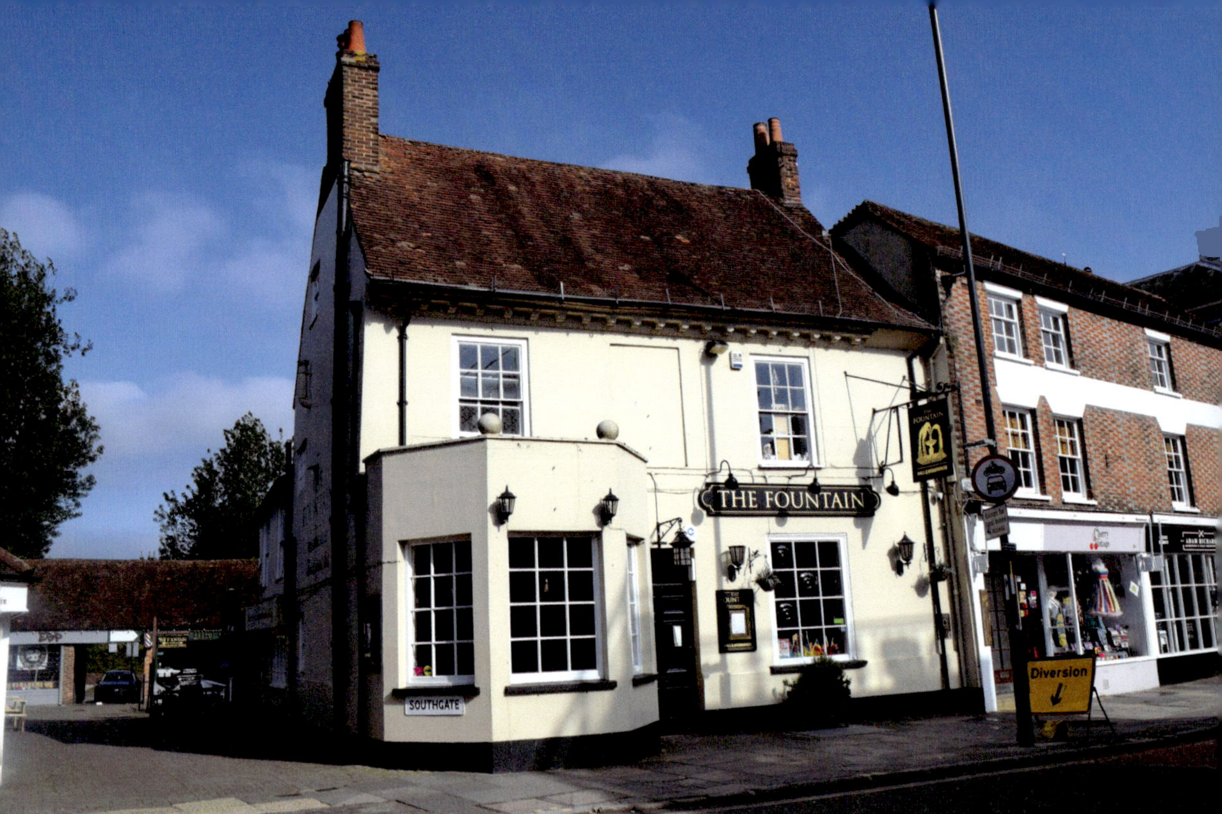

The Fountain Inn.

The pub underwent a major refurbishment in 2020, and is one of the popular venues for live music in the city.

25. Almshouse Arcade (1802)

Almshouses have been a feature of the site since the eighteenth century, initially housing six elderly widows. By 1786, they were deserted and dilapidated, repurposed as storage by local tradesmen. The present building dates to 1802, when the original six units were rebuilt by voluntary subscription into five small, self-contained tenements. Martha Dear, a wealthy spinster, also bequeathed £1,000 to the new almshouses in 1807 to provide for maintenance of the building, as well as an annual allowance for the five residents. Initially consisting of only a single storey, an upper floor added at a later date provided each of the five units with a second room, and small private gardens were also provided.

Aside from Martha Dear, after whom the Dear's Almshouses were named, the Corporation of St Pancras was (and remains) among the greatest benefactors, providing an annual Christmas meal and parade each December, with gifts for all the Old Dears, as the residents were affectionately known.

In 1960, the almshouses needed modern replacements once more, and four new units were built on a new site off Riverside in 1970, when all the Old Dears moved

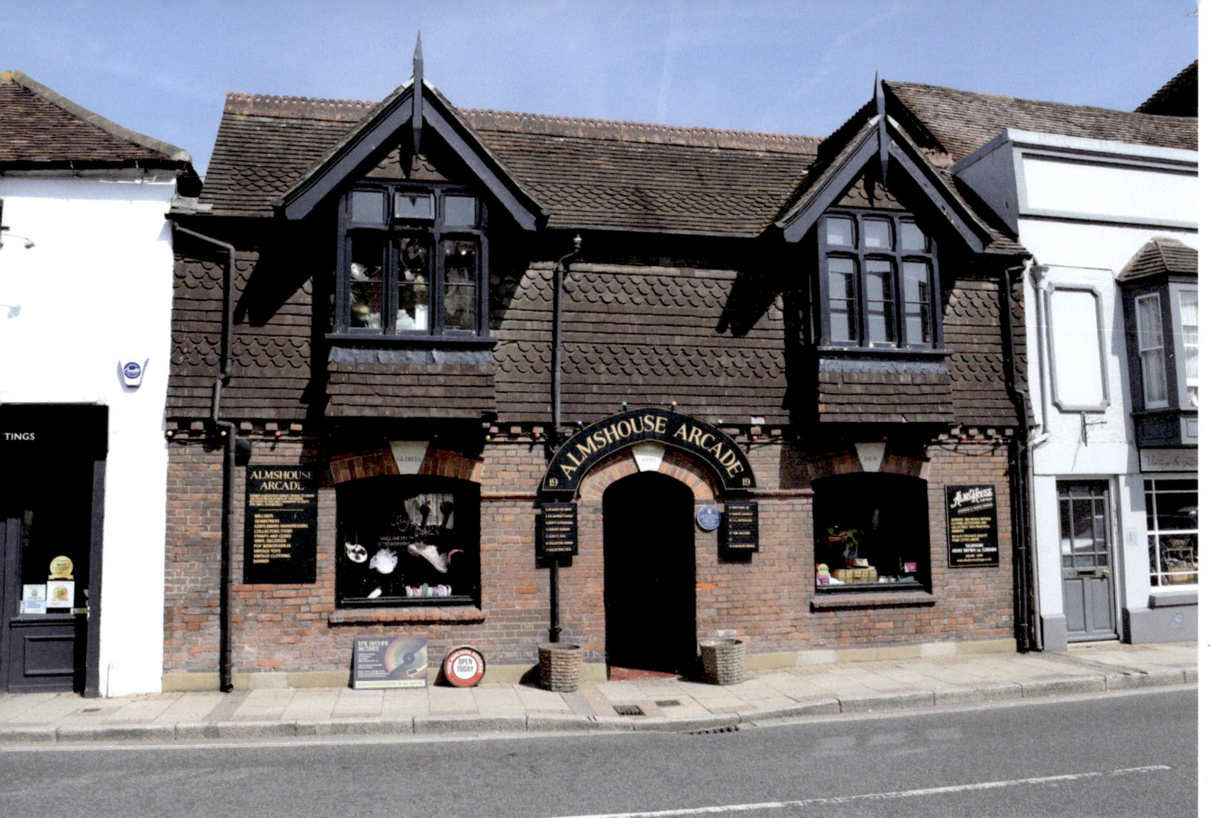

Almshouse Arcade.

into their new accommodation. A further four units were erected at Riverside in 2021, and the charity has since merged with St Mary's Hospital Almshouses, which manages all the Old Dears sites.

With the almshouses vacant, the building saw another conversion into a shopping arcade for twelve small shops in the 1970s, and is now just one of two surviving shopping arcades in Chichester, along with the Butter Market.

26. Ship Hotel (1804)

Known as the home of Vice-Admiral Sir George Murray, the house had been started by Thomas Cobden before being sold to Murray in May 1804 in an unfinished condition.

Admiral Murray had been born and raised in the city, rising rapidly through the ranks and becoming close friends with Lord Nelson. Having distinguished himself at the Battle of Copenhagen in 1801, he had been Nelson's personal choice to captain HMS *Victory* at the Battle of Trafalgar in 1805, but had to miss the opportunity owing to the death of his father-in-law. Nelson refused to appoint another captain, famously saying 'no one but Murray would do'.

Murray remained in Chichester until his death in 1819, having been elected as mayor in 1815.

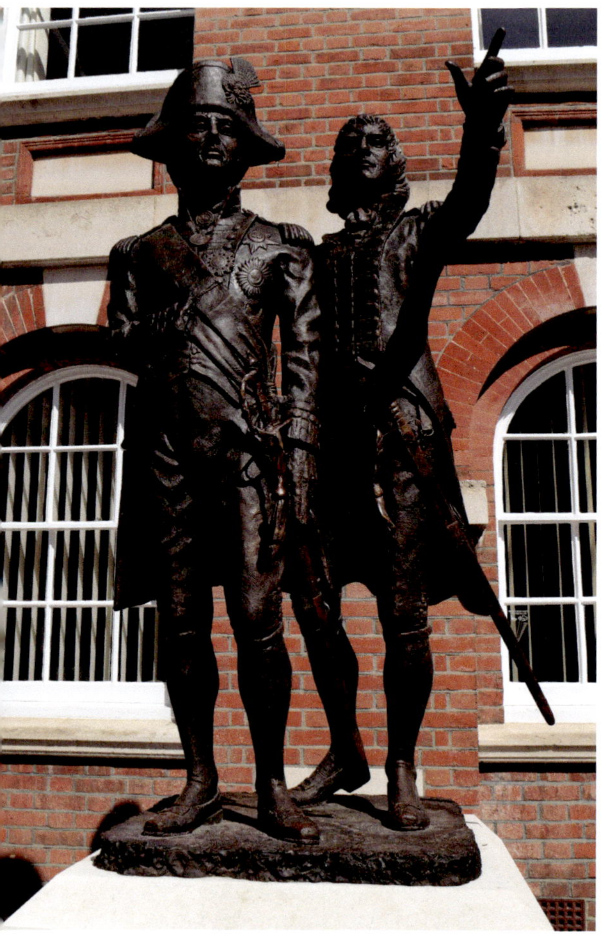

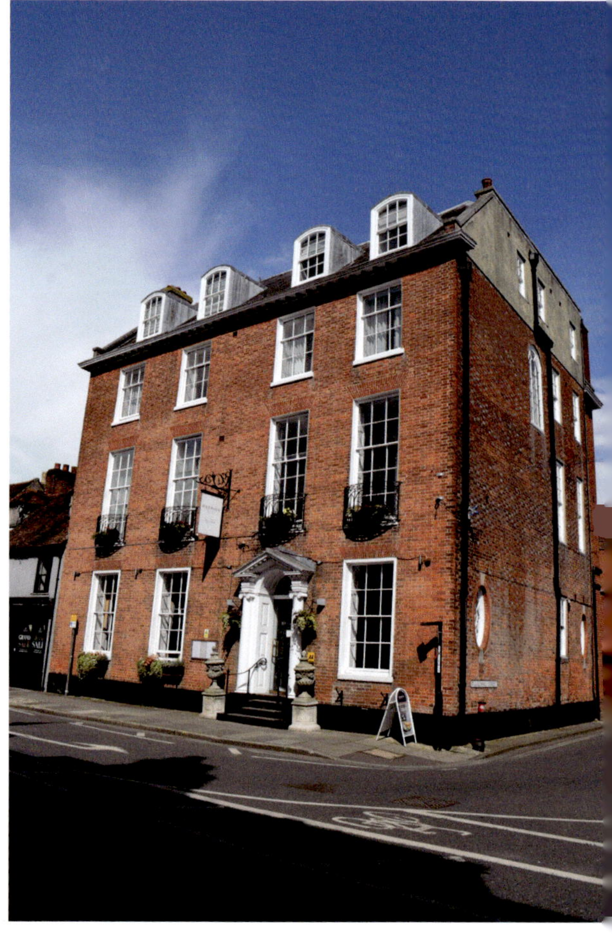

Above left: Statue of Vice-Admiral Murray and Lord Nelson.

Above right: Ship Hotel.

The house remained as a private residence until 1931, when it was converted into an art gallery. It was then converted into The Ship Hotel in 1939, having undergone renovations and extended at the rear.

The hotel was chosen as the venue for the meeting of General Eisenhower and Field Marshal Montgomery, as well as other senior officers, in the preliminary stages of planning for D-Day. The general stayed there for three days between 19 and 21 April 1944, using it as a base from which to conduct tours and inspections of nearby military camps and airfields.

Extended again in 1964, and once more in 2001, outrage met the new owners, Harbour Hotels, in 2015, when the hotel was rebranded as the Chichester Harbour Hotel. Just five months later, it was renamed again in April 2016 to Harbour Hotels | The Ship Hotel, to pay homage to the previous name.

27. Butter Market (1808)

Built by John Nash in 1808 as a larger replacement for the Market Cross, the single-storey indoor market gave small traders a place to sell their wares sheltered from the wind and rain. However, to compensate for this, traders had to pay a toll to offset the running costs of maintaining the building. Although undoubtedly a more comfortable location to trade, merchants did not have a choice but to set up here, since the arches of the Market Cross were barricaded with railings in order to prevent traders from avoiding paying the Butter Market tolls.

The upper storey seen today was added in 1900 to provide premises for a technical institute and art school; the latter vacated in the 1960s and moved to Worthing College.

Eventually, the open-plan nature gave way to individual units being made by bricking up between the support columns to create small shops and giving the interior a very bleak and industrial appearance. However, a complete refurbishment and redesign took place in 2010–11 (necessitating the complete closure of the building), fashioned after Burlington Arcade in London.

Butter Market.

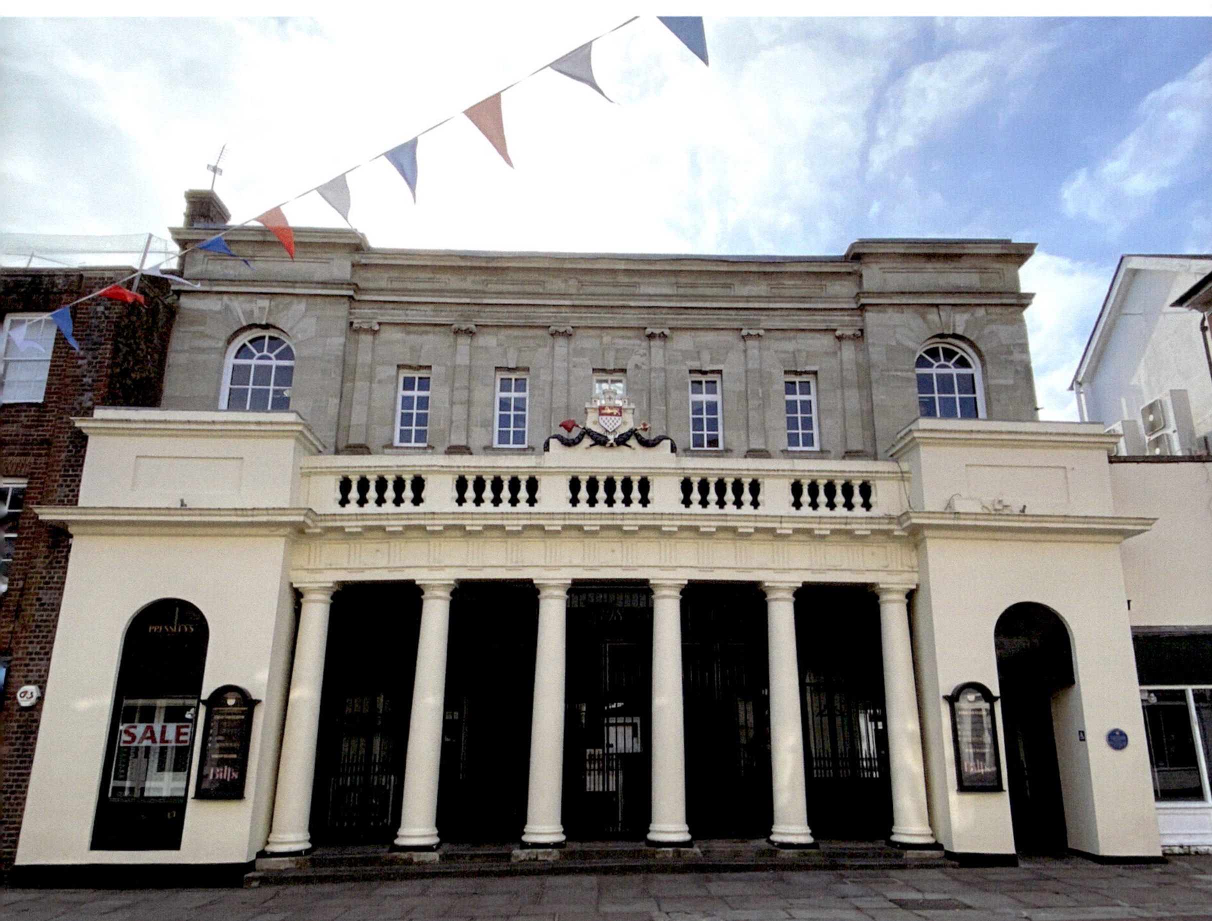

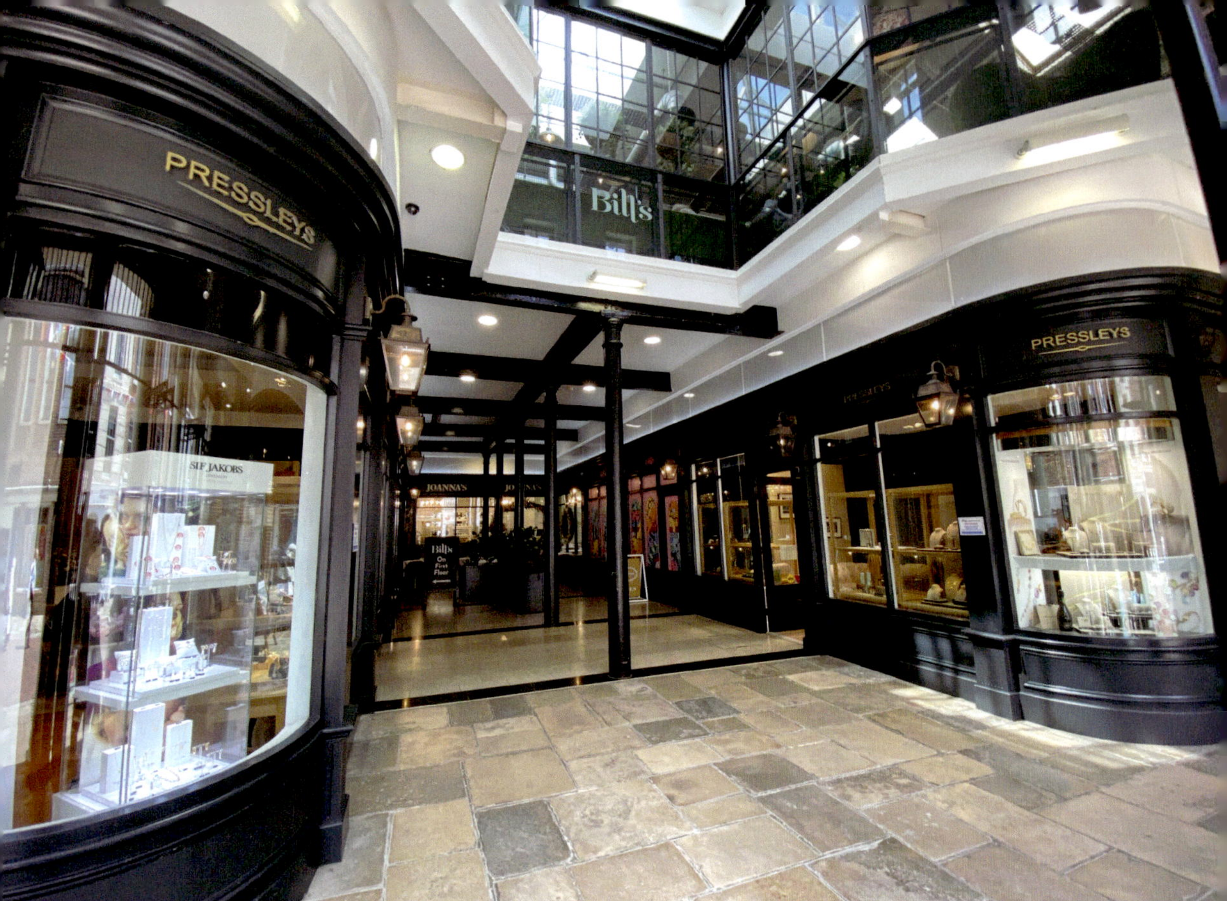

Butter Market interior.

With a far grander, elegant, and better lit space, the ground floor accommodates a number of independent retail shops, whilst the upper floor has been converted into a restaurant.

28. St John the Evangelist's Church (1812)

In 1808, the New Town area of Chichester emerged on land that once belonged to the Blackfriars monastery (dissolved in 1539). Within three years, the scale of building drew concerns about the lack of provision for worship in this rapidly expanding part of the city.

Built of white brick to an octagonal design by James Elmes, the new evangelical chapel, or 'preaching house,' opened in 1812, complete with American black birch furnishings and an impressive bell turret inspired by the Choragic Monument of Lysicrates in Athens.

From the outset, the church had a very shaky financial foundation, having been built by subscription and relying on pew rental to pay the minister's wages. The interior architecture centred on evangelical preaching, with a three-tier pulpit for

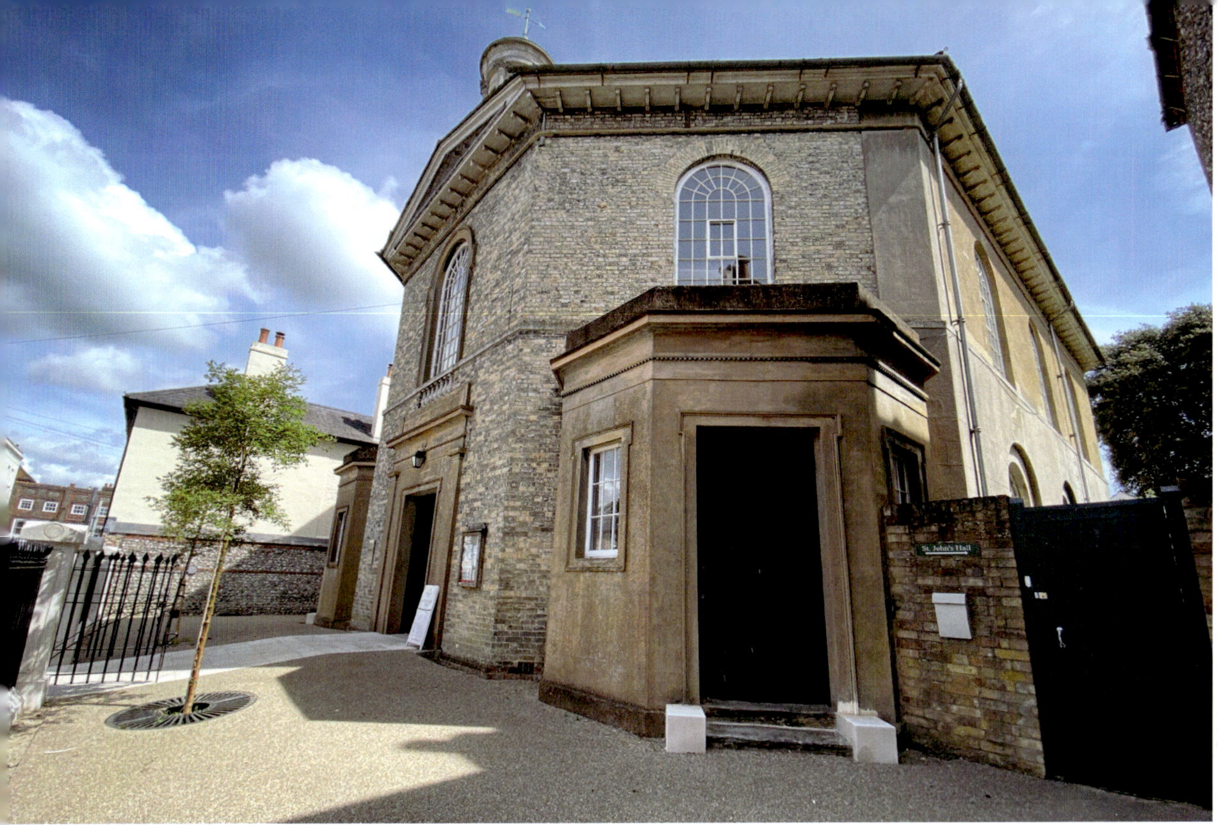

St John the Evangelist's Church.

visibility, a clock to ensure sermons lasted at least an hour, and a private upper gallery for wealthier congregants.

Despite reaching a peak of up to 600 members of the congregation in the early Victorian era, financial struggles resulted in the church's closure from 1871 to 1875. Although reopened, declining numbers persisted into the twentieth century, and the building sustained some damage in 1944, as well as having its outside railings removed for scrap metal during the Second World War. Ultimately becoming unsustainable, the church closed for good in 1973 and was deconsecrated.

The building underwent major restoration in 2003 and now enjoys a new life as an active live music venue, as well as being open to visitors every day and available for hire.

29. St Bartholomew's Church (1824)

The ancient circular church of St Sepulchre, modelled after the Holy Sepulchre in Jerusalem, stood on this site, atop a small mound, from *c.* 1397 until destroyed in the siege of 1642. The new church of St Bartholomew did not come into being until 1824, although financial issues meant that it was not completed until 1832.

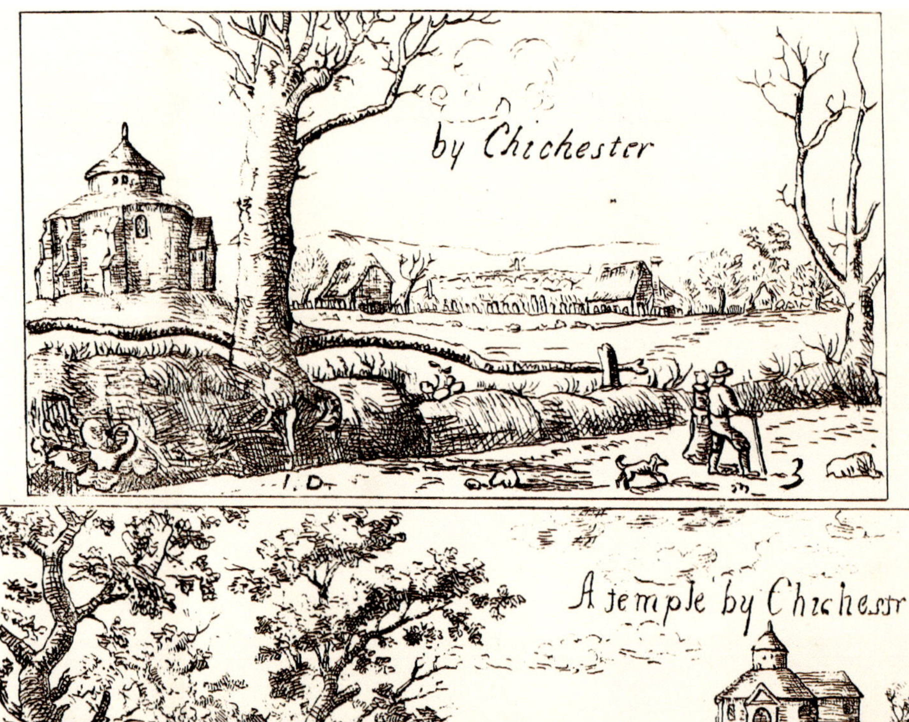

Two late seventeenth-century engravings of the original round church. (*Sussex Archaeological Collections* Vol. 7)

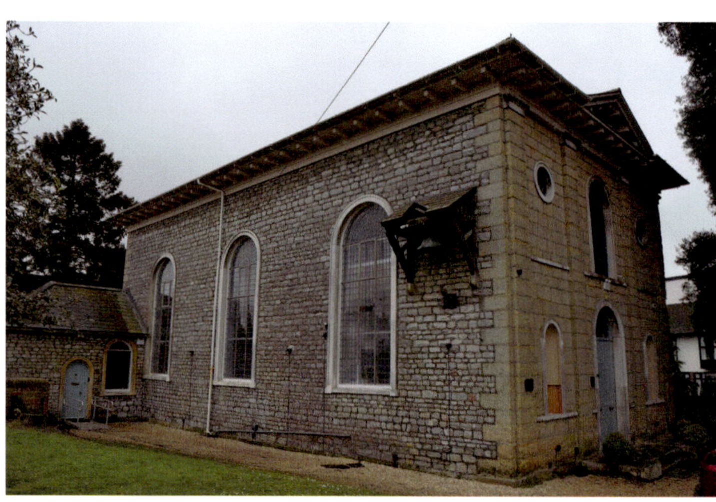

St Bartholomew's Church.

Originally consisting of a small entrance lobby and the main hall, a small churchyard and a two-tier bell tower, later extensions included the organ loft and chancel in 1878, and later a vestry. At some point, a connecting corridor linked the vestry with the chancel, cutting across tombs in the rear churchyard – by this stage no new burials had taken place since 1860, and with the exception of a burial in the early 1900s and the internment of ashes in the early 2000s, no burials have taken place since. Major alterations were then made in 1929, when MacDonald Gill had the bell tower removed and lavishly decorated the interior, including the chancel ceiling. A small memorial to the fallen of the First World War was added onto the front wall beside the main doors.

St Bartholomew's was deconsecrated in 1959 and taken on as the chapel of the Chichester Theological College until 1994. By 2002, a small group of nuns from the Servants of the Holy Cross took up residence nearby and used the chapel for daily worship; four of them have their ashes buried in the front burial ground. Soon after, it became the Chaplaincy Centre for Chichester College from 2005 until 2015, when it stood empty for many years.

In 2021, the building was purchased by the Chichester City Arts Centre LLP, which has been restoring the former chapel since 2022 into a community venue and home of the Rosemary Bell Academy of Dance. Upon taking ownership, much of the furniture and other items had been left behind from its former life,

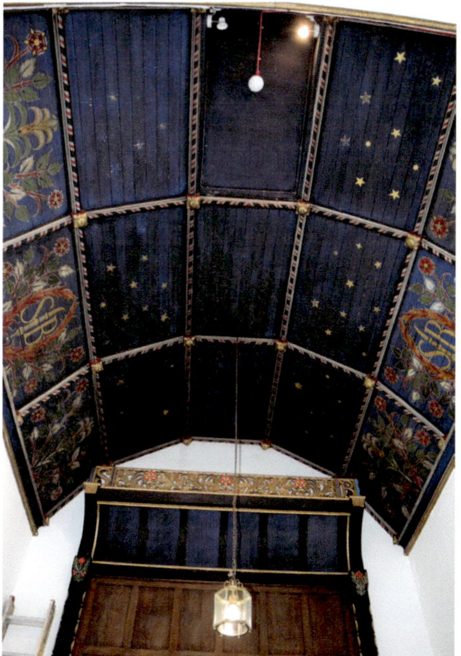

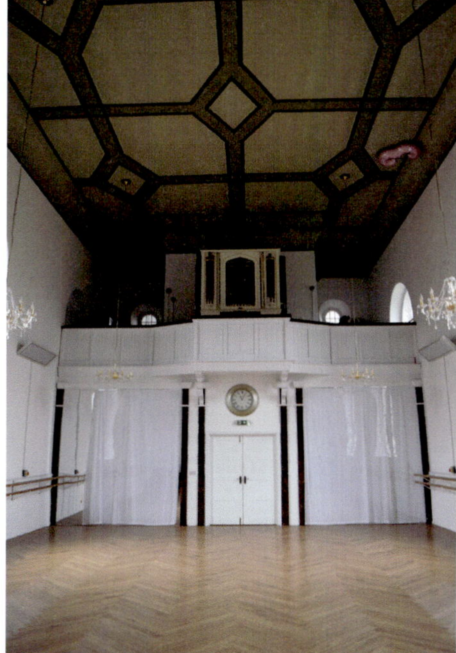

Above left: MacDonald Gill's painted chancel ceiling.

Above right: Former nave.

including vestments, boxes of candles and chairs. The venue is now available for hire for private and community events, and regularly hosts exercise classes, film screenings and parties.

30. Royal West Sussex Hospital (1826)

A series of cottages on Broyle Heath were converted into the Chichester Dispensary in 1784, founded by Revd William Walker and Dr Thomas Sanden. With an increasing population, it became evident by 1822 that a larger institution was required. The fundraising effort, led by Dr Sir John Forbes, resulted in a new forty-bed hospital, opening in 1826 as the West Sussex, East Hampshire and Chichester Infirmary and Dispensary.

Dr Forbes operated strict discipline during his tenure from 1826 until 1840, forbidding patients to consume alcohol or smoke, and banning visitors. Upon admission, patients had to agree to write a thank-you letter to the hospital when discharged and to attend church on the first Sunday afterwards to offer thanks.

Increasing demand required a new wing in 1833, followed by another twenty-bed wing in 1838 as a gift from Charles Dixon, a wealthy local landowner.

With Dr Forbes gone, his rules appear to have been relaxed by his successors, since a brew house was built in 1851 to supply beer to the patients, which was considered to be safer than the water. Further expansion came with a new

Original infirmary, 1836.

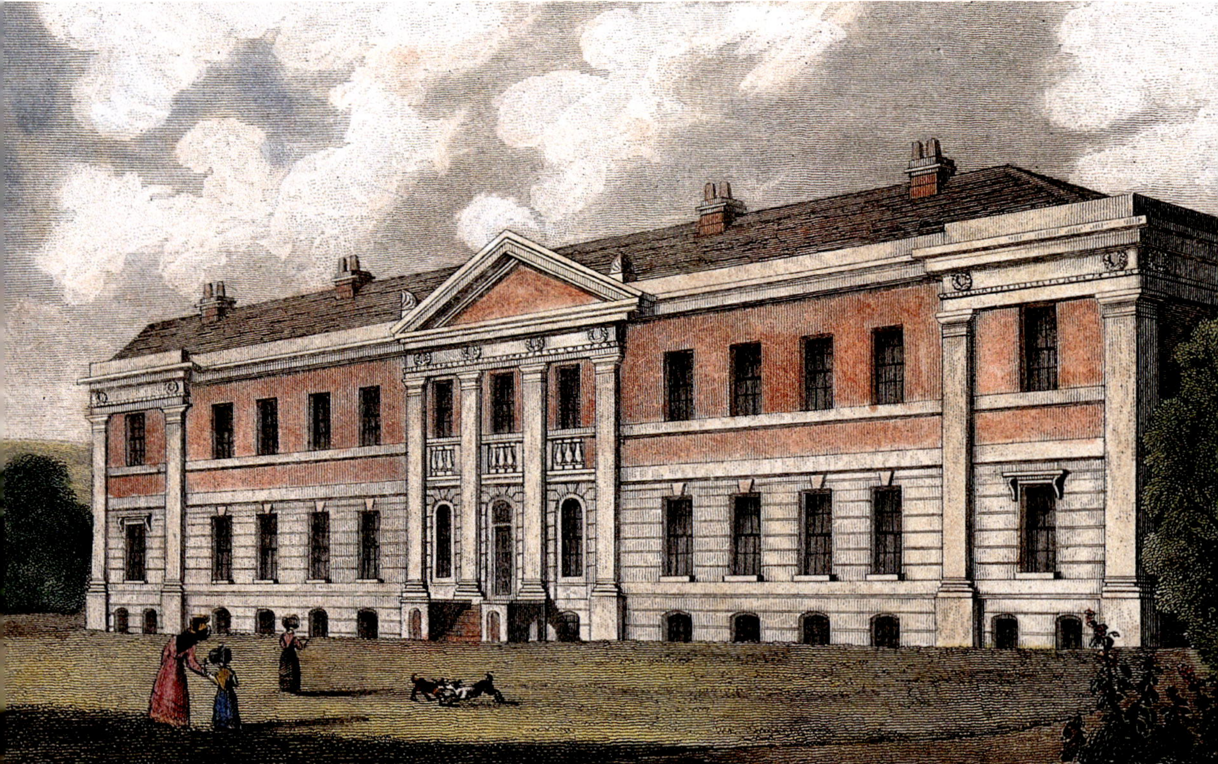

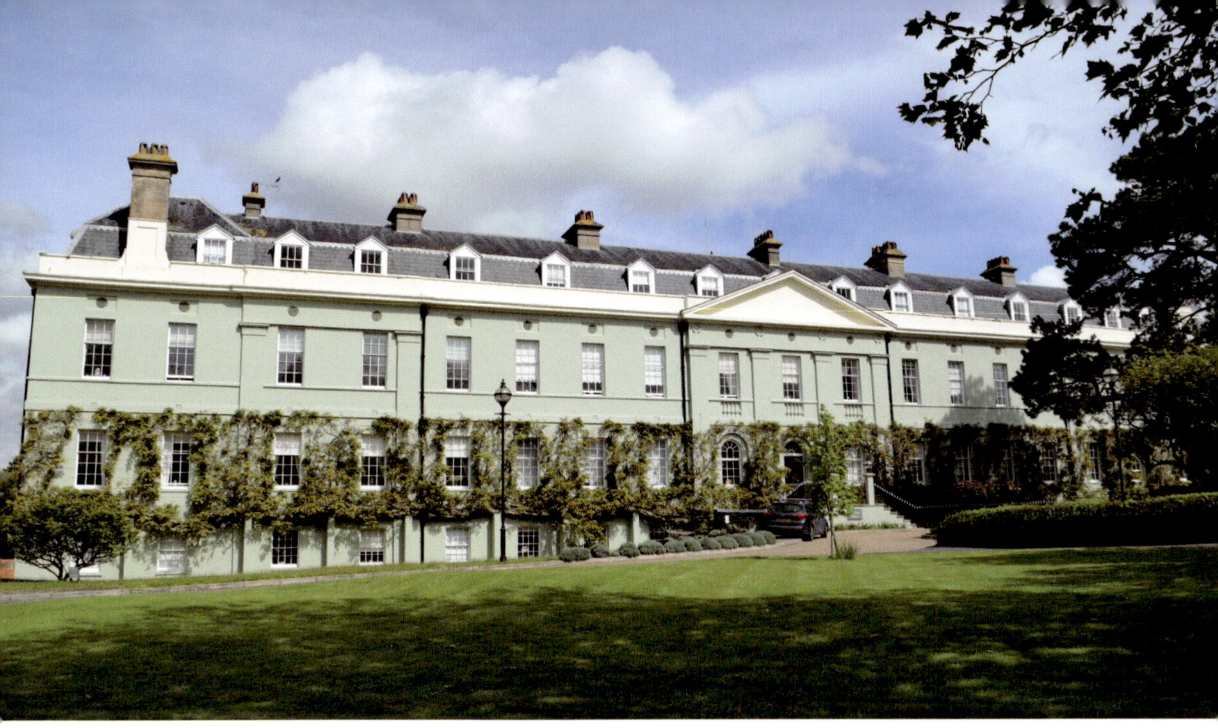

Former Royal West Sussex Hospital.

operations room added in 1869, and the first children's ward opened in 1879 (the supply of alcohol to patients having been stopped in 1872).

As medical and technological advances continued, the entire hospital was remodelled in the early 1900s and reopened in 1913 by George V, giving it the new name of the Royal West Sussex Hospital. Soon after, it became a military hospital between 1914 and 1919 to treat the wounded returning from France, the first patients arriving on 27 October 1914 in a convoy of twenty-one cars.

The military use continued in the Second World War with a further 200 beds provided in five hutted wards in 1940, which were still in use in the 1970s. Following a fiscal crisis, the hospital closed in 1995, and the building was sold and converted into flats.

Of particular note is the wisteria enveloping the front façade of the building, planted between 1825 and 1828 by, it is believed, the first matron, Mrs Rogers, who served from 1826 to 1857; it is thought the plant was a gift to Mrs Rogers from China, and is the oldest wisteria in Britain.

31. Corn Exchange (1833)

Until the Council House was built in 1731, the city's corn exchange took place in the undercroft of the former wooden market house on North Street. When this was replaced by the Butter Market, the corn merchants desired a place of their own and, in 1832, funded the new Corn Exchange in East Street, the first one of its kind in England.

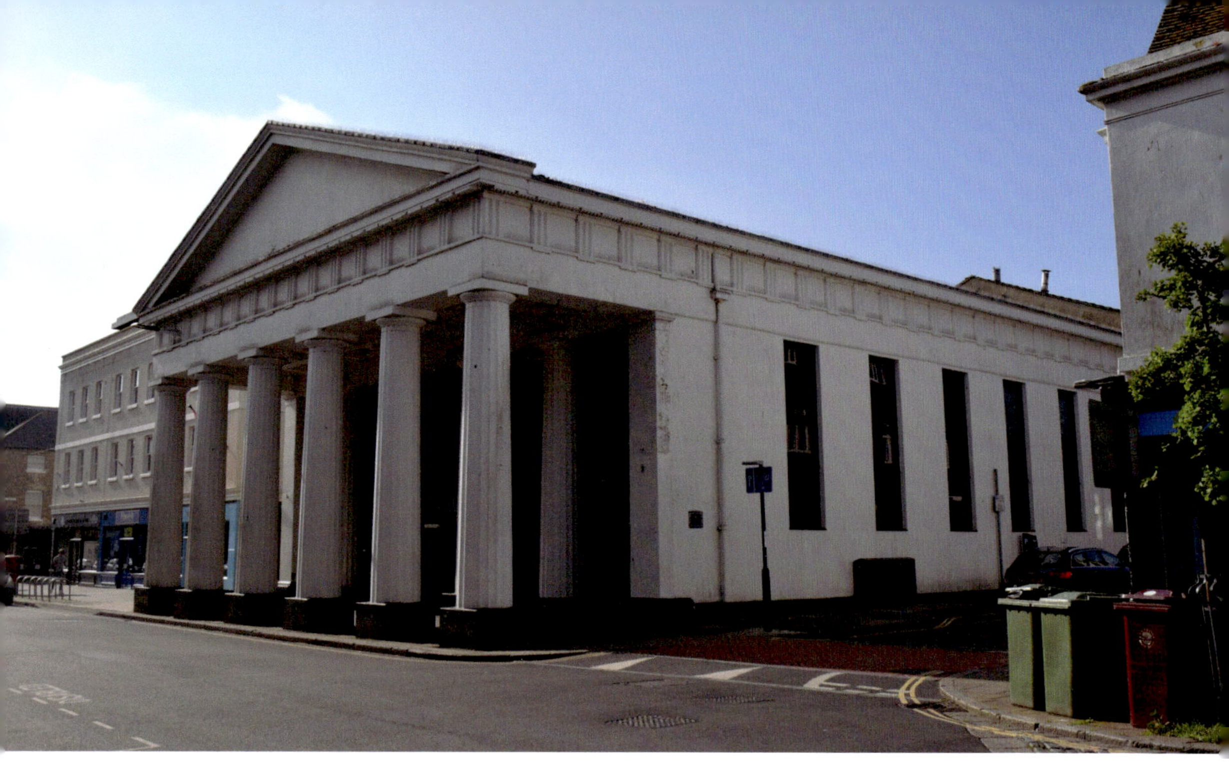

Corn Exchange.

Opening to a shaky start in 1835, when the roof was discovered to be unsafe and in need of a complete rebuild, it only lasted in its role as the corn exchange for fifty years, despite a three-storey corn store being erected at the rear. As demand for corn markets declined towards the end of the century, parts of the building began to be hired out to the community for other uses from 1883.

Rear offices.

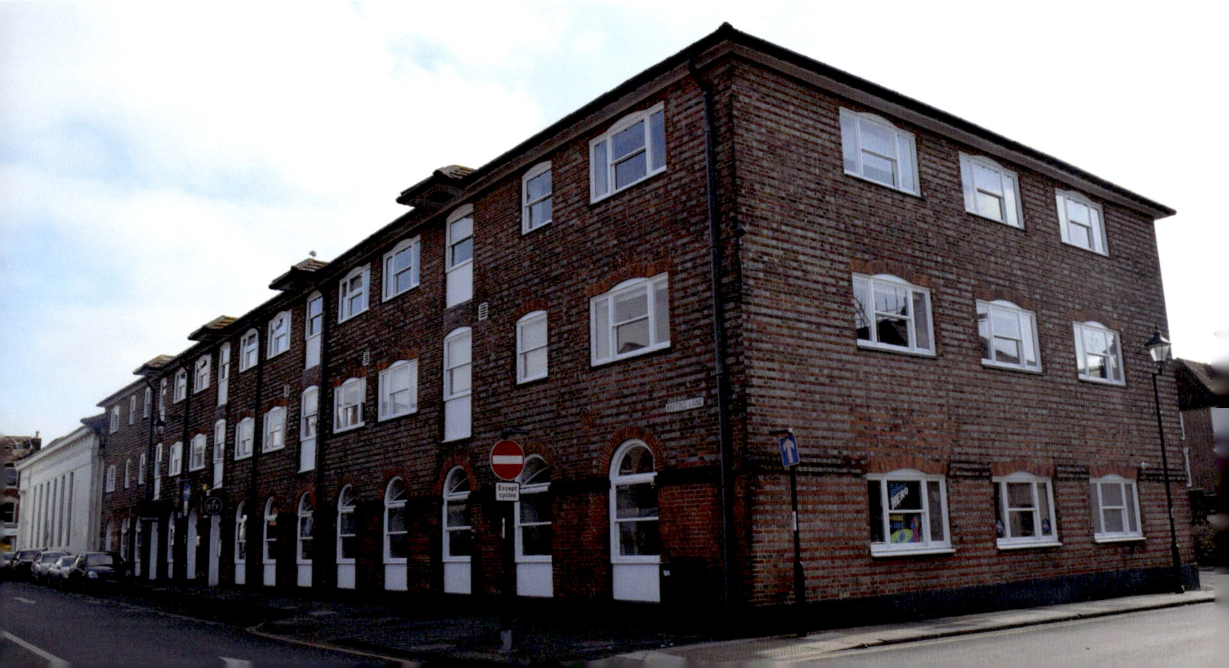

History was made on 26 December 1896, when Maggie Morton hired the building for a travelling film show, marking not only Chichester's first ever moving picture show, but heralding a new life for the Corn Exchange. By 1910, regular screenings were taking place here, and in 1922 it finally opened as a full-time cinema and ballroom. Renovations in 1927 saw the Corn Exchange become the Exchange Cinema, which lasted until it was taken over by Granada in 1948 and renamed as the Granada Exchange.

By 1960, this had become the only cinema operating in Chichester, but in 1977 Granada, who had already sold off the rear part of the building for conversion into offices in 1967, tried to turn it into a bingo club. With planning permission declined, the company chose to shut the cinema in 1980, closing its doors with a showing of *Star Wars: The Empire Strikes Back*.

Sitting dormant and empty for six years, McDonalds opened a restaurant in 1986 before selling to Next in 2005. New Look took over the premises in December 2021, and Boston Tea Party has also established a tearoom in the rear of the building.

32. University of Chichester (1849)

University House and the Old Chapel form the oldest part of the modern campus, dating to 1849. Bishop Otter's Training College, set up in memory of Bishop William Otter who died in 1840, provided training for schoolmasters. The following year, the training college moved to another location, and the site was renamed as Bishop Otter's College or the Otter Memorial College, depending on

University's main entrance.

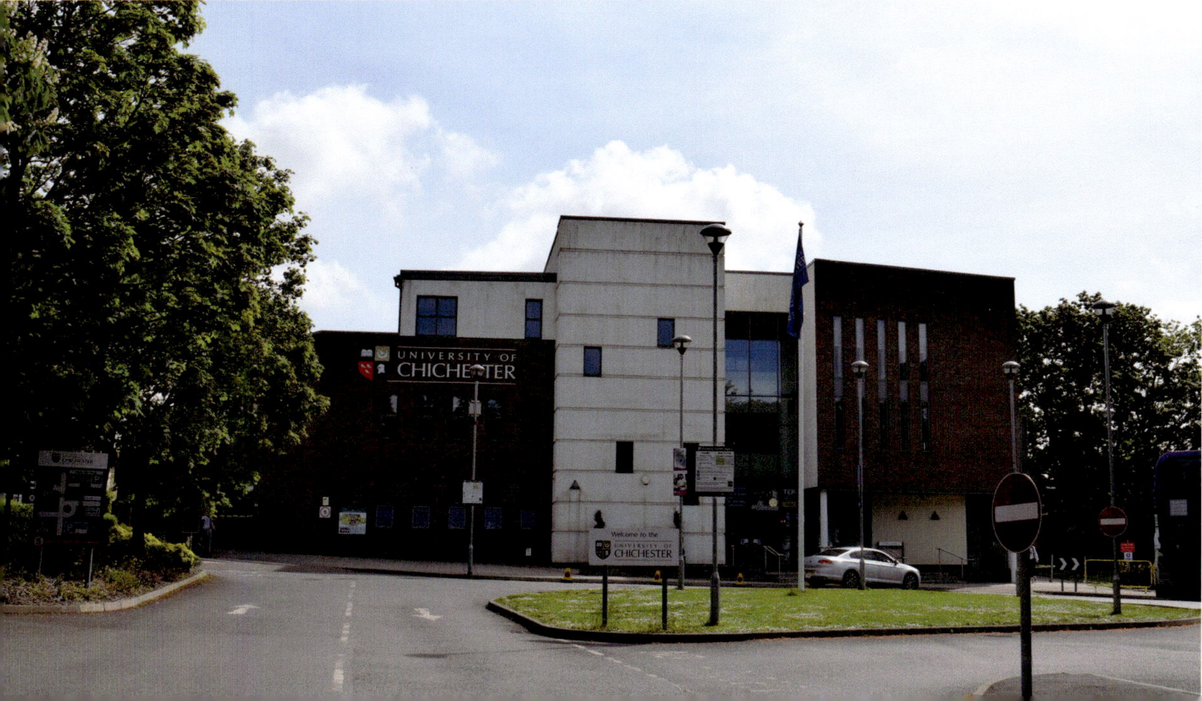

the source. The college failed in the late 1860s and was taken over as a training college for women in 1873, remaining a female-only college until 1957.

The staff and students were forced to vacate to Stockwell College, Bromley, in February 1944, as the RAF requisitioned the buildings to become the operations room for Tangmere. A special observation gallery for senior officers was erected in the lecture hall to overlook the plotting table tracking the movements of aircraft over the south coast, which proved vitally important on D-Day when it became the central nerve station for airborne operations over Normandy, controlling the movement of fifty-six squadrons in Sussex, Surrey, Hampshire and Berkshire. Later, from January 1945, it remained in use as an Emergency Operations Room to direct the interception of V-1 flying bombs.

Returning to civilian use after the war ended, the Otter Memorial College merged with the Bognor Regis College of Education in 1977 to form the West Sussex Institution for Higher Education. A number of subsequent name changes reflected the adapting nature of the college, becoming the Chichester Institute of Higher Education in 1995, then to University College Chichester in 1999. Recognition as a full university came in October 2005, since when it has been known as the University of Chichester – one of the top-ranked universities in the UK.

33. Convent of Our Lady of Mount Carmel (1870)

The Carmelites had a turbulent start to their new life in England. The site just south of Chichester had been chosen in the 1860s, and construction commenced in 1870, with the aim to move in once the building had been finished, but events forced a change of plans. Owing to the outbreak of the Franco-Prussian War in 1870, the nuns were forced to travel to England prematurely and took up residence in a private house in North Mundham for almost two years before the convent could be completed. Even so, the project overran the budget, meaning that the chapel could not be completed. Another part of the convent underwent changes to convert it into a makeshift chapel, and the nuns finally moved into their new home on 28 April 1872.

Being a closed order, the nuns segregated themselves from the outside world as far as was possible. With the convent chapel also doubling up as a public place of worship, an iron grille separated the nuns with any contact from the outside congregation attending services, and alms were given through a hatch in the door.

The community thrived, with a dedicated chapel finally built in 1930. The population also grew to reach a peak in the 1970s, but changing times in later years spelled the end for the convent. By the early 1990s, the number of sisters had fallen to such an extent that the building became too large and expensive to run. In 1994, the remaining nuns sold the site to a recruitment agency, who used it to house migrant workers working in nearby farms until 2007, and the siters moved out to Sclerder Abbey in Cornwall.

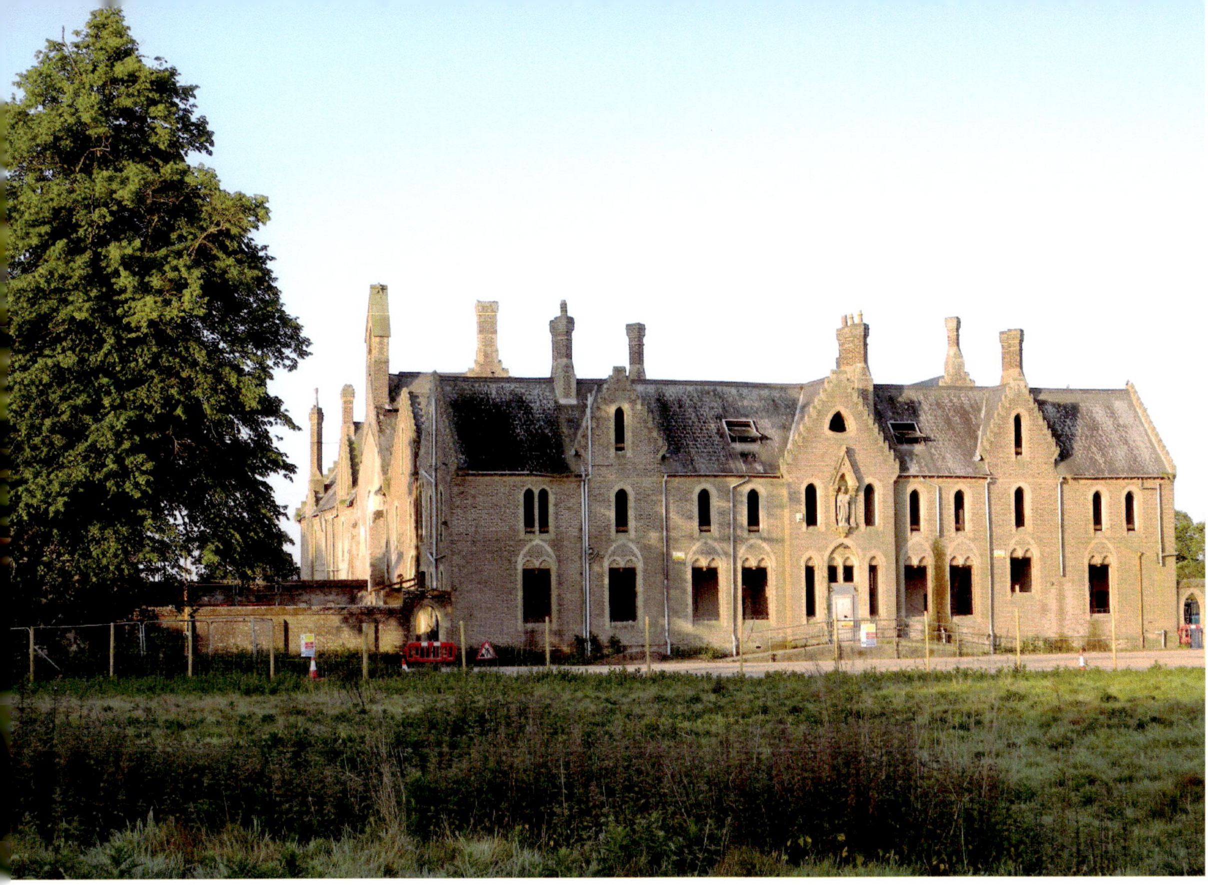

Above: Convent prior to renovation. (Chichester Free School)

Below: Chapel fire. (Chichester Free School)

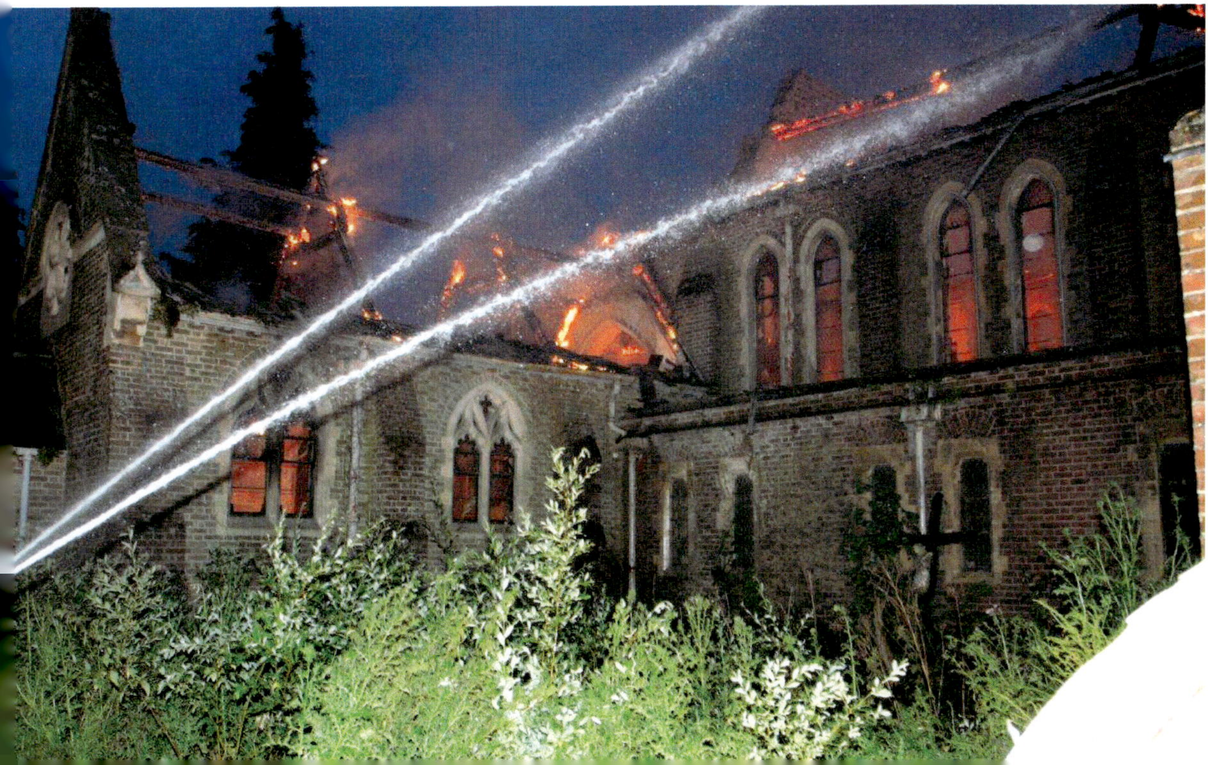

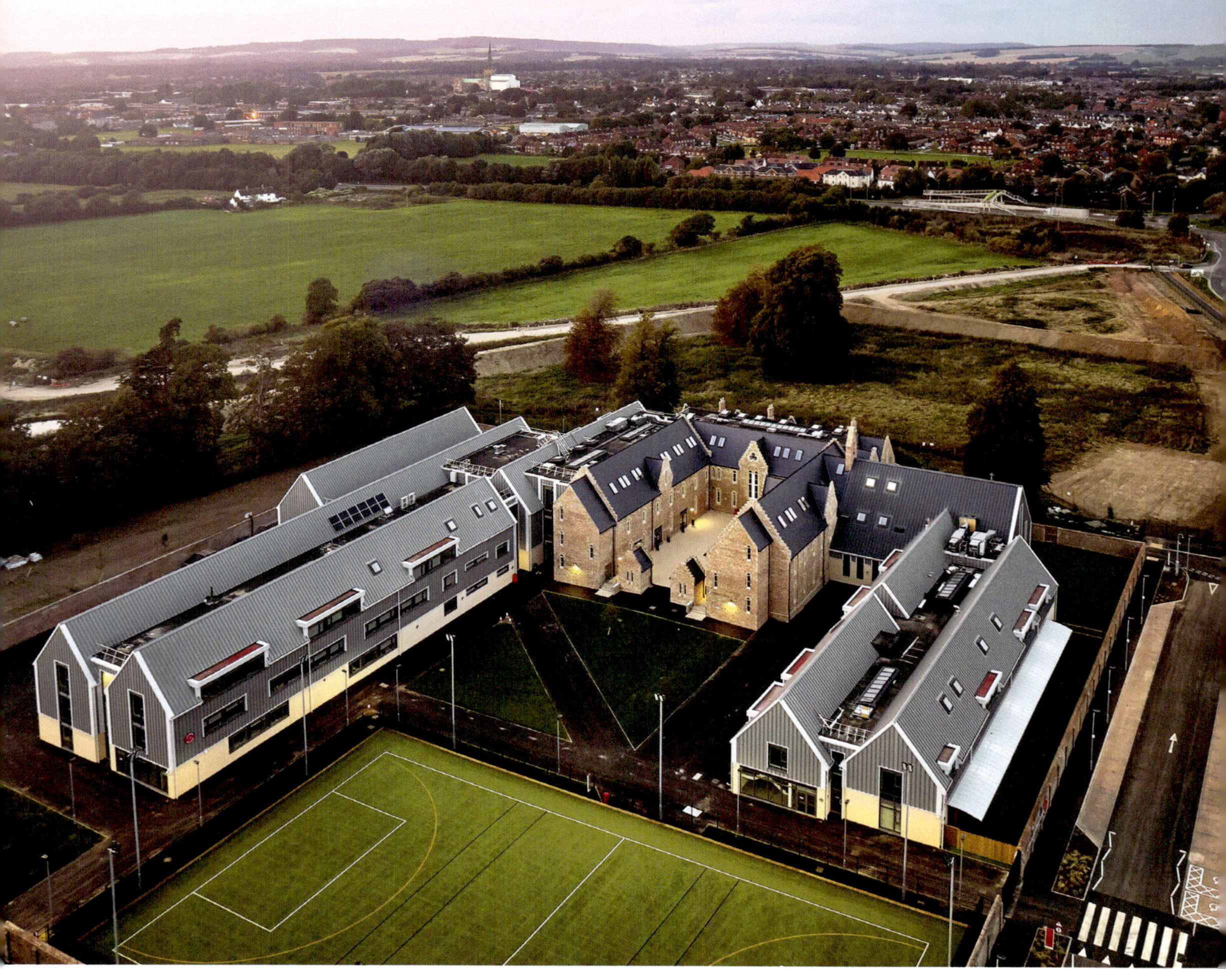

Chichester Free School. (Chichester Free School)

Left empty, an arson attack on the chapel in 2009 destroyed the roof and much of the interior, although no one has ever been caught. Continuing to be left to fall into decay for several more years – and becoming a popular target for urban explorers – Chichester Free School announced plans to convert the former convent into a new school in 2014. Extensive renovation and extensions to accommodate the 1,280 students meant that the school finally opened in 2018, bringing the convent back to life and giving the once neglected buildings a fresh start.

34. Roussillon Barracks (1875)

Roussillon Barracks, established in 1875, originated as a tented camp in Chichester in 1795 due to fears of a French invasion. The camp transitioned to wooden huts in 1803 and housed French prisoners during the Napoleonic Wars. These prisoners built a flint and brick boundary wall in 1814, parts of which still stand. The barracks became home to the 35th (Royal Sussex) Regiment of Foot, the 107th (Bengal Infantry) Regiment of Foot, and the Royal Sussex Light

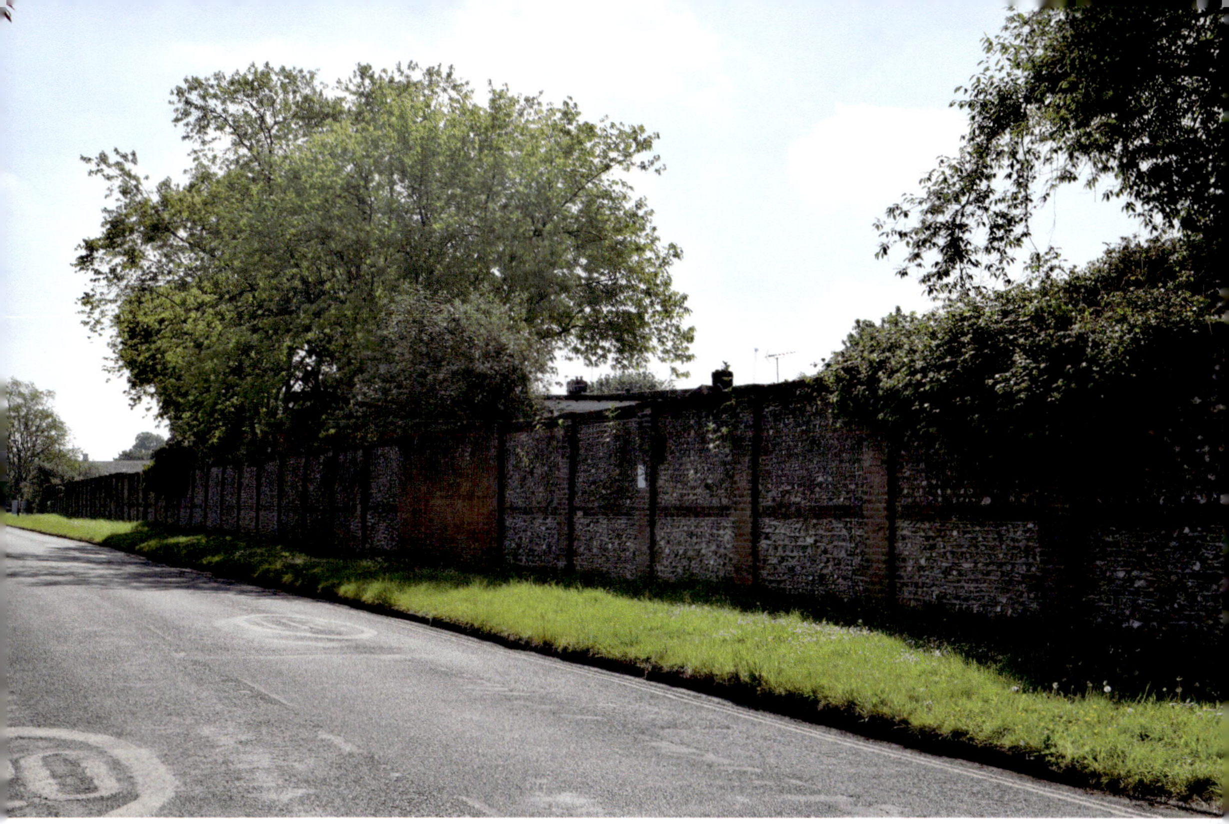

Above: Wall built by French POWs.

Below: The Keep.

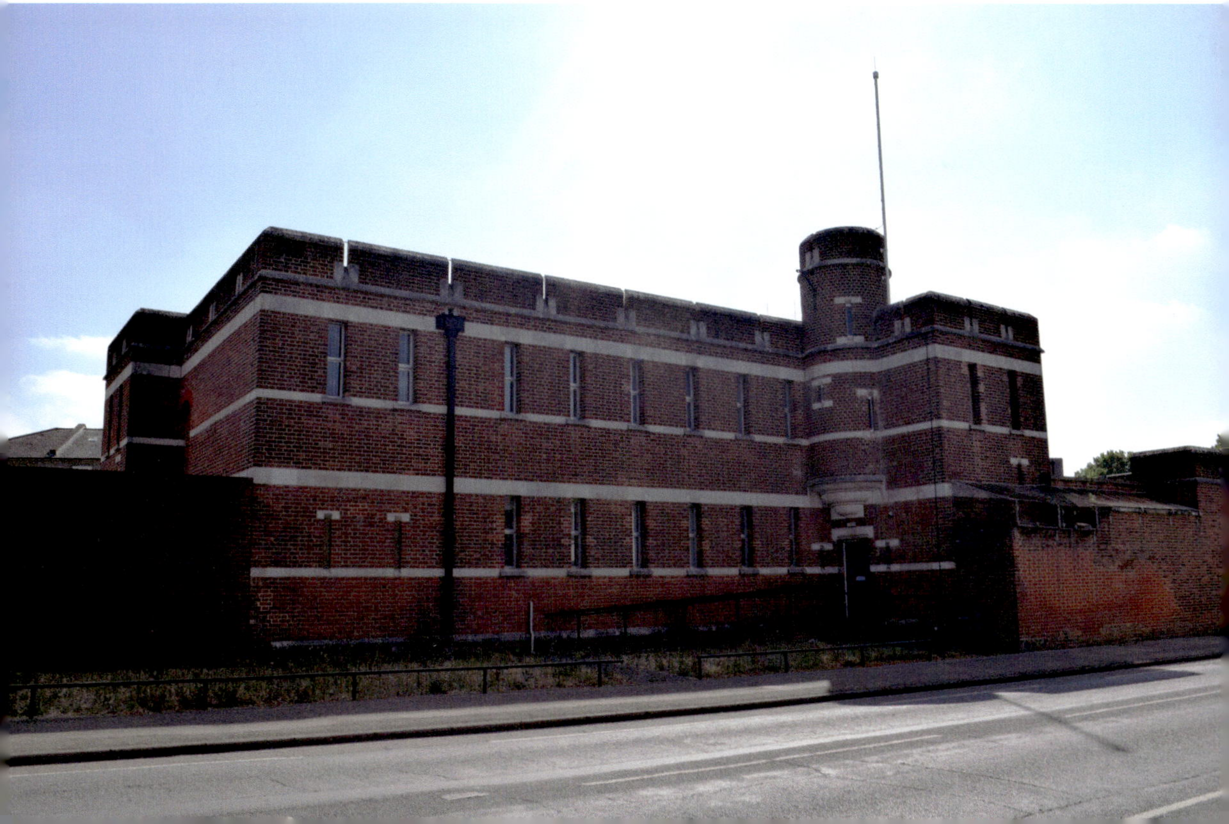

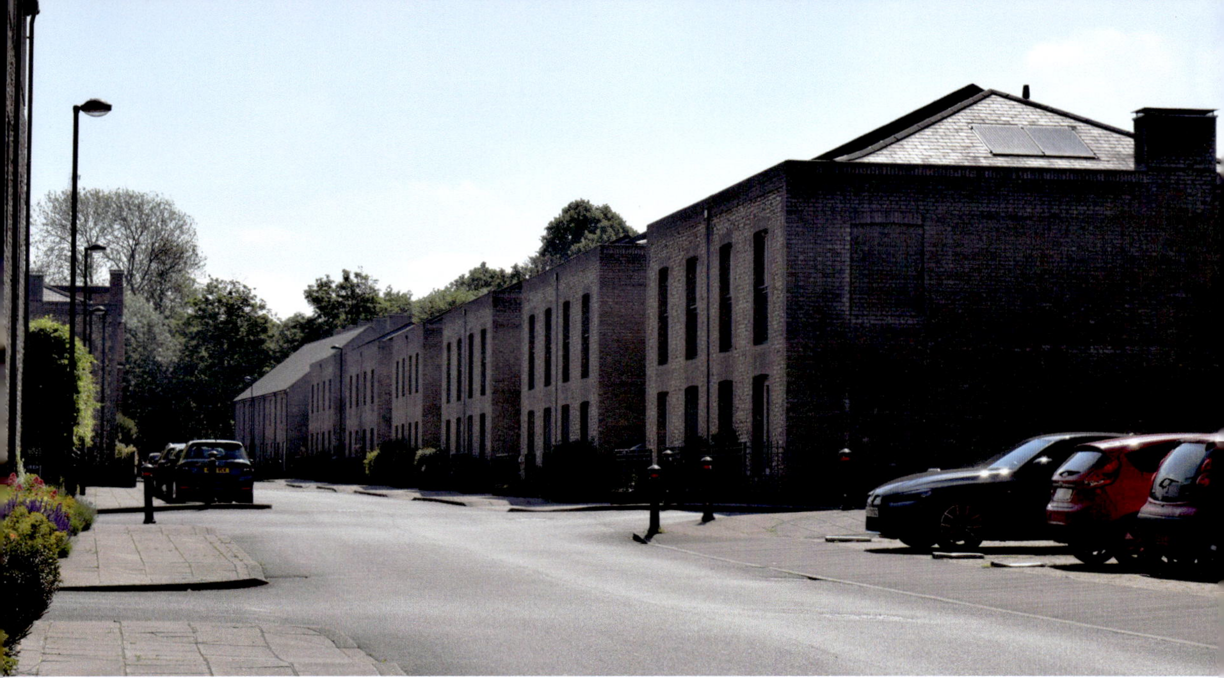

New housing on the former barracks.

Infantry Militia in 1872. The first permanent buildings, The Keep and a chapel, were added in 1875. The barracks became the depot for the newly amalgamated Royal Sussex Regiment in 1881.

The site underwent modernisation in the 1930s, replacing wooden huts with permanent structures. It was renamed Roussillon Barracks in 1958 to honour the 35th Regiment of Foot's actions during the Seven Years' War. The barracks became a station of the Home Counties Brigade in 1959, with the Royal Sussex Regiment departing in 1960. Major rebuilding occurred before the Royal Military Police arrived in 1964, staying until 2005.

The Keep served as a prison for Argentine Lieutenant-Commander Alfredo Astiz, implicated in the 1977 kidnapping, torture, and murder of several people, and captured in the Falklands War. He was later repatriated to Argentina and convicted of crimes against humanity in 2011.

The Royal Military Police left in 2005, and the site was sold for housing in 2011. A development of 252 residences was built between 2012 and 2018, preserving the Keep, parade ground, chapel, and parts of the boundary wall and War Department stones.

35. Graylingwell (1894)

Named for the Grayling Well pond, the 138.5-acre Graylingwell Farm site was purchased in 1894 for a new psychiatric hospital, opening in 1897 complete with a superintendent's house, farm, theatre and chapel. The latter, designed by Sir Arthur Blomfield & Sons is almost wholly original to the 1890s.

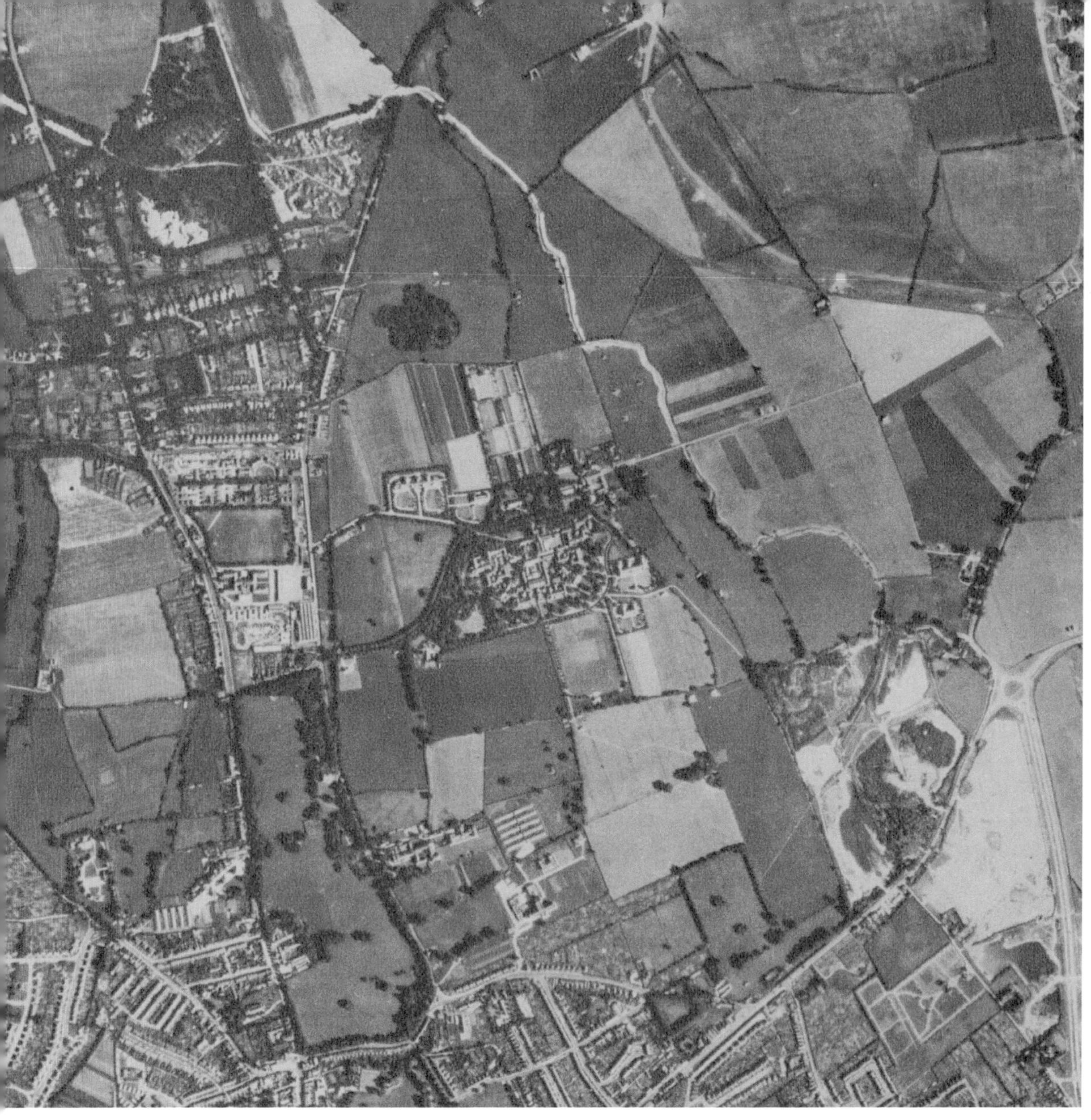

The extent of the Graylingwell estate is clear in this Luftwaffe image from 1942. (NARA)

The grounds and gardens laid out in 1897–99 included a tennis court, sporting facilities and open spaces to keep the patients occupied. The main building complex, large enough to accommodate 1,000 patients, contained a large number of day rooms and workshops for cobbling, tailoring and plumbing (for which patients were paid a special token for use in the hospital shop); the site remained almost entirely self-sufficient until the 1950s, when the farm and livestock were sold. However, the patient population grew such that three additional wards needed to be added in 1902. Despite this, it took until 1911 before a children's ward appeared.

Requisitioned by the military in 1915 to become Graylingwell War Hospital, all 742 patients were removed to other asylums in March to make way for the wounded, although twenty patients remained to maintain the estate, living in the farmhouse.

Only enlisted men were admitted to Graylingwell, with over 29,000 passing through by the time the military hospital closed in 1919. Owing to the high, number of casualties during the Battle of the Somme, officers began to be admitted to Graylingwell from July 1916.

Returning to civilian use in 1919, the next major event came on 25 February 1929. Leaving her music lesson on St Paul's Road, eleven-year-old Vera Hoad disappeared without a trace during her fifteen-minute walk home. A male patient found her body, partly covered in snow, at the side of a field in the grounds of Graylingwell. Police found signs of struggle and an adult boot print at the scene. Naturally, suspicion fell on the patients until staff were able to account for everyone's whereabouts at the time of Vera's disappearance. The case remains unsolved.

The hospital underwent further expansion in the 1920s and 1930s, including the addition of Summersdale Hospital to the north-west of the main building in 1933 and a nurses' accommodation block.

Graylingwell remained open throughout the Second World War, but the Summersdale Hospital block was requisitioned to treat servicemen with PTSD. A further two wards were also brought into military use following D-Day in 1944.

Expansion continued in the post-war years, and it was transferred to the NHS in 1948. Upon closure in 2001, all the hospital's furnishings and equipment were auctioned off, and the buildings sold for housing in 2010. Much of the site fell to the bulldozers, but the water tower, chapel, superintendent's house, nurses' block and Summersdale Hospital all survive.

The water tower among the modern housing. (David Martin)

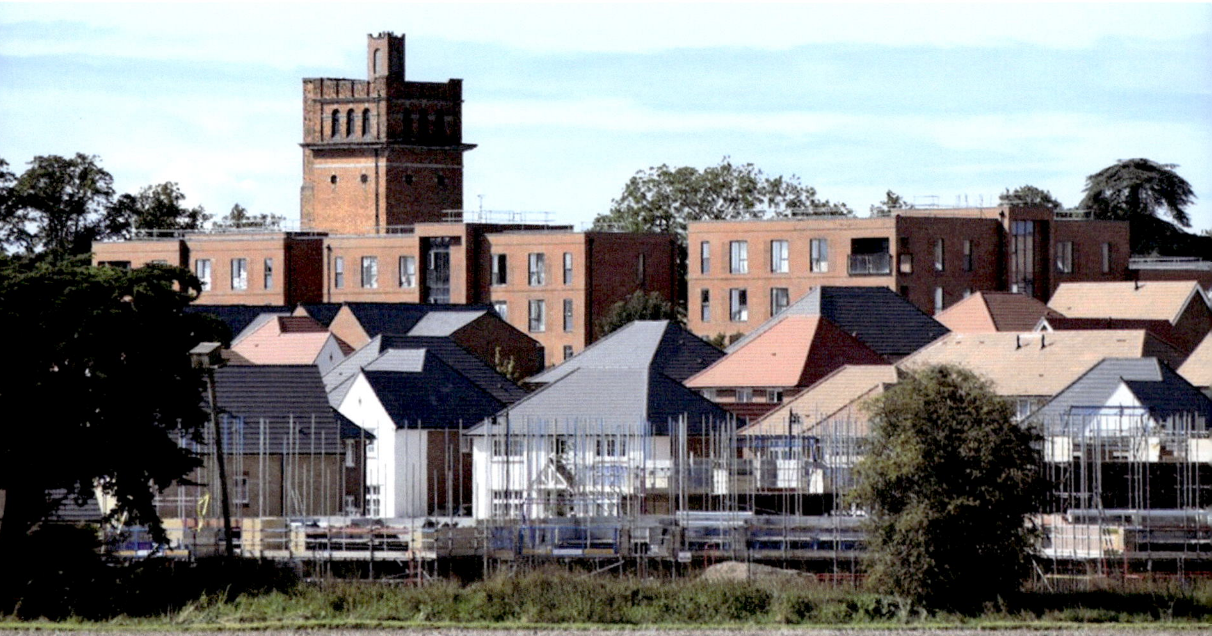

36. Oliver Whitby School (1904)

The eponymous Oliver Whitby left his fortune to the founding of a new school for twelve poor boys from Chichester, Harting and West Wittering in a will dated 16 February 1703. Aside from leaving his money, he also left instructions on the uniform the boys were to wear and that the principal subjects were to be reading, writing and mathematics.

The building on West Street was first rented in 1712 and then purchased outright in 1721. A carved wooden Blue Coat Boy (now at The Novium), just under 3 feet tall, stood outside the front door of the school from 1725 to encourage passers-by to make donations.

The school had a number of extensions from time to time, but by the turn of the twentieth century had become unsuitable. The buildings were demolished to make way for a brand new school in 1904. The right-hand wing of the new building became the headmaster's residence, whereas the left-hand wing housed the matron and other domestics. To the rear, playgrounds, classrooms, a garden, a woodwork room and, added later, a gym provided both education and play for the boys.

On 10 February 1943, a bomb hit the rear of the school and the new gym before bouncing into Chapel Street and exploding. A number of windows in the main building were broken and the gym all but demolished.

Former Oliver Whitby School buildings.

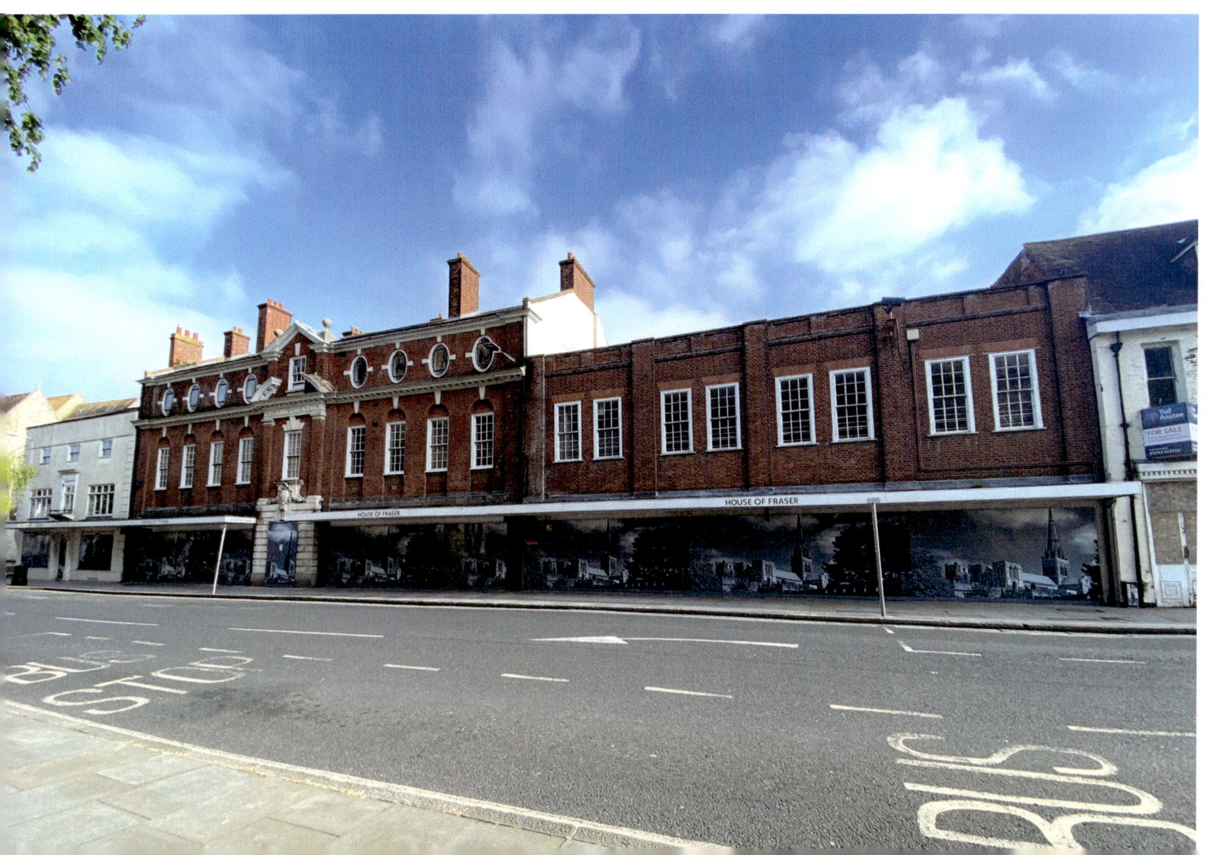

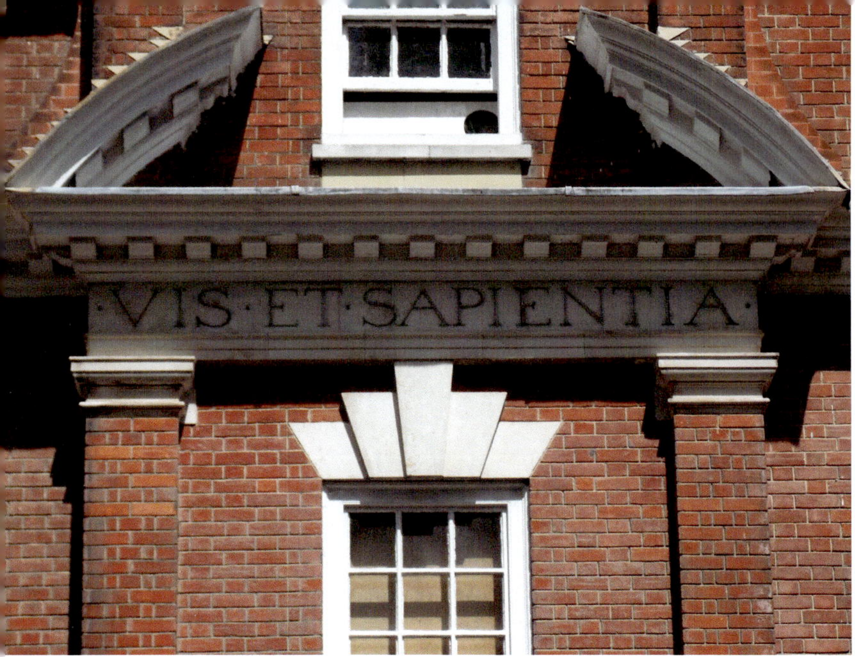

The school motto.

Although surviving the remainder of the war, the decision to close the school came in 1950, with all remaining pupils transferred to Christ's Hospital, near Horsham. The Oliver Whitby School later became a branch of House of Frasier until 2019, and it has sat empty since.

37. Shippam's (1912)

The first shop opened in Westgate in 1786 by Charles Shippam. His son, George, moved the shop to North Street in 1832 and then to East Street in 1851 to accommodate the growing business. Starting out selling groceries, the company expanded into production of its own pastes, spreads, soups, and canned and jarred meats from 1892, when a factory was added behind the East Street shop. As a pioneer and innovator in the meat preservation industry, a brand-new factory had to be built along the East Walls in 1912–13 to accommodate the demand for Shippam's products.

By now the company had become one of the major employers in the city, often recruiting staff from multiple generations of the same families. Gaining two royal warrants in 1948 and 1955, the factory became a tourist destination and attracted many visitors to Chichester; more than 15,000 people took the factory tour in 1959 alone.

Naturally, such a successful business attracted the eyes of the major corporations, and an American company purchased the Shippam's name in 1974, marking the end of the family-run nature of the business. A number of other takeovers followed throughout the 1990s, with the last member of the Shippam family resigning in 1996. The end of the factory finally came in 2001, when Princes purchased the business and closed the East Walls factory, instead moving to a new site on Terminus Road in 2002.

The East Walls factory was demolished in 2005, but the south- and east-facing façades were retained and rebuilt into the new retail units that replaced the factory.

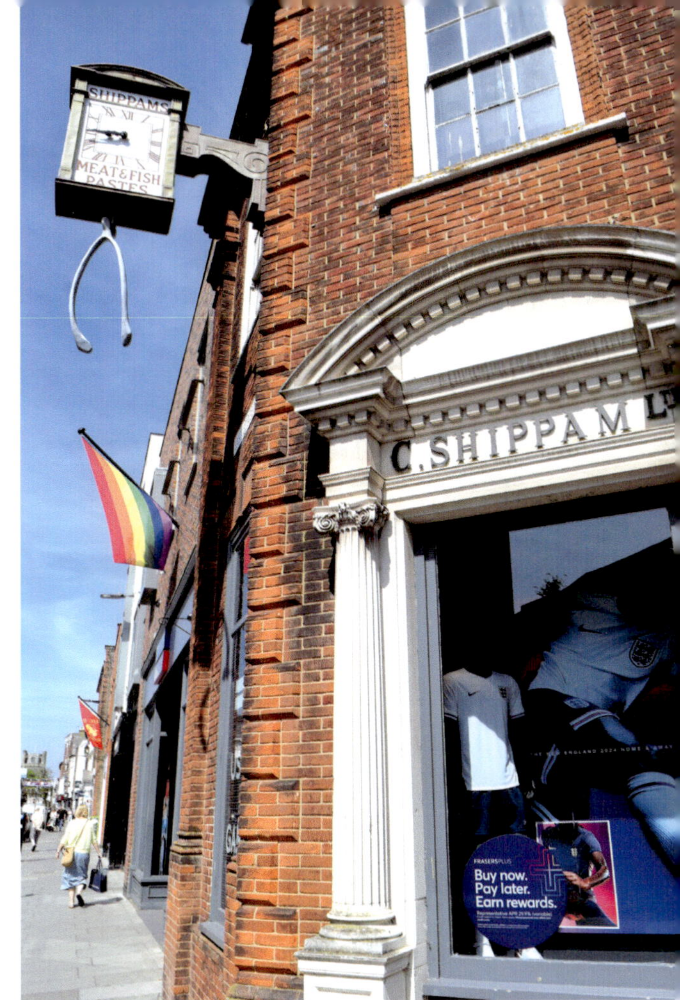

Right: Main entrance, clock and silver wishbone of Shippam's.

Below: The remains of the East Walls factory.

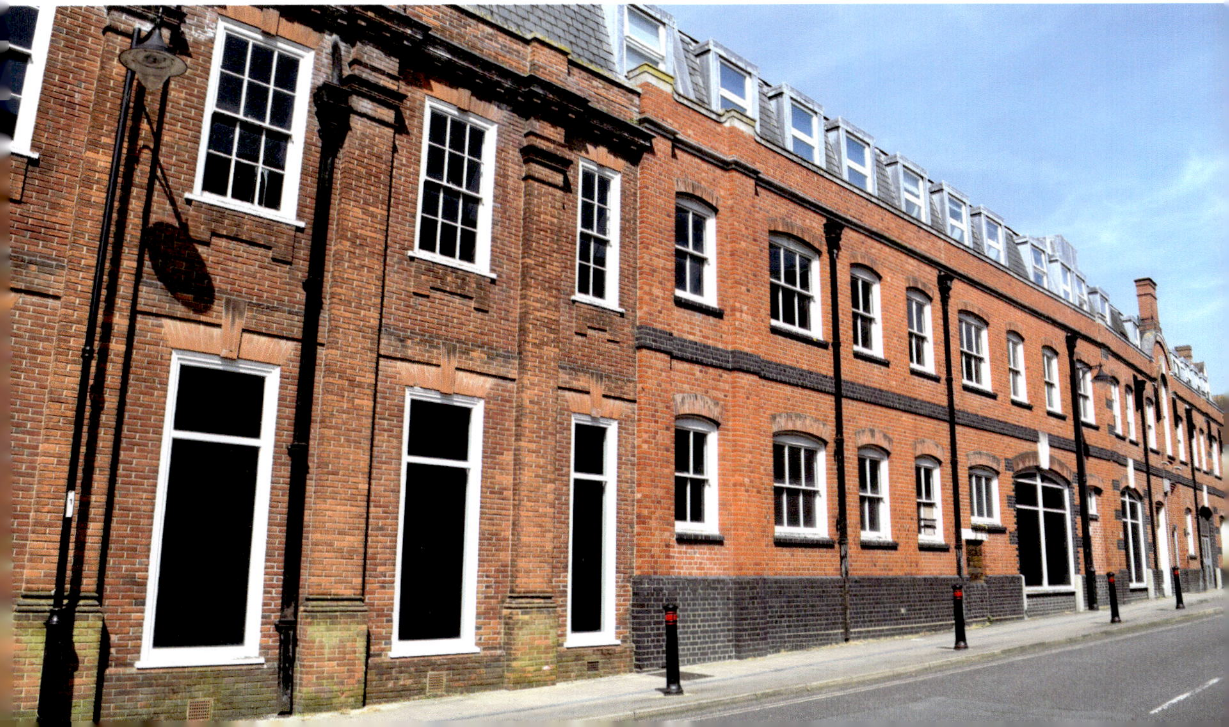

38. War Memorial (1921)

Originally located in Eastgate Square, the memorial to the city's fallen soldiers of the First World War was unveiled in a solemn ceremony in 1921 by Field Marshal Sir William R. Robertson – the most senior officer in the British Army at the time, and the only person to have ever served in every rank from private to field marshal – and dedicated by the Dean of Chichester. It stood here for nineteen years before changes to the road layout forced it to move. The chosen site, Litten Gardens, had up to this point been a disused burial ground, closed in *c.*1871 when Portfield Cemetery opened.

Initially bearing sixteen stone tablets with the names of 353 men of the First World War, four more stones, bearing a further 255 names from the Second World War, have been added in recent years. New names continue to be added as research uncovers more details of the city's wartime history.

In 2018 a chainsaw sculpture made from Sussex oak of a Tommy was installed close to the memorial to mark the centenary of the end of the First World War, in addition to a stone commemorating Lieutenant Colonel Wilfrith Elstob VC, who was born in Chichester in 1888 and killed in action near Saint-Quentin on the first day of the German Spring Offensive on 21 March 1918.

A further statue was added on Remembrance Sunday 2019 of Lance Corporal Maurice Patten of the Royal Sussex Regiment. Lance Corporal Patten died of

War memorial.

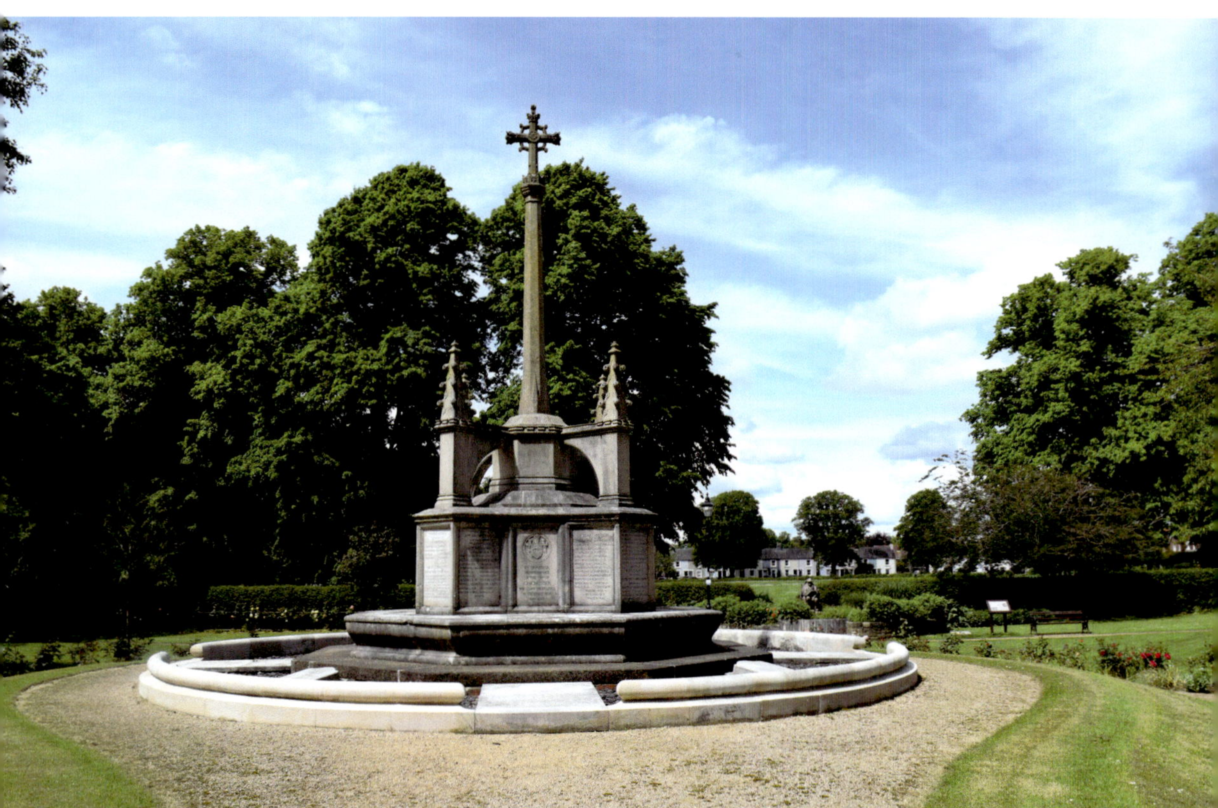

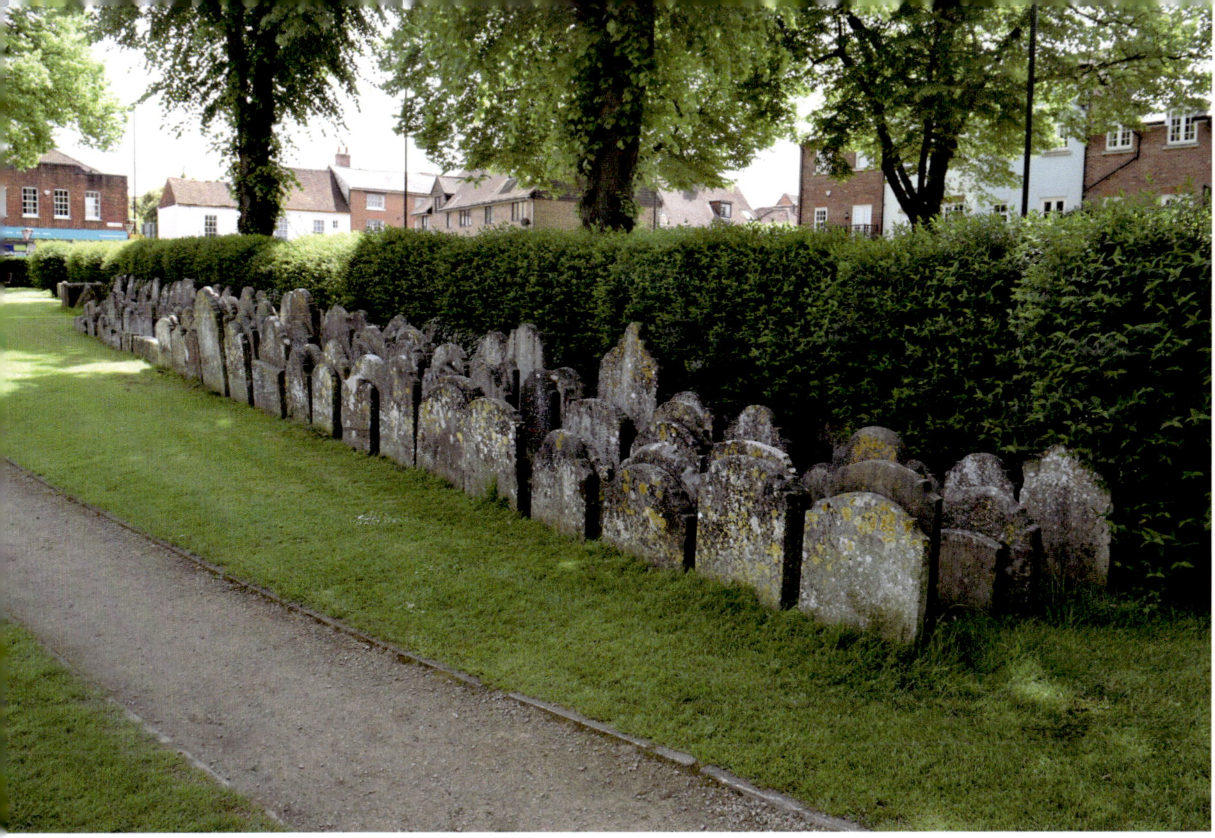

Above: Gravestones removed from the former burial ground.

Below: Wooden sculpture added in 2018.

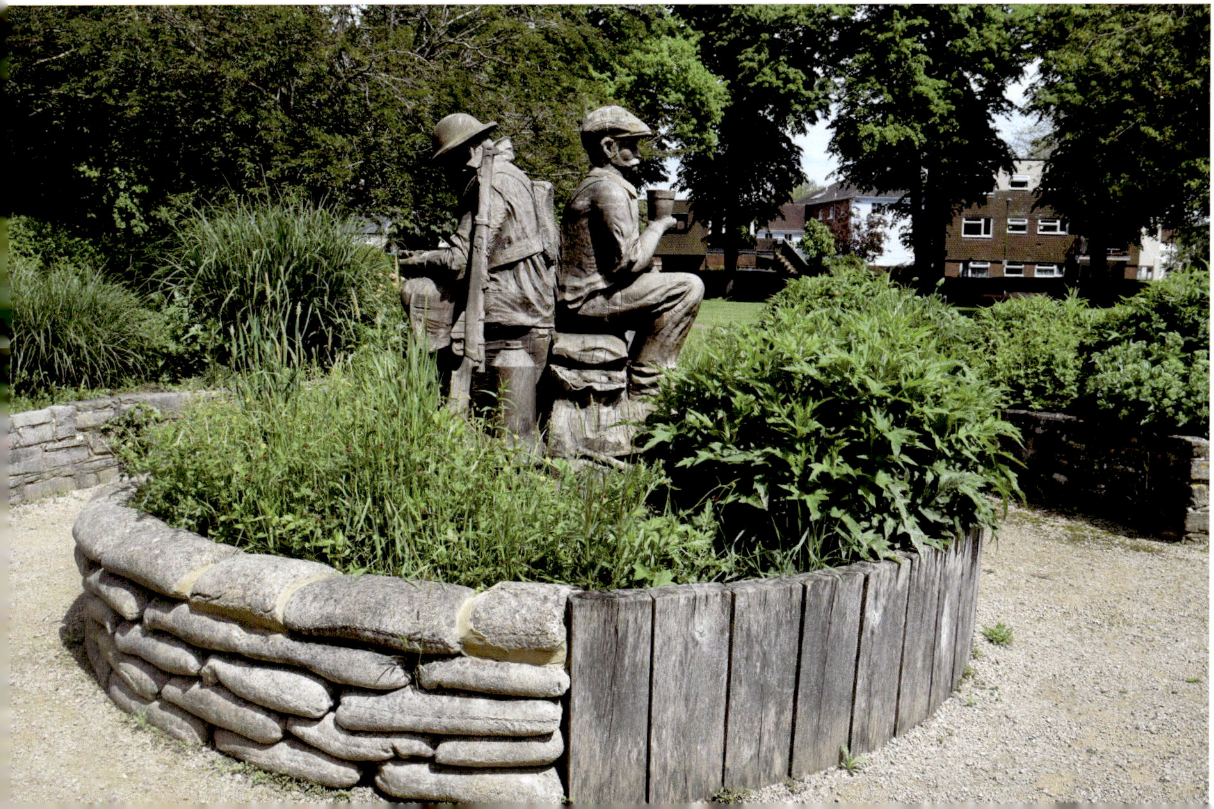

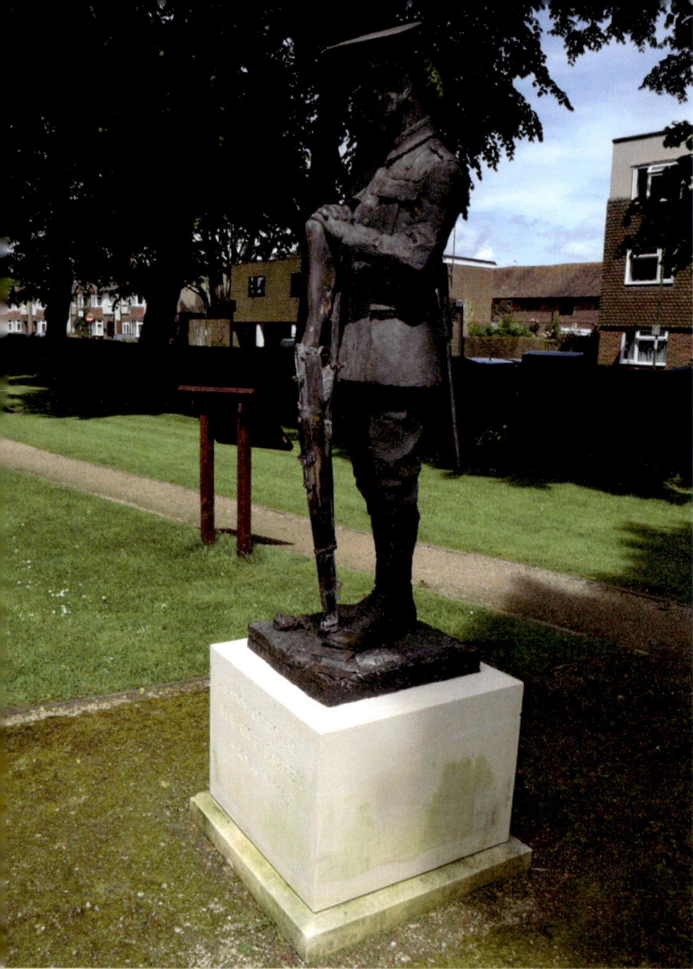

Statue of Lance Corporal Maurice Patten.

wounds sustained on 13 January 1916, aged just twenty-four. The statue depicts him standing in the resting-at-arms-reversed posture of official mourning, facing towards the war memorial, with cast replicas of his tobacco pouch, silver watch, and family bible.

39. County Hall (1933)

The 30,000-square-foot building that is County Hall began life on paper as the work of County Architect Cecil G. Stillman and was built between 1933 and 1936 to replace the offices in Edes House. In the 1960s, a Victorian mansion known as The Grange was acquired and absorbed into the site, being replaced with a large office block in 1962.

Perhaps the most interesting feature of the building is the County Control Centre created in the basement just prior to the outbreak of the Second World War. Manned continuously day and night throughout the war, the staff recorded every report of bombing, gunning, and aircraft crashes from across West Sussex in real time, and oversaw the response to incidents.

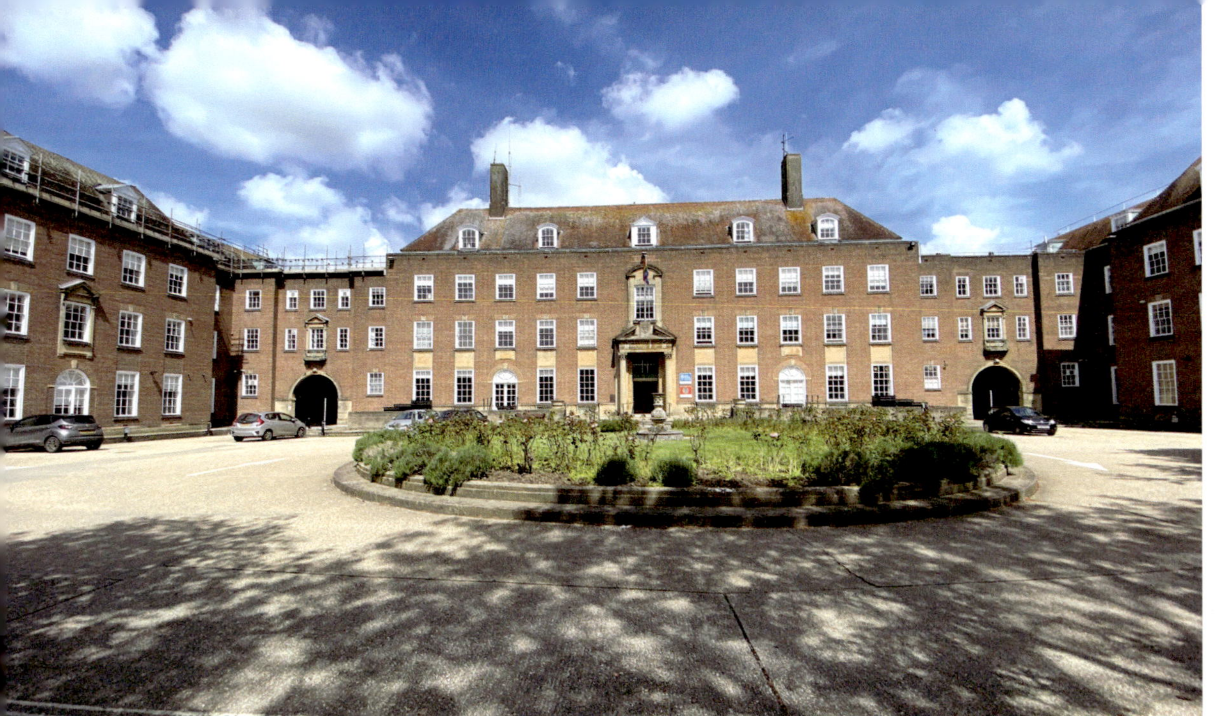

County Hall.

In the 1960s, with the threat of a vastly different kind of warfare, the centre was altered to become the Emergency Control Centre to oversee the civil defence operations in the event of nuclear war. Ironically, the centre never received any reinforcement to be able to survive a nuclear blast, nor protection from fallout or gas.

Access to the Emergency Control Centre is via a door behind the main reception desk and down a narrow flight of stairs. With the exception of the SX2000 County Emergency Communications Network switch cabinet installed in the late 1980s to allow direct communication with other control centres, the centre is largely as it was in the 1960s – it even still holds a stock of over 400 radiation monitors from 1979.

Now used to manage any large-scale disaster, the centre effectively operates as a central hub for the planning of responses to emergencies, containing an array of maps, boards, charts, and tables. A radio room installed in the 1960s now stands empty as the technology has moved on, with mobile phones now the go-to mode of communication.

40. Police Station (1937)

In the early days, policing in Chichester was haphazard, relying on several part-time constables funded by the city council. The Guardians of the Poor introduced a small number of nightwatchmen in the early eighteenth century to patrol the dark streets. They operated from a purpose-built watch house opened in 1821.

Chichester City Police, established in 1836, marked the appearance of a professional police force. Crime prevention fell under its authority, with a

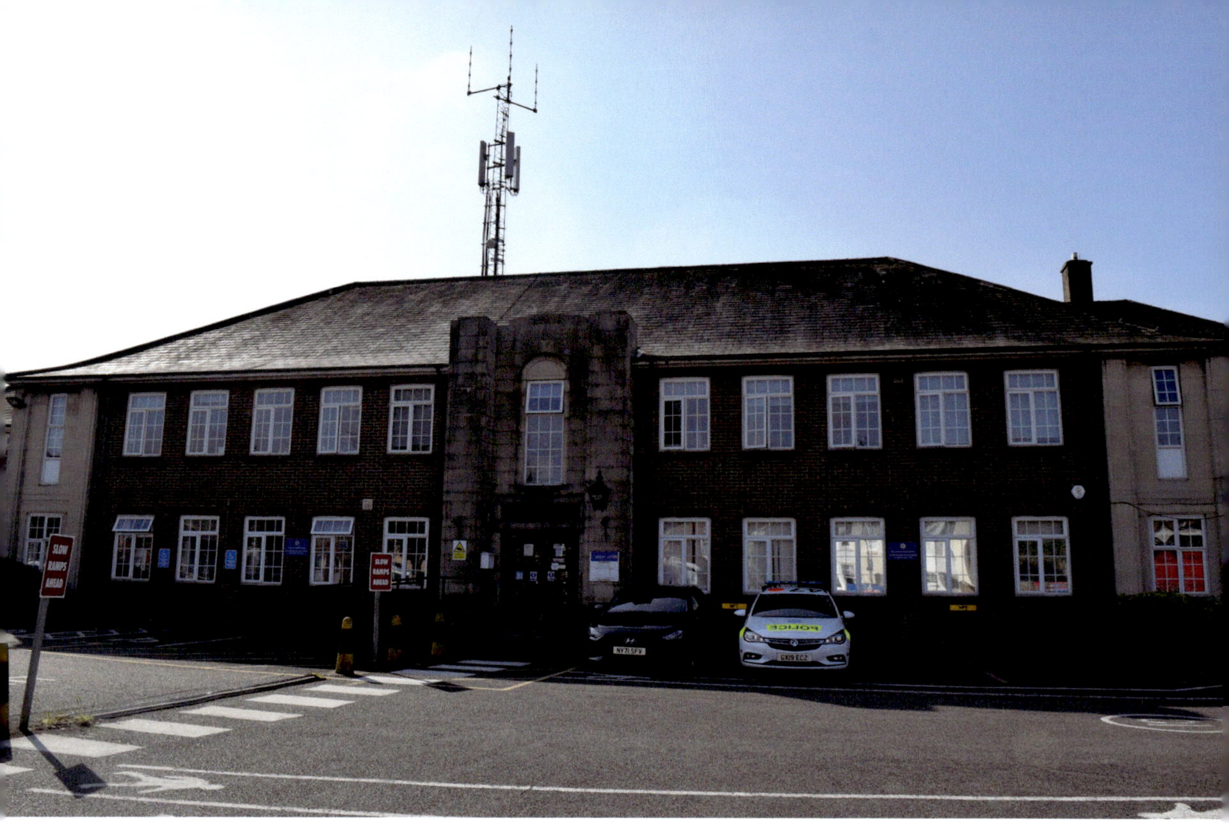

Above: Chichester Police Station.

Below: Custody Suite.

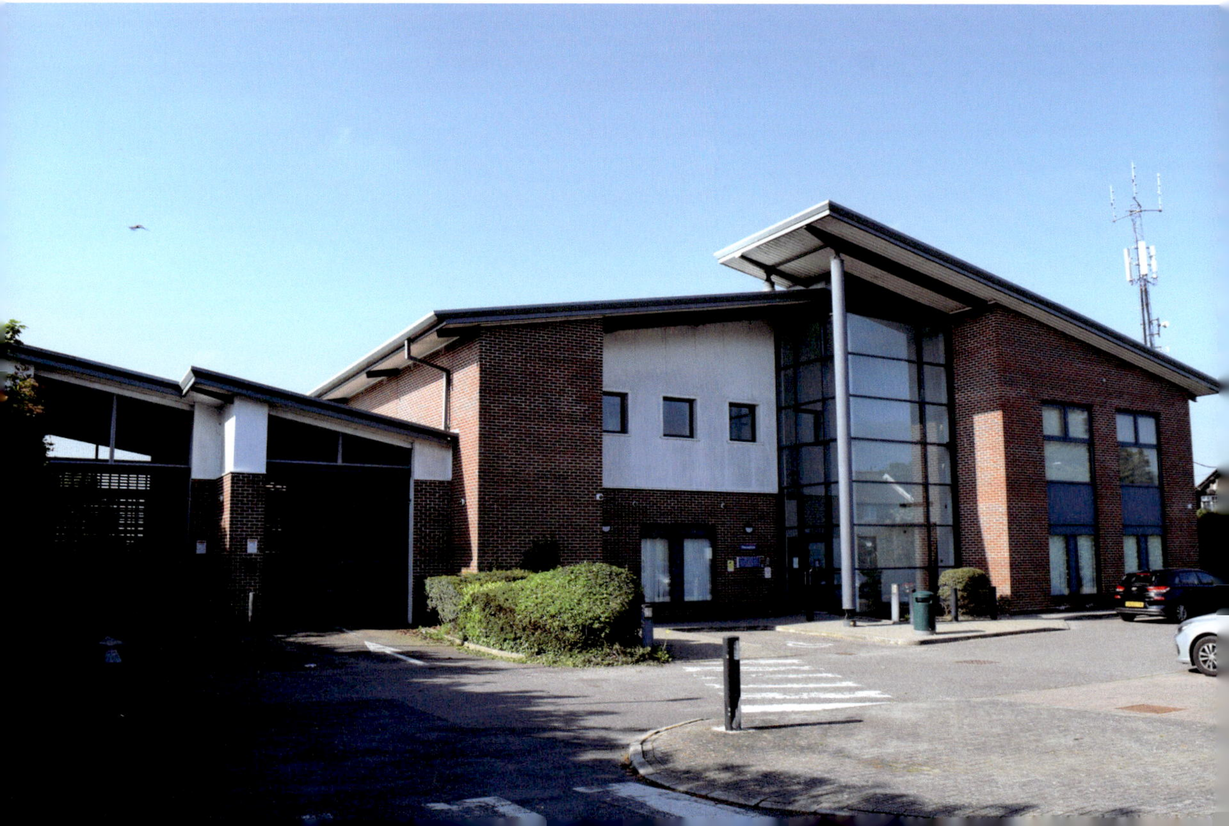

police station located at the city gaol in Eastgate. Interestingly, the West Sussex Constabulary emerged separately in 1857, operating from a new police station at Southgate near the railway station. These two forces remained distinct until their merger in 1889 at the Southgate station. Chichester became the headquarters of the West Sussex Constabulary in 1922.

To accommodate growth, a new police station opened in Basin Road in 1935. Lord Leconfield laid the foundation stone in April 1932, and the former Eastgate station was demolished (though one gaol door was preserved). Before the Second World War, an extension above the cells provided a billiards room, library and bar for officers. A sports field behind the station offered leisure opportunities during shifts. Later, a section house and training school were added.

Controversially, a custody suite opened in a separate building in 2001 under a thirty-year PFI contract, costing £11.6 million annually. The Chichester Custody Centre became the least utilised in the county, closing in November 2018. It briefly reopened between September 2020 and the summer of 2021 during upgrades at other centres.

41. St Richard's Hospital (1938)

Named for the Bishop of Chichester from 1244 to 1253, West Sussex County Council built St Richard's Hospital between 1938 and 1939 to provide 194 beds for the elderly and infirm.

A&E main entrance.

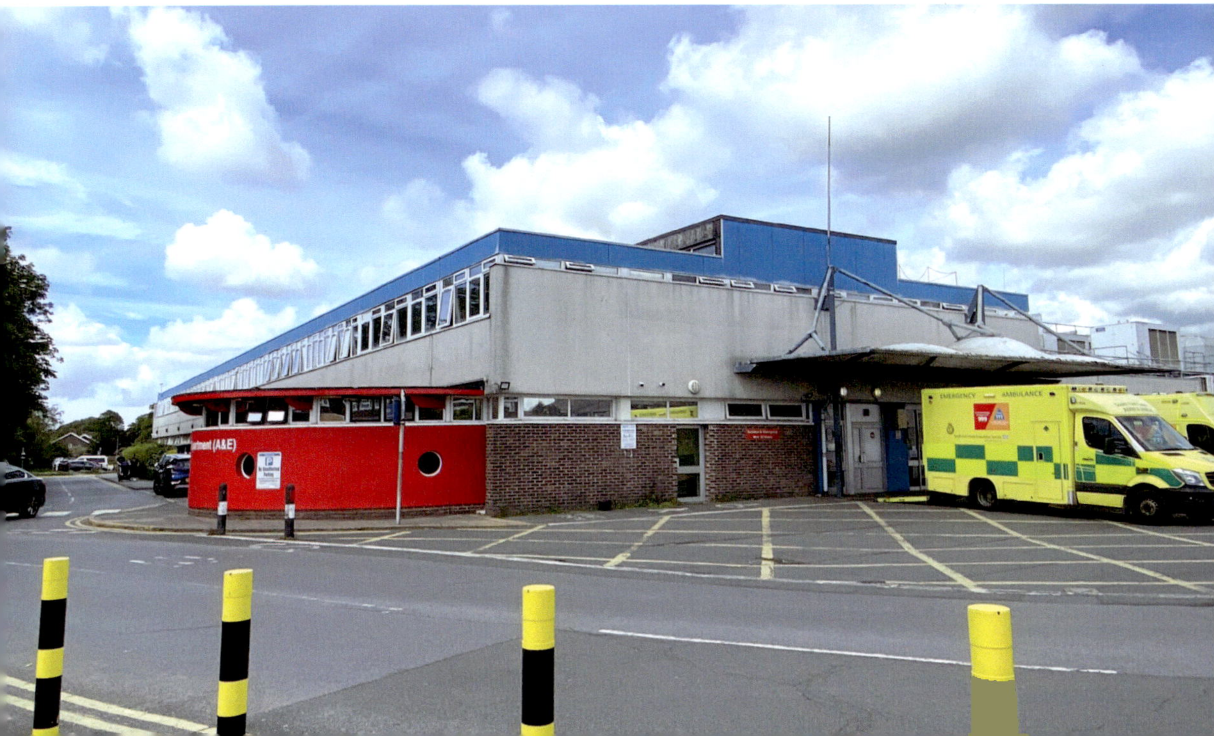

Shortly upon opening in 1939, the government declared St Richard's as an Emergency Medical Service General Hospital, bringing it under direct control of the state, with ten hutted wards added in 1940 for an additional 400 beds.

Although remaining a civilian hospital, all patients were moved to other hospitals in the lead-up to D-Day in 1944, in expectation of the enormous number of casualties; the hutted wards were also emptied and set aside to receive wounded German prisoners of war. Beginning on 6 June, wounded servicemen began arriving almost every other day for several weeks, and additional civilian staff from the London hospitals had to be brought in, alongside military medics units stationed in the area.

The post-war era saw further changes and rapid expansion, starting with joining the NHS in 1948. A postgraduate medical education centre opened in 1966, followed by the accident and emergency unit, outpatient's department, X-ray department and maternity department, all opened in 1970, in addition to a further two operating theatres. Donald Wilson House, a neurological rehabilitation unit, opened in 1975, followed by the intensive care unit in 1976.

St Richard's became an NHS Trust in 1994, again undergoing rapid changes and expansion to create a new, larger hospital in 1996. It was downgraded to District General Hospital status in May 2008, the same year that Donald Wilson House was replaced with a modern, eco-friendly building and a new cancer day unit added. A new children's ward opened in February 2011.

As with all hospitals, St Richard's was on the front line of the pandemic in 2020, performing above and beyond and overcoming countless challenges.

42. Unicorn Inn (1938)

The original Unicorn dated to *c.* 1670 following the rebuilding of the Eastgate area after the Civil War. Soon after, the inn became the headquarters for the Corporation of St Pancras upon its foundation as a drinking and dining club in 1689, in celebration of the ascension of William of Orange to the throne and the overthrow of the Catholic King James II. The Corporation brought like-minded individuals together for social events and fellowship, meeting at the Unicorn every year from 1689 until the pub closed in 1960 for its infamous Christmas meal. The nature of these meals is evident in the adoption of the nickname the Wheelbarrow Club due to the legend that members would have to be carried home in wheelbarrows. Since 1897 the Corporation has held charitable status and still exists as the UK's oldest dining club. To mark the Diamond Jubilee of Queen Victoria in 1897, the Corporation bequeathed money to the residents of Dears Almshouses, and provided the ladies with a Christmas meal. This proved so popular that this became an annual tradition that still survives to the present day. Until 1971, the Corporation marched in procession to the almshouses each Christmas day, carrying food and gifts, but upon the relocation of the almshouses

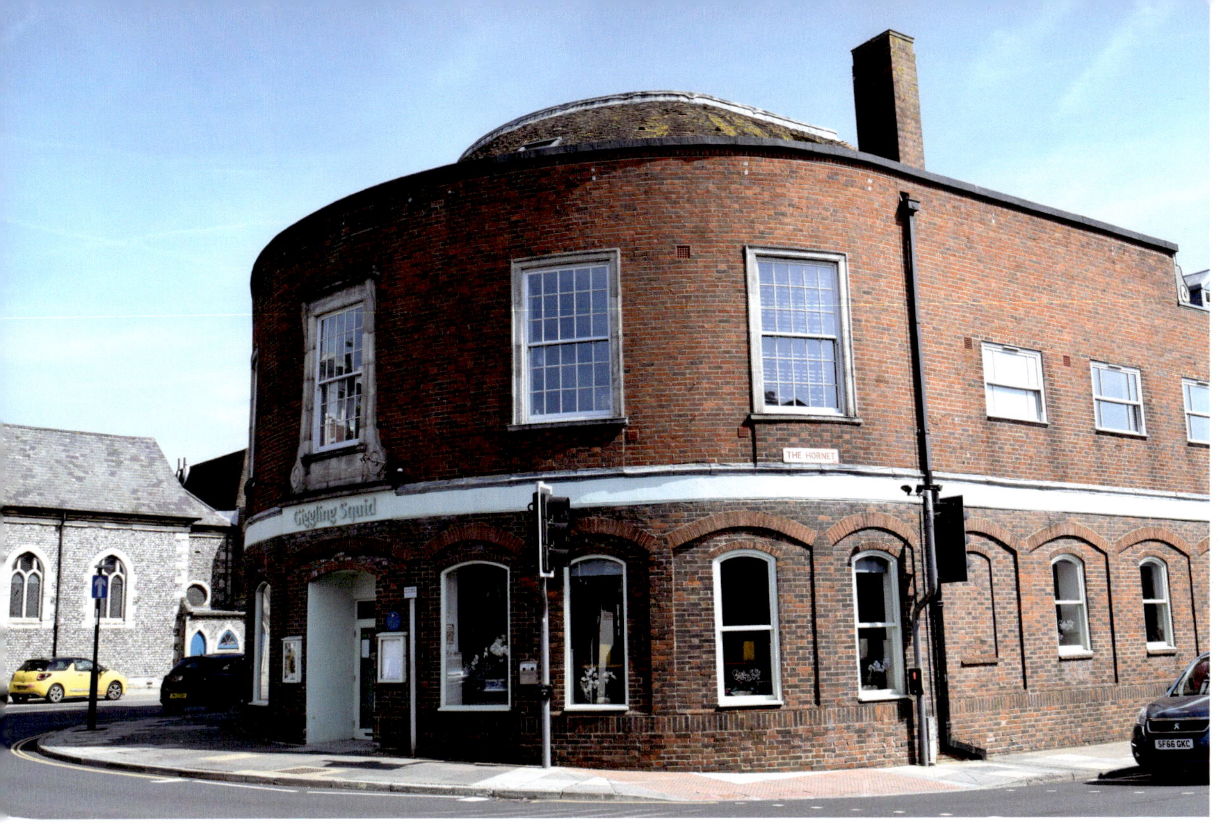

Former Unicorn Inn.

to Riverside, the date of the procession moved to a Saturday before Christmas to allow all the residents to be free to spend time away for the holidays without having to miss out on the festivities.

The present building dates to 1938 when the Eastgate Square area was remodelled to allow for road widening. Upon the outbreak of war, the hotel became one of the favoured drinking holes for the wealthier RAF officers at Tangmere, especially members of 601 Squadron – the co-called Millionaires Squadron. A gallery of famous airmen festooned the walls for several years in the 1940s.

The hotel closed down in 1960 and was leased for many years to Chichester Festival Theatre for use as its Minerva Studios from 1962 to 1994. The *Chichester Observer* then took on the building for its offices until 2015, after which it remained empty until converted into the Giggling Squid Thai restaurant in 2018.

43. Chichester Crown Court (1940)

The Sussex Quarter Sessions courts, established in 1940, evolved into the Crown Court by 1972. The building closed in 2017, but reopened as a temporary Nightingale court in 2020 to alleviate a backlog of cases during the pandemic, remaining operational since.

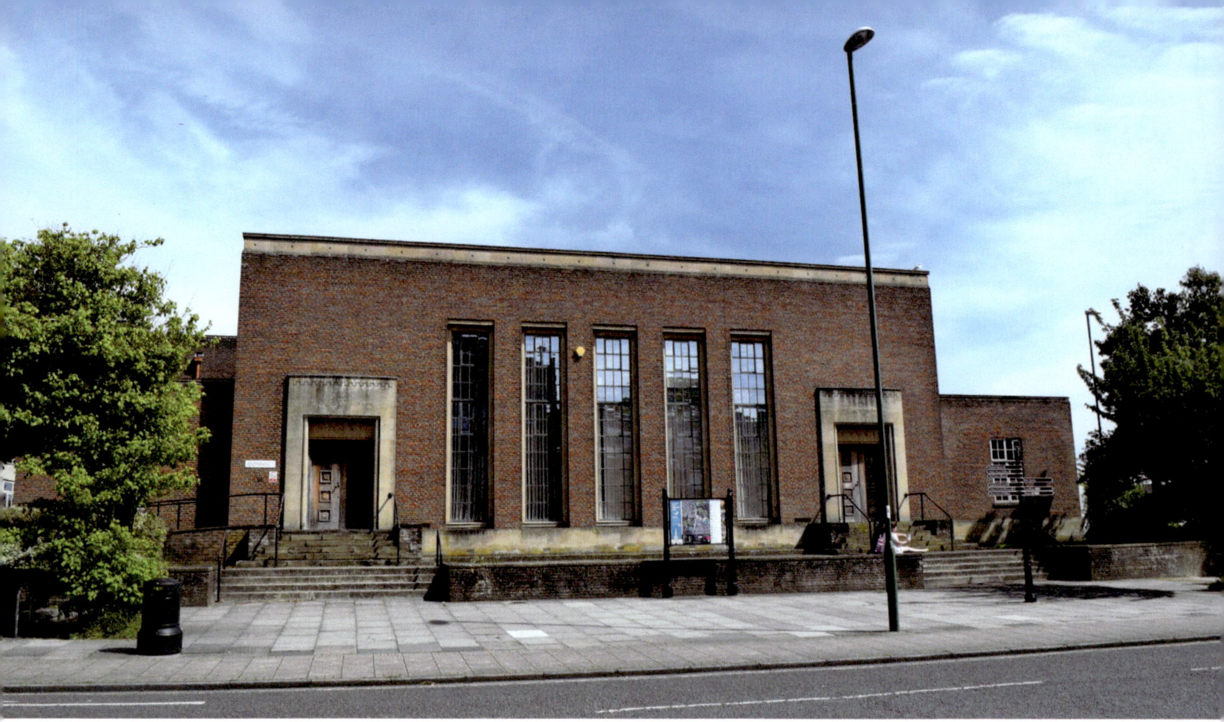

The court house.

Perhaps the highest-profile case to come before the magistrates was that of Mick Jagger and Keith Richards for drug offenses in May 1967. Richards had purchased the Redlands estate in West Wittering in 1966 and hosted a party there in February 1967 attended by a number of high-profile names of the time such as art dealer Robert Fraser, photographer Michael Cooper, Marianne Faithfull, George Harrison and Pattie Anne Boyd, as well as David Jove, the 'Acid King'.

Following a tip-off from the *News of the World* to the police, nineteen officers raided Redlands during the party and subsequently charged Jagger, Richards, and Fraser with drug possession offenses.

Considered as subversive by the government, Jagger and Richards appeared before the Chichester Magistrates Court on 10 May, greeted by large crowds of screaming schoolchildren and teenagers. Inside, the pair pleaded not guilty, and the case referred up to the Crown Court. Found guilty, they were remanded to Lewes Prison to await sentencing, with Jagger receiving a three-month prison sentence and Richards a twelve-month sentence in June. They each spent a day in prison before being released on bail pending appeal by their barrister, Michael Havers (father of actor Nigel Havers). In August, both sentences were quashed.

44. St Richard of Chichester Church (1958)

From 1829 Catholic services were held in a room of the Bedford Hotel in South Street, before the Countess of Newburgh donated land sandwiched between Theatre Lane and Old Market Avenue for a new church in 1855. The small

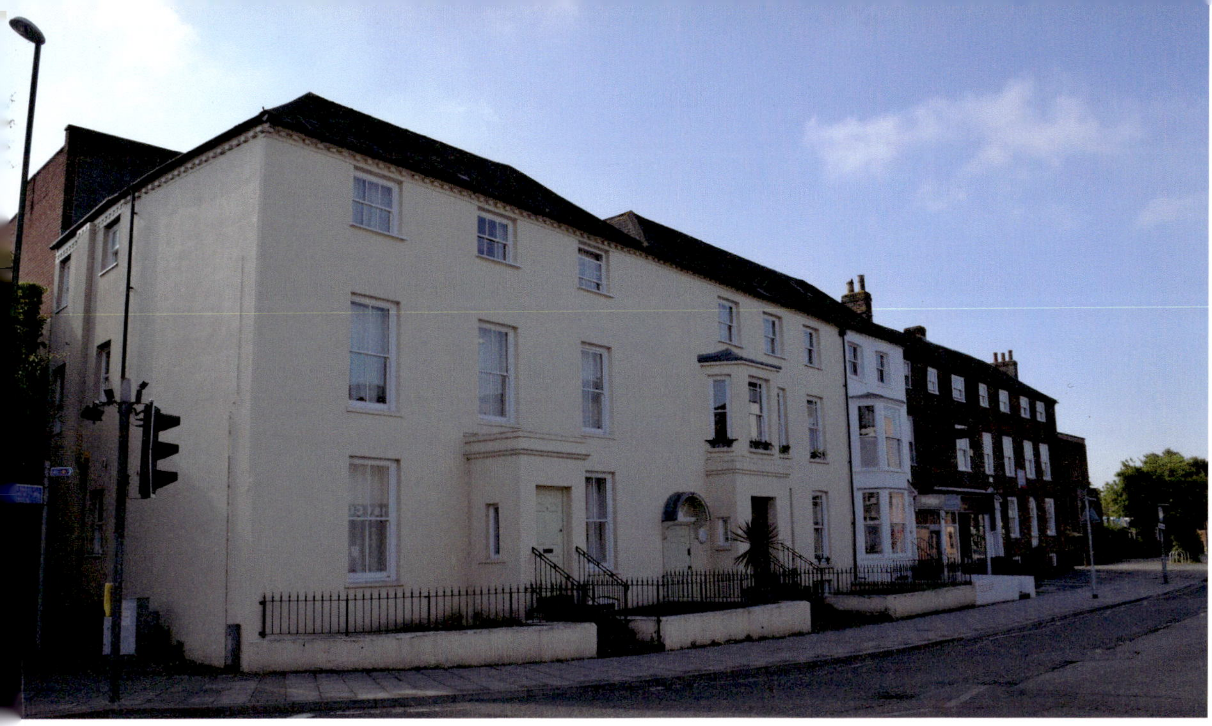

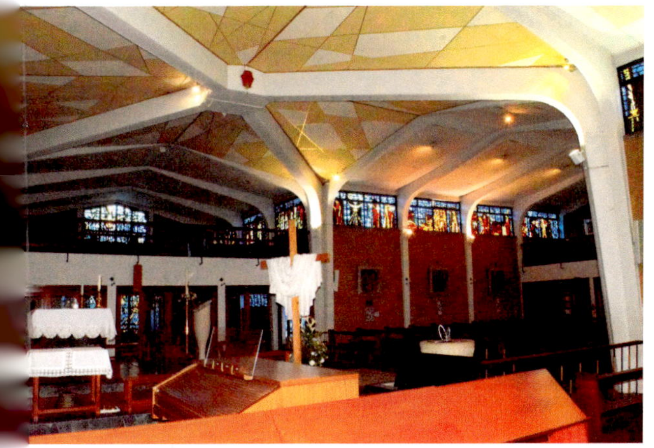

Former Bedford Hotel.

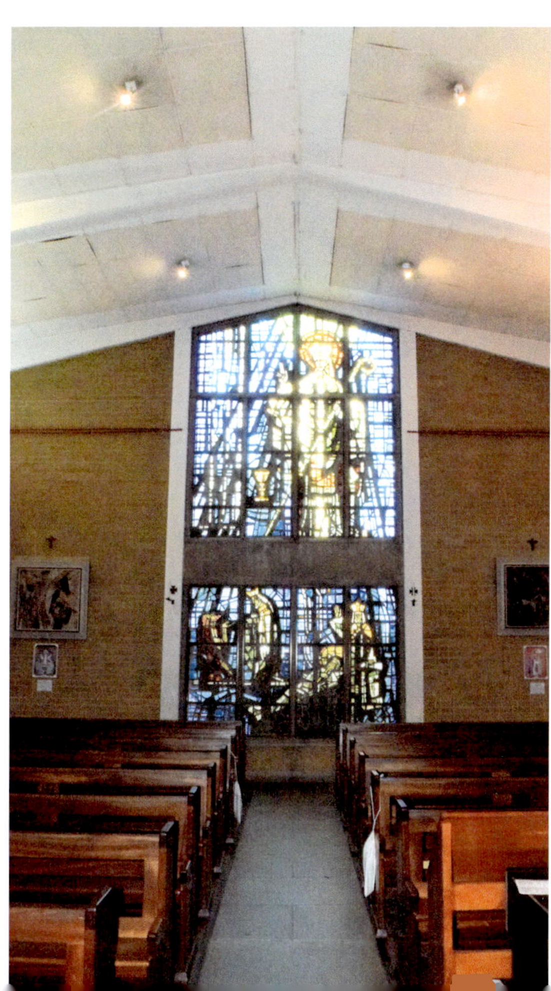

Above: Church interior.

Right: North-east Gabriel Loire window.

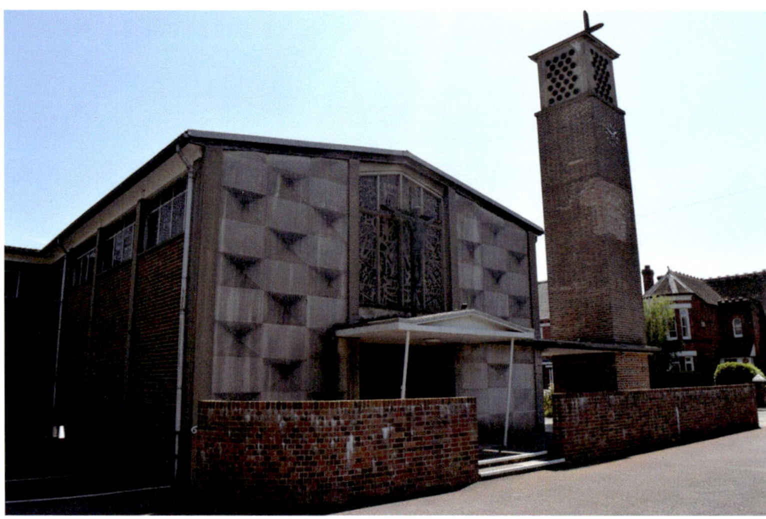

Main
entrance.

eighty-person, neo-Gothic church survived until 1958, with a number of monuments and artworks, including a stained-glass window depicting St Richard, St John the Evangelist and St Francis in memory of Revd J. Wilkinson.

The present church opened on 19 March 1958. It had been designed by Lawrence Tomei and John Maxwell in a modernist style. Until 1963, the interior remained as a plain shell until the marble, cladding, paintings, and stained glass were gradually added between 1963 and 1965, becoming home to the UK's largest collection of stained glass by the noted French artist Gabriel Loire.

Fundraising did not stop until 1981, when more than £750,000 had been raised for the church, as well as donations to six other Catholic churches and two schools in the Chichester District, as well as the city's first public swimming pool.

It was here that the small community of Carmelite nuns from the convent visited for the first time in 1994 to take part in a farewell mass before leaving for Cornwall.

The Bishop of Arundel and Brighton consecrated the church on 21 March 1998, with relics of St Richard and St Philip Howard placed into the altar stone. The latest addition was the Reconciliation Room, created out of engraved glass panel walls, installed in the side chapel in 2010.

45. Railway Station (1961)

A train station has existed on this site since the arrival of the railway in 1846, becoming a hub for the wealthy and prominent during the racing season at Goodwood. A new branch line to Midhurst opened in 1881, with the signal box being added in 1882 to control the traffic through the station. This increased in 1897, when the short-lived Selsey Tramway opened. Being prone to constant

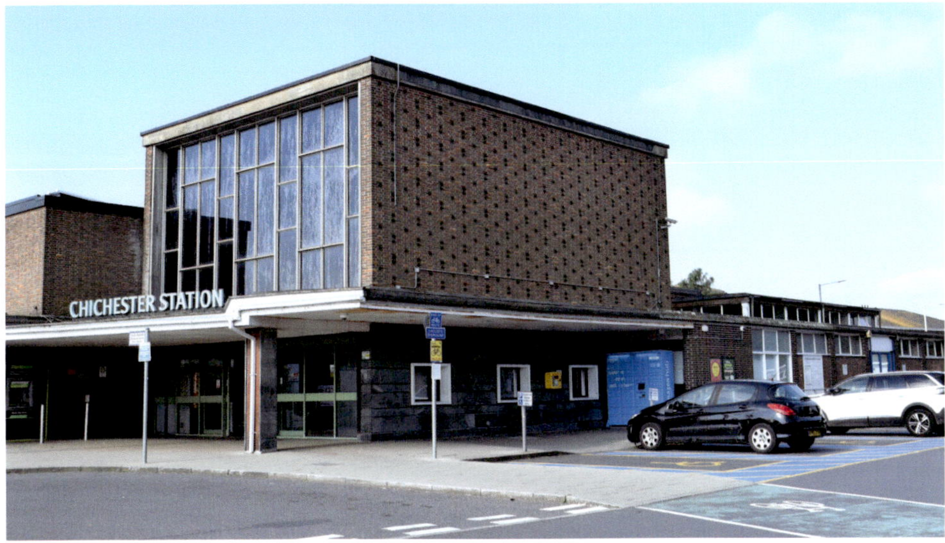

Chichester railway station.

delays and problems, this line closed in 1935, followed by the Midhurst Line in 1951.

The main station building fell into dilapidation and was finally demolished in 1958, to be replaced with a modern building in 1961, to the design of British Railway's Architect's Department. It remains one of the major stops on the Brighton-Portsmouth Line, servicing thousands of railway journeys each year.

In 1940–41, the railway also played its part in the defence of the city. A 9.2-inch railway gun was located on a stretch of track adjacent to Terminus Road, and later replaced by a pair of 12-inch railway howitzers set on trucks aimed at the RAF base on Thorney Island, ready to shell the airfield in the event it fell to a Nazi invasion, as well as targeting shipping in the Channel.

46. Chichester Festival Theatre (1962)

Designed by Philip Powell and Hidalgo Moya as a hexagon-on-stilts, the idea for a theatre in Chichester came to Leslie Evershed-Martin in 1959 when he learned of the Stratford Festival Theatre in Canada. Discovering that Stratford and Chichester shared a similar population size and demographics, he set about bringing the idea into reality.

Incorporating a five-sided thrust stage to give all theatregoers a view of the action regardless of where they sit, the theatre opened with a production of *The Chances* on 3 July 1962, with Sir Laurence Olivier as artistic director.

Becoming a major venue during the height of The Troubles in Northern Ireland, it is no surprise that a bomb threat was called in during a performance of *The*

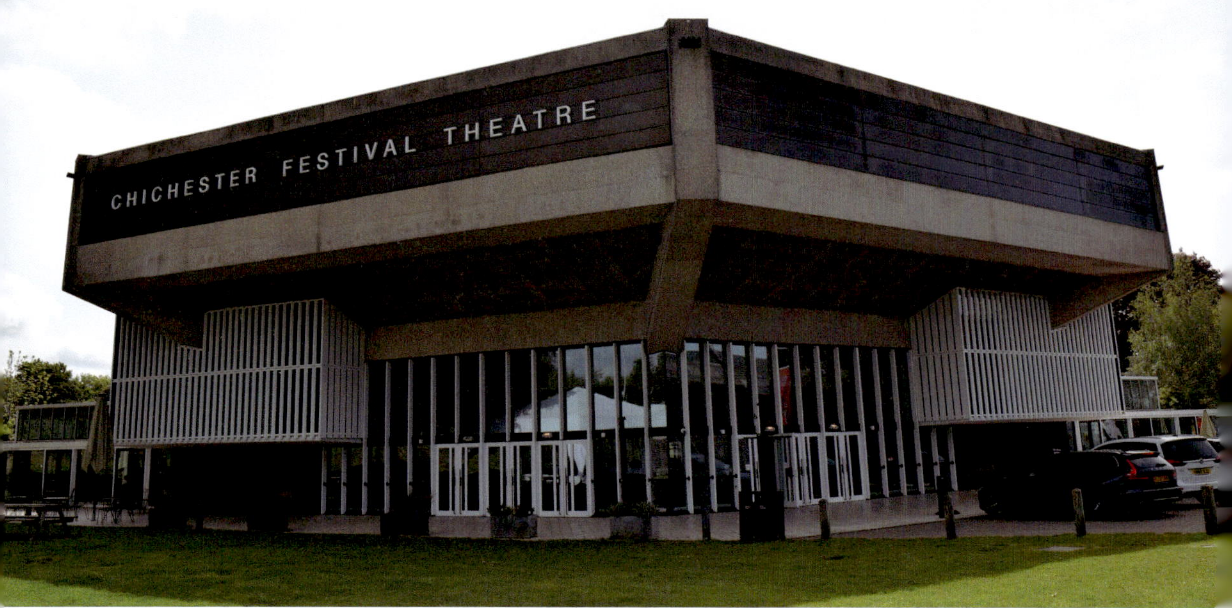

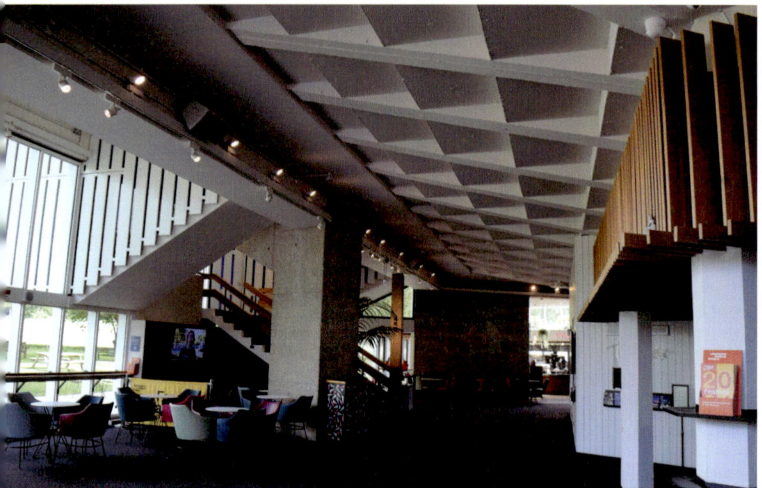

Above: Chichester Festival Theatre.

Left: Entrance lobby.

Below: Minerva Theatre.

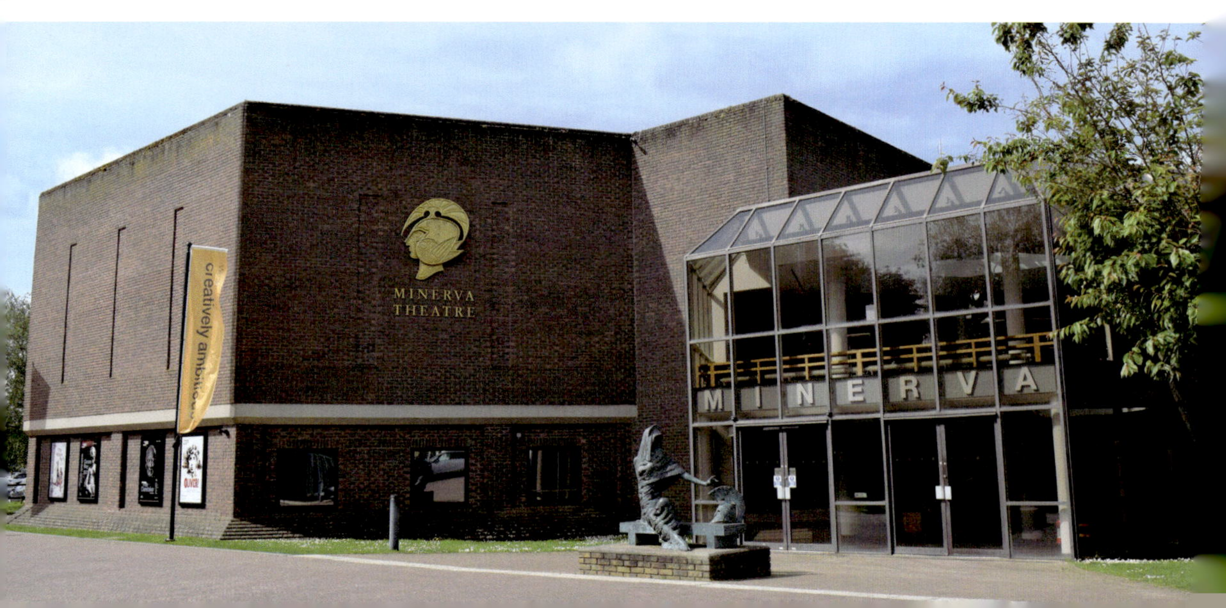

Rivals attended by Princess Alexandra, who had laid the foundation stone for the theatre ten years earlier. Evacuating the theatre and sweeping for the supposed bomb, it was found to have been a hoax call, and the show went on.

A big innovation came in 1983 with a temporary studio opened in a 140-person marquee set up in the park to attract younger audiences with experimental performances. The idea proved a tremendous success, and each year from 1984 to 1988 The Tent appeared before the Minerva Theatre was built in 1989 as a permanent space for young writers, directors, and actors to try out new pieces.

Closing for the first time in its history in 2013 for extensive refurbishment, a temporary tented structure once more arrived to provide a 1,400-seat theatre throughout the eighteen months of closure.

47. Marriott Lodge (1963)

A 1960s brutalist apartment block built as part of Chichester Theological College has perhaps attracted equal parts scorn and admiration for its rule-breaking design.

The college was founded by William Otter in 1839 as a centre of religious training under the oversight of the first principal, Charles Marriott. The original location was in Vicar's Hall at the cathedral, which housed the college's lecture room and library. Financial reasons almost forced the college to close in 1899 but fortunes reversed and a hostel in West Street was purchased. This was sold in 1919, and a new location in Westgate was purchased, being formally opened

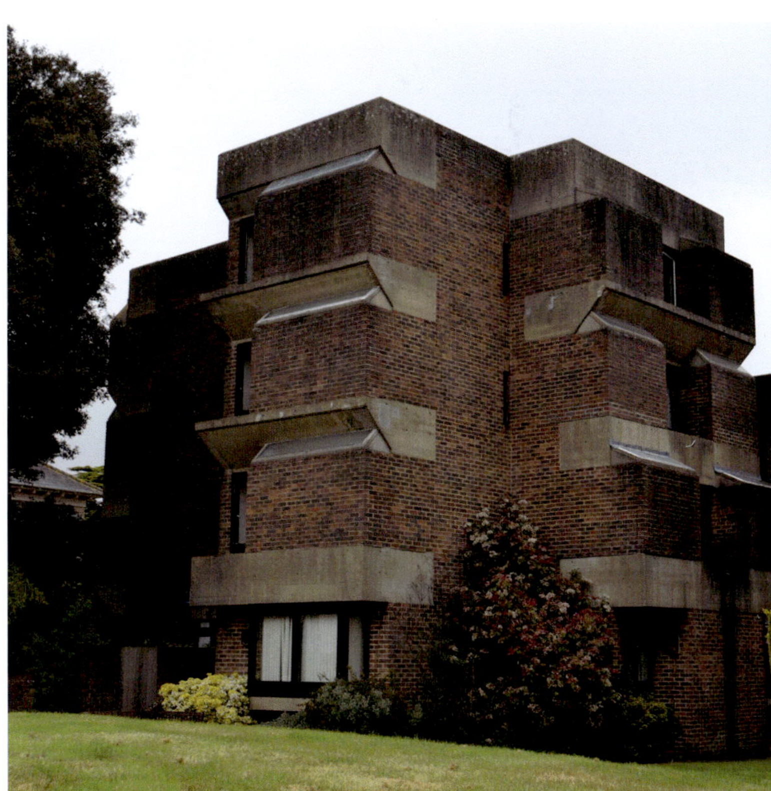

Marriott Lodge.

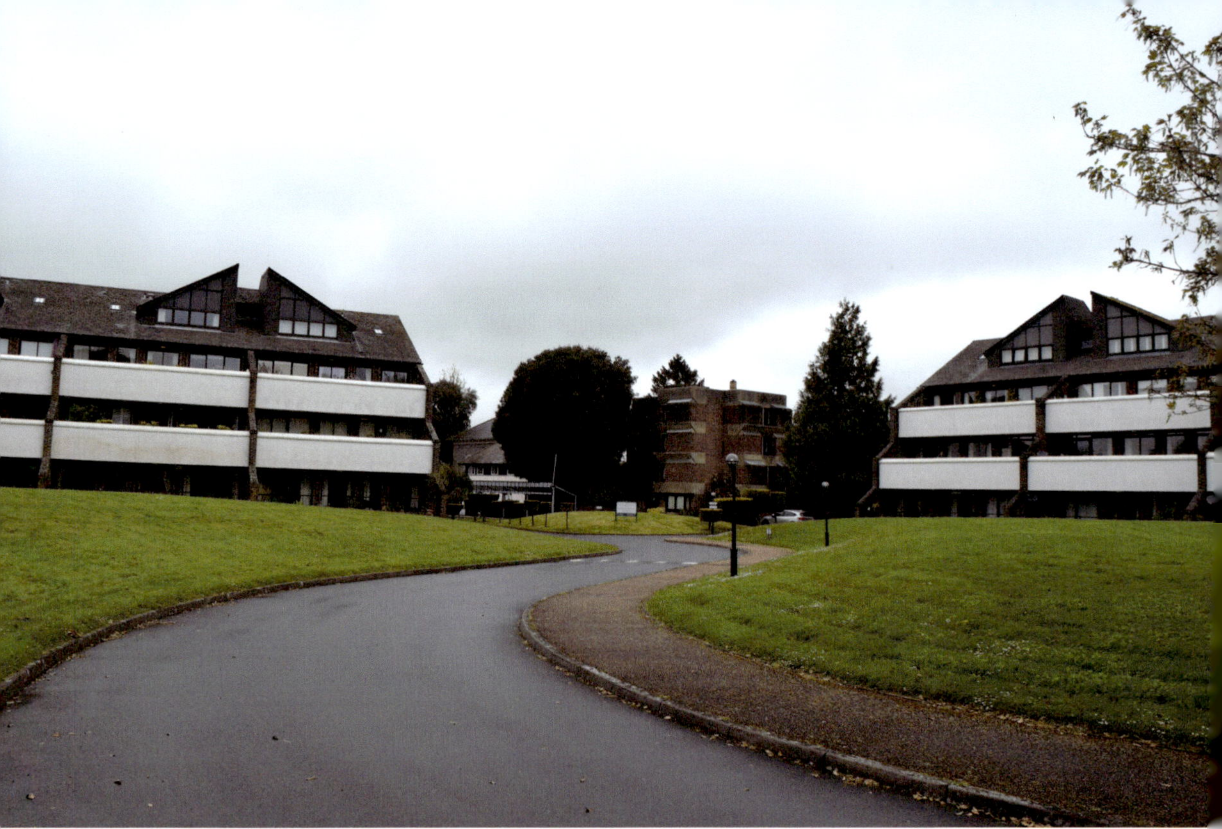

Barchester estate.

by Bishop Ridgeway; an ex-army hut used as a church for wounded soldiers in Brighton was re-erected at Westgate to serve as the college's new chapel.

The good times continued into the next decade, with a new wing built in 1927 and other properties in the area purchased throughout the 1930s for use as hostels.

In 1941, the college moved to Cambridge as the military took over the Westgate buildings. Perhaps facing financial uncertainty once more, all college assets except for Marriott House (now No. 3 Westgate) were sold off in 1945. The reformed college opened in Marriott House in 1946, with St Bartholomew's Church taken on as the chapel.

Better times returned in the 1960s, and a new site was purchased adjoining the chapel led to the Bishop of Chichester laying the foundation stone for Gillett House in 1963, opening to students in 1965 with a ceremony by the Archbishop of Canterbury. Additional buildings sprung up in 1987, but the college closed for good in 1994.

Gillett House is a perfect example of the 'new brutalism' style designed by Ahrends, Burton and Koralek to provide a thirty-five-bed dormitory over three storeys, including three staff flats, a library, lecture room and two-storey chapel. The study-bedrooms were grouped into fives with a shared kitchen and bathroom per group.

Upon the closure of the college, the site was sold off and became the Marriott Lodge care home, operated by Barchester.

48. Library (1965)

Nicknamed 'the nuclear reactor', 'the gasometer' and 'The Albert Hall' during its construction by bemused spectators, the unusual circular design of Chichester Library provides a light, airy and open atmosphere that can be missing in other traditional libraries, as well as making the best use of the confined space available on which to build it, being tucked snugly between County Hall and Tower Street.

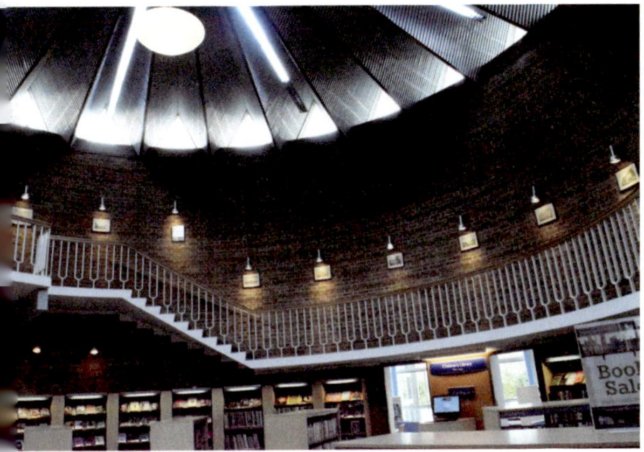

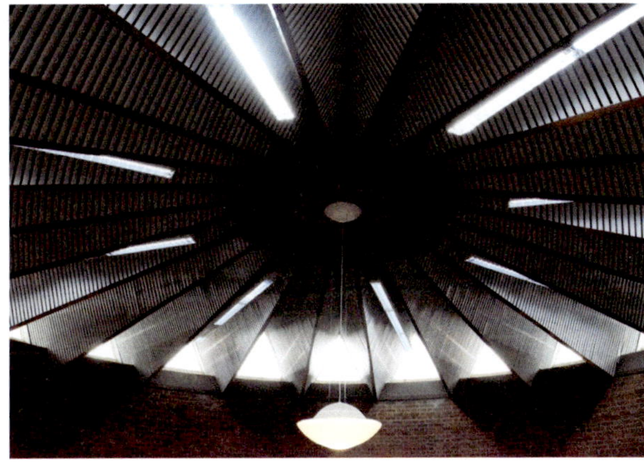

Above left: Central brick drum.

Above right: Library ceiling.

Below: Chichester Library's main entrance.

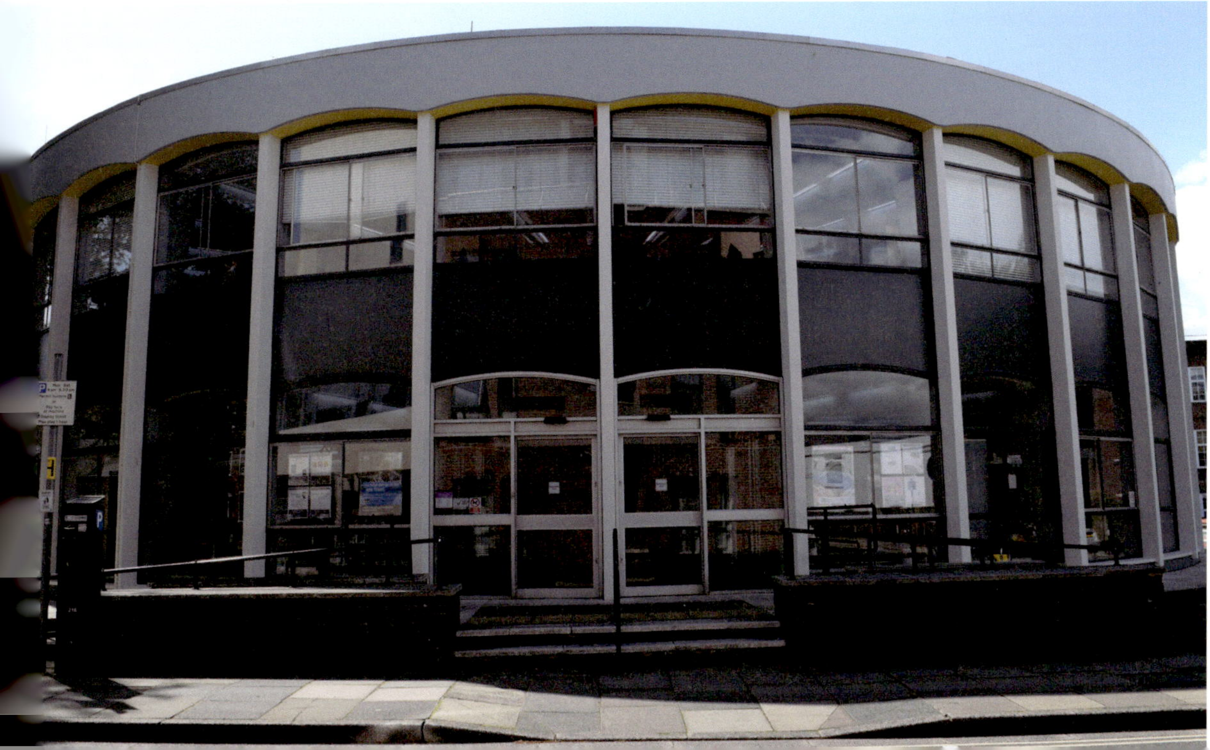

Built as the new West Sussex Library Headquarters in 1965–66 by Ove Arup and Partners to a design by the West Sussex County Council county architect, F. R. Steele, the building consists of seventy-two prefabricated concrete portals erected around a central red brick 'drum'. A loosely spiralling staircase around the inner circumference of the drum leads to the upper floor, where panoramic views across to the cathedral can be seen and admired.

The vice-chancellor of the University of Sussex formally opened the library on 24 January 1967, which also housed the UK's first electronic computer issue system. An extension added to the south-west in 2009 created a sizeable children's library entered through a pair of brick arches from the central drum, with offices created above it on the upper floor.

The Grade II listed library hosts regular community art displays and meet-ups, with the wall beside the staircase lined with a changing array of artwork and old photos.

49. Avenue de Chartres Car Park (1991)

Located in an extremely sensitive historic context, the design brief from Chichester District Council for a new 900-space car park with a footprint larger than that of the cathedral, certainly brought out some of the best talents of the architects behind Avenue de Chartres Car Park, Birds Portchmouth Russum.

Outer wall and stair tower.

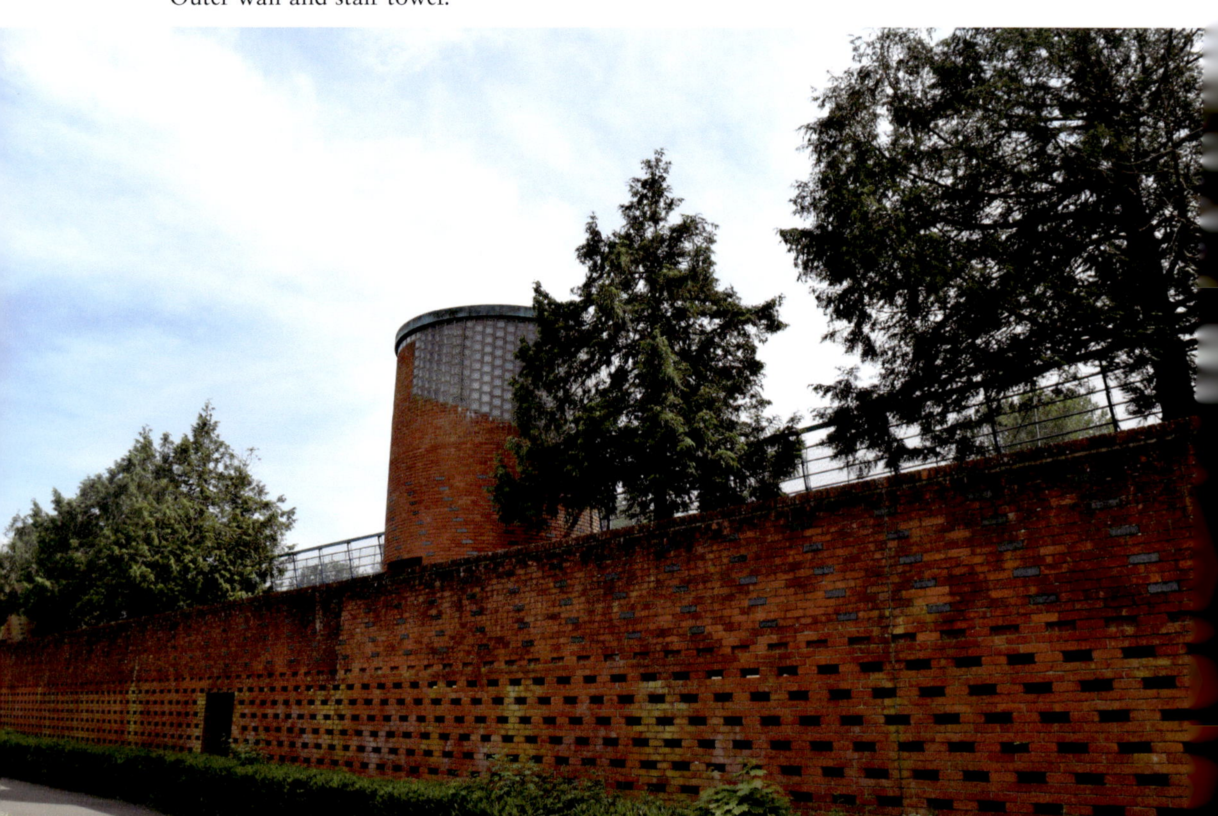

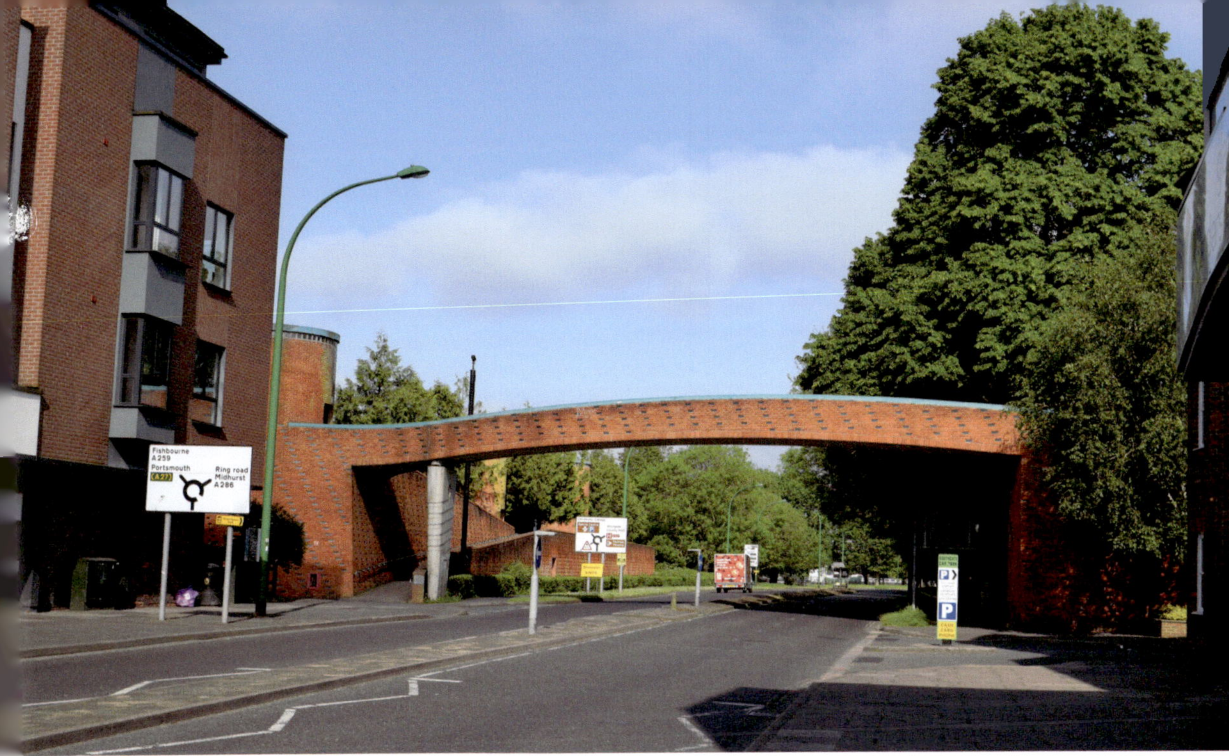

Integrated footbridge 'portal'.

Taking inspiration from the surroundings, the car park forms a new city wall supporting an elevated tree-lined walkway screening the car park from the street, and forming a new entrance portal into the city. The innovative, fortress-like building has gone on to win no fewer than six prestigious awards for its architecture and design.

Circular castle-like towers providing access to the new city wall walkway at the first floor level, and honeycomb brickwork providing a convenient mix of natural light and ventilation for exhaust fumes in an eye-pleasing way are but some of the features that have brought acclaim, as well as the internal design being fully accessible from the outset without the need for lifts. It is no wonder that it made it into the 'World's Ten Best Car Parks' in a vote by *The Guardian* in 2014.

50. The Novium (2012)

Built around the ruins of a Roman bath house, The Novium is the latest incarnation of the city's museum.

Dating back to 1831 when Dr John Forbes set up the Philosophical and Literary Society at the Royal West Sussex Hospital, including a space set aside for a natural history museum, the museum had a somewhat chequered history until the 1960s. In later years, the society moved firstly to a house in North Pallant and then to premises in South Street, but went into steady decline by the turn of the century.

In 1914 the South Street property was requisitioned by the army, with all the exhibits gradually being sold off over the next decade.

A temporary exhibition in the Guildhall in the 1930s of some items that had been saved and stored away eventually led to a new museum setting up there until 1962, when a larger building was purchased in Little London. This became the home for the museum for the next fifty years until the purpose-built Novium opened to the public in 2012.

Designed by Keith Williams following a competition, the story of Chichester is told over three floors, with regular special exhibitions on a variety of subjects held on the top floor throughout the year.

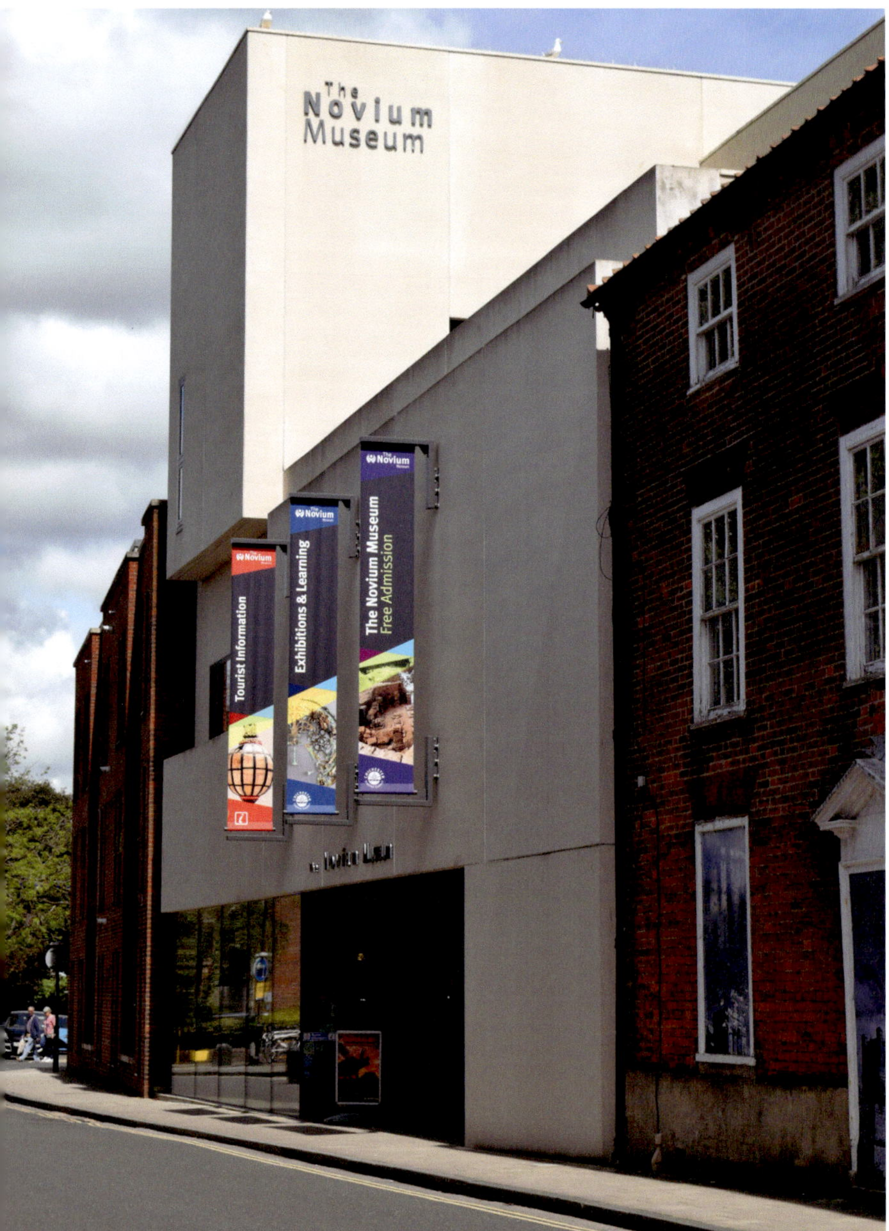

The Novium.